ECONOMICS AND INFORMATION

Economics and Information

Edited by

Pascal Petit

KLUWER ACADEMIC PUBLISHERS
BOSTON / DORDRECHT / LONDON

A C.I.P. Catalogue record for this book is available from the Library of Congress.

ISBN 0-7923-7571-8

Published by Kluwer Academic Publishers,
P.O. Box 17, 3300 AA Dordrecht, The Netherlands.

Sold and distributed in North, Central and South America
by Kluwer Academic Publishers,
101 Philip Drive, Norwell, MA 02061, U.S.A.

In all other countries, sold and distributed
by Kluwer Academic Publishers,
P.O. Box 322, 3300 AH Dordrecht, The Netherlands.

Printed on acid-free paper

Printed in the Netherlands.

TABLE OF CONTENTS

On the authors 7
Acknowledgement 9
Introduction 11

Part One : Information theories

Chapter 1 Economics of Information or Economics of Information Systems? (Jean-Louis Le Moigne) 17

Chapter 2 What Economics Borrows from the Statistical Theory of Information (Pierre Garrouste) 33

Chapter 3 Structure and Role of Information and Beliefs in Game Theory (Bernard Walliser) 49

Part Two : Information and market .

Chapter 4 Information and Prices (Alan Kirman) 61

Chapter 5 The Self-centred Logic of Financial Markets (Andre Orléan). 83

Chapter 6 Theory of Information: from Bounded Rationality to Interpretative Reason (Olivier Favereau) 93

Part Three : Information and organisations.

Chapter 7 Information, Knowledge and the Evolutionary Theory of the Firm (Patrick Cohendet) 121

Chapter 8 Information in the Theory of Organization (Jacques Crémer) 139

Chapter 9 On the Codifiability of Knowledge : Technical Change and the Structure of Cognitive Activities (Robin Cowan and Dominique Foray) 155

Part Four : Perspectives and conclusions.

Chapter 10 The European Policy of Promotion of the Information Society (Michel Catinat) 167

Chapter 11 Screening the Information Economy Through Theories of Information (Pascal Petit) 189

Index 217

ON THE AUTHORS

Michel Catinat	Advisor to the General Director of DG III, European Commission, Brussels.
Patrick Cohendet	Professor Louis Pasteur University, BETA, Strasbourg.
Robin Cowan	Professor Western Ontario University, research officer at MERIT, Maastricht
Jacques Crémer	Director of Research CNRS/GREMAQ and IDEI, University of Social Sciences, Toulouse.
Olivier Favereau	Professor Paris X University, FORUM, Nanterre
Dominique Foray	Director of Research CNRS/IRIS, Paris IX-Dauphine University.
Pierre Garrouste	Professor University Lumière, Lyon I.
Alan Kirman	Professor Aix-Marseille III University, EHESS/GREQAM.
Jean-Louis Le Moigne	Professor Emeritus Aix-Marseille II University.
André Orléan	Director of Research CNRS/CEPREMAP, Paris.
Pascal Petit	Director of Research CNRS/CEPREMAP, Paris.
Bernard Walliser	Professor Ecole des Ponts et Chaussées, CERAS; Paris.

ACKNOWLEDGEMENT

This work is in great part an adaptation in English of a more voluminous book published by La Découverte, Paris, in 1998 under the title "L'économie de l'information : les enseignements des théories économiques". *At the time it was a question of publishing the proceedings of a monthly seminar organised on the initiative of the Commissariat Général du Plan (an economic advisory committee to the French government). The difficulties presented by the analysis of contemporary economies, often qualified as information economies or knowledge economies, was the motivation behind this publication. The publication of this adaptation in English continues to benefit from the same circumstances : the statutes given to information and knowledge in various economic theories help to understand some objective strengths and vicissitudes of the "New Economy" and the still very partial character of the analyses which have been made of it.*
We would like to thank the Commissariat Général du Plan for having supported this project and also our colleagues who participated actively in the debates.

****

INTRODUCTION

The notion of information is multifaceted. According to the case, it is a simple signal or already knowledge. It responds to codes and is inscribed into a social relationship. There are clearly many perspectives which the social sciences can take to analyse the notion of information.
The economy cannot account for the majority of situations where, in the activities of production, consumption or exchange, the notion of information finds itself implied, although each school of thought has its own understanding of the notion of information.
This book takes this observation as a starting point and goes on to clarify a contemporary debate on the economy of information which remains quite vague, making use of the ways in which different theoretical approaches deal with information. To seize the nature and scope of the transformations in our societies, a consequence of our new ways of handling, stocking and circulating information in the workings of the markets like organisations, such a theoretical exercise seems useful.
The organisation of the book results from this choice. The contributions gathered in one part deal with the role of information in the functioning of the markets, those featuring in another are more interested in the organisations. To favour an enriching cross-reading of approaches developed in the two sections already referred to, we have preceded these with a section gathering approaches (which are more transversal) developing different theories of information (according to perspectives which are, respectively, systematic, statistical or strategic).

These three sections are followed by a conclusion which is more particularly centred on the way in which the contributions to the present work allow to have a better grasp of the questions being faced by our economies both because of the use of information and telecommunications technology and the accumulation of knowledge.

How, indeed, are we to characterise *ex ante* this notion of the information economy which the three parts of the book will allow to clarify ?

The notion is used to signify several things. Most often it seeks to qualify an historical phase in the development of our economies when they developed a new relationship with information. For certain people, this relationship is directly linked to the dissemination of a full technical system centred on information and communications technology (ICT). For others, the major element has less to do with technology than with the accumulation of knowledge resulting, in the first place, from the rise in the level of education, but also from the constitution of numerous forms of expertise (re. Foray, Lundvall 1996). With this in mind, we will accept that in a first definition, the notion of the information economy refers to one of the major characteristics of contemporary

P. Petit (ed.), Economics and Information, 11–16.

developed economies, underlining the scope and the diversity of the uses of information and knowledge which allow each economic agent to broaden the field of his strategies. This broadening differs, of course, according to the initial abilities of the agents but it nonetheless has the general consequence of increasing the weight of certain external features.

However, the list of commonly held definitions of the notion of an economy of information doesn't stop there. Some speak of an economy of information in a more restrained but just as legitimate sense to designate the activities of a sector which produces information and disseminates it where it is in demand, in both market and non market contexts. We will not be making use of this sector based dimension but will take note that this area of information has seen its importance grow in the contemporary historical phase and that this development is, by nature, very linked to the development of a so-called economy of information in the first sense of the term.

This questioning of the new historical phase of development is also grounded in the observation of a certain number of structural changes.

Four evolutions, respectively affecting the dissemination of new technology, accrued internationalisation, the development of the service sector and the continued increase of the general level of education and the stock of knowledge, are profoundly transforming the conditions of production and exchange. These evolutions are, moreover, largely interdependent.

The dissemination of new information and communications technology, driven by the growth in storage ability and the processing of information has had spectacular aspects. The continued miniaturisation of microprocessors (which double their strength every 18 months) has allowed to multiply the possibilities for the computerisation of processes and products. The parallel development of generations of software has contributed to the modification of communication and organisational structures, giving rise to a new organisation of work not only inside firms but above all between firms. The new forms taken on by internationalisation (with the development of communications and intangible exchange) and by the development of the service sector (with the development of services to companies) attest to these transformations in the division of labour.

Even if this equipment only represents a small fraction of investments (11.6% of fixed assets in 1993 in the United States according to Sichel 1997) its impact on the organisation of production and exchange is important.

The rise in the general level of education and intangible investments (another way of spotting a part of the growth of stored knowledge) is contributing just as fundamentally to giving the impression that our economies have reached a stage of development where information and knowledge play a major role.

More than fifty per cent of each age group now reaches higher education in the most developed countries of the OECD. The part of intangible investments made by firms has grown by about 50% (in terms of GDP points) in a decade. Thus, between the middle of the 70s and the middle of the 80s, the percentage of these investments as part of GDP has gone from 2.6% to 3.7%, while at the same time tangible investment went from 17.6% of GDP to 15% (OECD 1992, p.113). As such, this is a small part of what a stock of knowledge and learning might be.

But identifying these major structural and complementary transformations, affecting technology, the nature and the localisation of economic activities and the accumulation of human resources and knowledge, does not suffice to qualify the manner in which economies of information develop, whose paradoxical aspects remain numerous. We will address three of these : the often evoked paradox constituted by the contemporary slowing down of productivity gains in the dissemination of new technology, that which represents the hazards of the profitability of investments in education (marked by the rapid obsolescence of training and the importance taken by the personal qualities and networks) or finally, that hidden by the stability of the structure of the final demand of households which has been little modified by the new universe.

The explanations given for these paradoxes oscillate between an emphasis of the quite particular qualities of the period just gone through, and the just as particular difficulties of the organisational co-ordination required at present (as much in a firm as between firms or when dealing with households). The past was a period of catching up for European countries where the model for production techniques as for norms of consummation was American and where the still quite protected national markets were only opened to competition following the rise to power and efficiency of the concerned production devices.

In the immediate future, the synchronisation and intermediation which the compatibility problems of new technology and its codes will require, the individualisation which the detention of knowledge will lead to, or the marginalisation which allows for the substitution of an overall network into multiple independent networks, can be long and difficult to establish according to the yardstick of historical experiences. Paul David (1991) points out that the good fairy of electricity took fifty years to disseminate all of its benefits.

There is nothing to say that it will be the same case again, but to reach a level of strong and durable growth quickly, our economies have to adapt their institutions, regulations and economic policies so that the market dynamics developing in the new context do not exclude units of production or segments of population which might not have financial means or the necessary information and knowledge (re. Petit, Soete, 2001). Such a dualistic slide would strongly limit the potential of these knowledge-based economies where network phenomena make the participation of all a collective advantage.

Finding the means of favouring this solidarity without reducing the capacity for creative innovation is quite a complex contemporary challenge which requires a good understanding of development mechanisms.

This work seeks to contribute to this objective by taking into account different ways of handling information in certain contemporary economic approaches.

A reading framework.

In order to have a clearer idea of the diversity of approaches and their respective contributions it is useful to have an overview. The papers will be organised in three parts.

The first part of the present work brings gathers three approaches which are theorisations of what information is, in wider contexts than just economic activities. The second part presents three approaches to the role played by information in the workings of the markets. The third part deals with information in organisations.

This division should not obscure the continuities between the various approaches (whose interest will be recalled in the conclusion in chapter 11).

The theories of information (part 1).

Chapter 1. In his contribution "Economics of information or economics of information systems", Jean Louis Le Moigne first presents information in its three dimensions (sign, sense and context) and points out that a complete analysis of this complexity has to articulate three heuristics: the code/canal dialectic, relations between information and organisation and finally economics of information systems in the strict sense of the term.

Chapter 2. Pierre Garrouste carries on from there with an historical and critical reading of works which take communication problems as a starting point, (in the perspective of a code/canal dialectic echoing the previous contribution), to develop a "Statistical theory of information". He brings to light the limits but also the positive contributions in contemporary studies (initiated by biologists) on order through noise.

Chapter 3. Finally, Bernard Walliser addresses the theory of information in a completely different perspective, that of the theory of games where information exists both through the strategic dimensions which it offers actors but also through its capacity to create the context of action (through the representations which the agents of this reality make), in " Structure and Role of Information and Beliefs in Game Theory".

Information and markets (part 2).

Chapter 4. With Alan Kirman we leave theories of information in the strict sense of the term to specify the (central) place of information in a general pattern, that of the Walrassian general balance. Prices are taken to constitute condensed forms of optimum information but this property is not accompanied by any operative mode defining the way in which *de facto* information circulates. In his contribution, "Information and prices", Kirman examines the consequences of this incompleteness.

Chapter 5. In his contribution on the workings of the financial markets, André Orléan extends this reflection by analysing the preponderant role played by agents' beliefs which, in certain cases, become more important than the underlying realties. Hence the importance of knowing the manner in which the opinions of financial agents are formed and the hazards that this sometimes implies as in certain cases of imitation in behaviour.

Chapter 6. Olivier Favereau closes this series with an analysis of individual behaviour supposing not only that their rationality is limited but that the individuals know it is and act in accordance. Going from the perception of the signal to its transformation into meaning only takes place through certain "common" processes of decoding which at first glance emphasises diversity, contingency and, finally, uncertainty ("Theory of information : from Limited Rationality to Interpretative Reason ").

Information and organisations (part 3).
The contributions presented in this part look at information in the context of an organisation. Individuals are therefore, *a priori*, more localised.
Chapter 7. Patrick Cohendet's perspective is given by the title of his contribution "Information, Knowledge and the Evolutionary Theory of the Firm". The firm is going to be both an operator for information received from the outside, in particular from the markets, and an organiser of internal skills, themselves resulting from the flux of anterior information. The question here will be to be able to distinguish what pertains to individuals and what pertains to the collective operator, in other words the firm, in the learning processes mentioned.
Chapter 8. Jacques Crémer's contribution "Information in the Theory of Organisation" will develop different facets of the notion of information in the well contexted approaches which the New Industrial Economy knows how to deal with. The question of the frontier of this knowledge (the space of the cases that we know how to handle) becomes primordial.
Chapter 9. The last contribution in this series, "On the codifiability of knowledge : technical change and the structure of cognitive activities", by Dominique Foray and Robin Cowan, leaves the analysis of organisations and takes a more generic interest in one organisational feature : codification. According to the proprieties that can be established in such an economic analysis of codification, relations between what is tacit and what is codified, it is not a "localised" theory of information that we find but a full theory of information.
Perspectives and conclusions (part 4).
Chapter 10. In this last part of the book, Michel Catinat reminds us of the scope of what is at stake for Europe in the policies allowing to make the best of an orientation which is giving increasing importance to information and knowledge in economic activities.
Chapter 12. In the conclusion of the work, Pascal Petit emphasises the continuity and the correspondences between the questions raised in the various approaches and, in the framework of analysis thus constituted, outlines the principal features of the contemporary role of information and knowledge in developed economies.

REFERENCES

David P. (1991), "The Computer and the Dynamo: the Modern Productivity Paradox in a Not-Too-Distant Mirror" in OCDE (1991).

Foray D., Lundvall B.A. eds (1996), Employment and Growth in the Knowledge–based Economy, OCDE, Paris.

OCDE (1991), Technology and Productivity : the Challenge for Economic Policy, Paris.

OCDE (1992), Technology and the Economy. the Key Relationships. TEP Report, Paris.

OCDE (1996), Employment and Growth in the Knowledge-Based Economy, Paris/

Petit P., Soete L. (2001) « Is a biased Technological Change Fueling Dualism ? », in Setterfield M. ed. *Demand led Growth :Challenging the Supply-Side Vision of the Long Run,* Edward Elgar

Sichel D. (1997) The Computer Revolution : An Economic Perspective, Washington, Brookings.

Chapter 1

ECONOMICS OF INFORMATION OR ECONOMICS OF INFORMATION SYSTEMS ?

Some Systemic Modelling Considerations about a Complex Concept

Jean-Louis Le Moigne
Professor Emeritus, Aix – Marseille II University

Information can not be destroyed by use, it grows when shared and it expands when used. So Information offers few interesting features for the "normal mainstream" (T.S. Kuhn) or even the "enlarged-normal mainstream" (O. Favereau) Economics. The emergence of an "economics of information" (in the 1940's) needed semantic shifts for information to amount to either to an organisational transaction (as J. Cremer shows about the Coasian thesis, 1937) or to a class of stable and physically-materialised items which could be analysed as potential energy-carrier sub-particles (the "quanta of data" which should be treated as if it equated the energy-like dimensions, then with erg by degree!) as L. Brillouin (1956) desperately tried to demonstrate. Those exercises led to the very first formulations of an "economics of organization", of an "economics of transmission" (and to some extent - probably less so - to an "economics of communication") and an "economics of electronics" which allowed the transmission, processing and the storage of electric-signal systems (usually called "information technology"). While interesting, those exercises do not really allow to move towards a "standard economics of information"(a "normal science"), whatever the extent to which citizens and economists desire it.

For a long time, the latter used another semantic shift as a shelter, stating that the concept of information could be reduced to the concept of price. However, they were to take the "economics of information" as a tautology : Who could reasonably speak of an "economics of price"? As a result, "*the price and information relation was far from easy*" as A. Kirman recalled. Whenever there is an "oversimplification" of a fundamentally complex concept –which can not be reduced to a finite model- and a limiting of information to a category deeply-rooted in Economics or Energetic sciences, economists and politicians seem deadlocked, although they are witnesses to the social and cultural transformation which turns the "post-industrial society" into the "information society".

P. Petit (ed.), Economics and Information, 17–31.

1. AN INFORMATION IS NOT A (GIVEN) DATA[1]

As a result, resuming the original set of problems might be tempting, disregarding information as a given data or as a natural resource the agents would trade on a more-or-less perfect market in an attempt to determine reason-based allocations procedures. The economics of information may be different from others (e.g., raw materials, manufactured and agricultural goods, transportation, health) and an "isomorphism of structures", this assumption made by the economists and mathematicians[2] for featuring the nature of the "item" they want to interpret, is not guaranteed whenever phenomena are not endowed with steady and isomorphically-reproducible "structures". Instead of working desperately hard at applying a usual economics paradigm over an artificial-item class which is irreducible to a single identity, perhaps we can attempt to model that item class assuming the irreducible complexity of the information concept, and then to reconsider the epistemic and pragmatic paradigms as a fruitful source for a few interpretations, relevant here and now[3].

2. THE COMPLEXITY OF INFORMATION : A TERNARY SCHEME

The emergence of the "New Sciences" of information and communication highlighted the "essential" complexity of the information concept. The seminal papers by W. Weaver (in C. Shannon and W. Weaver, 1949) and C. Morris (1946) are frequently quoted while rarely simultaneously (except for R. Pages in his paper devoted to "*Communication processes*", reprinted in the editions series of the "Encyclopædia Universalis", keyword "Communication") : Information is a complex problem fundamentally made of three elements :

The physical form or pattern, called the Sign (*the syntactic component*) can not be separated either from the Meanings –with the sign as a potential carrier (*the semantic component*)- or from contextual actions generated by the reception of that sign, the meaning of which may differ (and may be unforeseen by the

[1] In French, the word "Data" is usually translated by the word "Donnée" , that is "Given".

[2] "*For the mathematician, identity is replaced by isomorphism and, for language ease, he identifies, unscrupulously, items with different natures whenever an isomorphism guarantees he just says the same thing with two different languages*", as A. Lichnerowicz reminds in l'Encyclopédie Pléiade "Logique et Connaissance Scientifique", J. Piaget Ed., Gallimard, Paris, 1967, p. 478.

[3] In the early 1970s, J. Marshack outlined this difficulty in two successive papers whose titles are – to my mind - significantly different: "*Economics of Informational Systems*", 1971 (JASA, March 1971, V.66, n°333, p.192-219), "*Economics of Organizational Systems*", 1972, paper presented at the Conference "*Man and the computer system*" held in Bordeaux in Sept. 1972 and formerly published by Heidelberg University. These two texts debate and interpret differences between the economics of information as proposed by statistics-economics and the one as proposed by the mathematical theory of communication. He, specifically, highlights how difficult it is to use a single model for expressing both production – as measured in value - and distribution – as measured in volume - of information. To conclude, I will underline the fruitful aspect of this slide from information to organization economics, as J. Marschack seemed to notice in 1972.

issuer, as well) depending on the context of reception (*the pragmatic component* for C. Morris, or *the effective component* for W. Weaver).

Those components can be distinguished to set them out, but cannot be separated or hierarchically organised when a piece of information has to be identified. For the receiver, a meaningless sign is not a piece of information. Considering only a sign-focused processing (even with electronic machines) as having nothing to do with either meanings or action provoked in one context at least, is a pure illusion (but, alas, a frequent illusion among computational-sciences theoreticians and practitioners).

This ternary or triad-like scheme (at least as old as the logician C.S. Peirce, 1839-1914, the first semiotics and pragmatism theoretician, i.e. the "Peirceian triangle" and the "*teirceity*") may not boil the information down to an usual category but allows an easier interpretation in a discursive style[4]. Natural language does know how to manage those recursive concepts which express an action and its result as well - the operator and the operand. Energy, organization, game, decision, communication and information are intelligible concepts which, moreover, can be modelled while they do not amount to a finite or to a close-ended model. Properly understood, they work with synchronic and diachronic operating and self-transforming modes which make them incompatible with the classical methods of deduction. Some modern logicians facing up the processing of the information concept are responsible for the emergence –or re-emergence– of reasoning modes compatible with the manipulation of those recursive concept, from a global standpoint –e.g., the abduction concept by C.S. Pierce, the transduction concept by J. Piaget and J.B. Grize and the retroduction concept by N. Hanson et H.A. Simon… As many reasoning modes, well-known to rhetoricians from Protagoras to Ciceron and Aristotle along the way, can be found, today, for embracing those complex recursive-concepts such as information. The surprising but relevant definition given by G. Bateson (1972) is often quoted : "*A difference generating a difference*": The emergence, in the course of time, of a "*new form, which formerly in-formed turns out to be in-forming*".

3. NOT SEPARATING DATA, KNOWLEDGE, AND INTELLIGENCE GATHERED BY INFORMATION

At first sight, the computer scientist as well as the economist may be deterred by this generic definition. Sometimes, to avoid that complexity, he offers to divide the raw data from the elaborated knowledge and from the intelligent knowledge. These puns, however, do not take anyone in for a long time; whatever its appearance, the analysed item is fundamentally the same whenever its global

[4] M. S. Feldman and J. G. March (1981) give a very good illustration of this in a paper that has become a classical one : "*Information in Organization as Signal and Symbol*", ASQ, June 1981, p.171-186.

dimension is considered. Data analysed - by the issuer- as a raw or primary might turn out to be, for a little time, knowledge and intelligent knowledge (source of power) for the receiver. Apart from assuming that a perfect dictionary might, one day, define a clear and a one-to-one correspondence between every conceivable sign and its single and exclusive meaning presumed to be intrinsic, no-one could prevent this "contextualising effect" (E. Morin, 1977) which will transform - sometimes in an unforeseeable manner - that "perfect information" when its receiver(s) meets it.

B.A. Lundvall has recently tried to make an intermediate distinction called "economic information" which would be the only one consistent with the economics of information. As a result, he offered a new ternary scheme relative to the information concept, valuable as it enlarges the Weaver and Morris classical model ("Sign, Signifying, Signified") : Cannot this "economic information", assuming things can be distinguished in this category without too many ambiguities, be divided up into three terms or forms of "knowledge" that might be featured according to the "use" economic agents make of it ?

- The "know-what", "fact-related knowledge" –"usually called information that can be broken down with bits". This information can be located in "data-bases" (or knowledge-bases) that "specialists and experts, working for specialized consulting -firms, frequently look for".
- "know-why", "scientific-principles-related knowledge ruling nature, society, and the human mind" : "Knowledge that organizations, such as universities, produce and multiply ".
- "know-how", "specific-skills-related knowledge implemented in any spheres of economic activity"...and which are " frequently tacit".

Concretely however, B. Lundvall concludes that the distinction among agents operating according to one of these three terms "*is not always a clear cut*", and that the informational complex, will be revealed with a synthetic word - he calls it "*know-who*"- given its lingering-conjunction with the What, the Why and the How of knowing. This draws us back to the issue the observer constantly meets in social-economic organizations : the economist and the management engineer is not interested in the information but in the attention (and the attention capacity) which turns out to be an invisible "scarce resource" (H. A. Simon still reminded it in his chapter entitled "*Economic Rationality*", 1981, p.25).

Because we lack modelling operators, allowing tremendous savings in our interpretation exercises, can we not assume an intelligible complexity, even with a discursive mode, instead of working out separately economics of sign, economics of knowledge and economics of knowing (or economics of intelligence) ignoring the fundamentally complex and tangling feature of the "*information-form-informing-which forms itself*" ?

Recursive interactions phenomena, like "end x means" or "what ? x for what? x how ? " type, can best be grasped with a discursive mode –without both splitting or linearising them up and constraining the economic agent to ignore the information which is under consideration contained in the what ? the why ?

or the how ? While this teleological-modelling exercise is rather unfamiliar to statistician economists, although E. Kant, two centuries ago, invited us to consider it in our reasoning processes, in the "*Critic of Judgement* ".

As it calls for a synthesis, the three-knowing model (what, why, how ?) that B. Lundvall (1995) offered, seems to express a dual mode portraying the question the economic agent usually raises: he does only seek information (i.e., data, knowledge and knowing) and, as a result, he does rather wonder about the three dimensions of his search process: what to know ? and why to know ? and how to know ?

This duality reveals the confusing complexity of the information concept whenever we aim at grasping its global dimension –without any simplification- and suggests search processes as well –some modelling heuristics by which our systemic representations of information might be enlarged.

4. FIRST MODELLING HEURISTICS : THE "CODE / CHANNEL DIALECTICS" (KNOW WHAT)

Indeed, we are not as unprepared as one might fear to tackle the economics of information, defined as such,: the definition suggests a few modelling heuristics as the forerunners of new sciences of information strongly imagined it to be. C. Shannon and W. Weaver's follow this line –information and communication can not be divided up; and vice-versa nobody can conceive of information that would be potentially communicable to no receiver even if the latter is the very issuer. C. Shannon (1949) did perceive the benefits to be drawn from this aggregation : as he modelled communication in the supposedly-easy case of "message" transmission–expressed in a "train-of-signals"-coded form- with no feed-back process through a standard channel, he presumed he might suggest a few arguments relevant for working out our intelligence of information. This was a well-grounded assumption that his "*Mathematical Theory of Communication*" witnessed (made up in 1945-46 and published in 1947-48) and which was rapidly presented as the "*Theory of Information*". His world-wide spread view will not be presented here, but the emphasis will be on the interpretation of "*the basic theorem for a discrete channel with noise*", theorem 11 - following both C. Shannon who qualifies it as a basic one and W. Weaver, his preface writer, who will further this interpretation.

This theorem states : a "*coding system*"–that is to say an artificial mode of expressing the information contained in a message to be transmitted from the issuer to the receiver- can always be designed in such a way that whatever the constraints imposed on by the transmission channel (i.e., a noise), the error frequency (i.e., an ambiguity) of transmission lies beneath an arbitrarily-fixed small value. (The theorem makes a distinction between cases where the information "flow" –expressed in bits per second- is over the channel "capacity", and those where it is below). If this statement is to be interpreted as a heuristics, modelling the communication of information, then we are to consider that :

- On one hand, the receiver gets the result of "*an interaction between a channel and a code*" –or a coding system- but not a fixed –coded- message which might be white noise.

- On the other hand, the issuer may use, in a strategic manner, coding systems and the channel choice for "effectively" transmitting a particular message, given that he knows that transmission feature.

Following C. S. Shannon (p.74), the proof of theorem 11 has, without any doubt, flaws inherent to "*proofs of pure existence*" : If the existence of a coding system relevant for a particular channel is proved, the invention process of that "ideal coding" system is left without any demonstration. However, interpreting information-communication as a dialectical choice for some code and channel might be a potentially-innovating work. If another "appropriate" coding system for communicating a message is imagined as an alternative to the one which is initially possessed -no matter whether it is constructed or acquired- then we should be induced to search for it...and sometimes to find it...to benefit the freedom of the channel choice we in fact have. This is what we usually do when we observe that "*a diagram is (sometimes) worth ten thousand words*" (Larkins J.H. & Simon H.A. (1987), tackled the complex cognitive reasons of this phenomenon in a very convincing way).

While attention is usually drawn to the prospects of an optimising choice of some channel –given an invariant coding (the "purpose of any organization chart" and, more specifically, of hierarchical trees, are just optimum because they lack loops: whatever the message, there is only one way to link two agents), social communication engineering systems tend to ignore the extraordinary resource given by the design and the choice of a coding system, as well as tone of a voice, winks, iconography and alphabets. Indeed, that "Scheme Production" of adequate coding systems freedom (following J. Piaget) can hardly be expressed through formal communication models, whereas communication channels ease network modelling with graph theory. However, there is a risk that socio-economic communication theory will become highly impoverished by limiting it to "*a game on channels*" for the sake of an attractive theory, forbidding "*the game on codes*" it can play, while it has a still-little-theorized resource, "*the game on coding systems*" and, moreover, the complex game of interactions between codes and channels.

E. Morin still perceived this distinction as he offered to differentiate "*generative information*", called organizing information, from "*flowing information*", called organized information too (*Method,* T.1, 1977, translated 1992, p.322+). A mainstream economist, as a computer engineer, would clearly say he would accept that second kind of information only – information that could be processed as any other usual resource both assuming its invariant value (i.e. its contextual meaning) and avoiding every transformation imposed upon by coding systems at stake in this circulation. But, to do this he should not mind that "*generativity and circulation are the two moments of information*" (E. Morin, 1977 p.341). Each coding generates information because it changes the information shape exposed to radical transformations of reception contexts. H. von Foerster (1981, p. 131) will go further, stating that "*a computer will never be the same once it has computed*" –which deepens an observation made by the biologist Th. Dobzansky (1961, p.335). "*As he changes what he knows about the world he knows, man changes the world he knows; by changing the world where he lives, man changes himself*".

There is no real ground to make a lingering division between "generative information" and "flowing information" as soon as information must –or can-regenerate, be exposed to some different coding systems within unsettled contexts –for information to flow.

5. SECOND HEURISTICS : "INFORMATION FORMS THE ORGANIZATION WHICH FORMS IT" (KNOW WHY)

Self-Organization theories and "Complexity from Noise" theories gave us another heuristics source for modeling which we can use to enlarge our intelligence of the economics of information. Today, the founding papers written by H. Quastler (1956), H. Von Foerster (1959), H. Atlan (1972, 1979) and F. Varela (1979) are all but as famous as C. Shannon and W. Weaver one's, and going over these theoretical developments may be unnecessary. For the sake of demonstration, I could resume them stating that "*Information forms the Organization which forms it*". Thus, modeling the "*Organization-Information interaction*" can be coupled with *the "Communication-Information interaction*" as defined by Shannon and Weaver. Unfortunately, we must –at this point-forgive the tangible, and so, cheering references of the Shannonian theory and its hydraulic metaphors dealing with channels and message flows, if we want to come into the purely conceptual world of representations and representation of representation. The organization is not endowed with a "*structure power*" of invariant frameworks. "*The organization, the organized thing, the organizing activity and the result of that action are hard-wired*" as P. Valery perceived it in his Cahiers (1930). At this stage and for a few years, the economist has no longer felt disoriented, thanks to K. Arrow and, above all, H.A. Simon, not to mention E. Morin. He is forging his own modeling experience of the non-deterministic complexity of the evolving socio-economic organization : The conception of collective action that is much more a trial-and-error proceeding (i.e. "*procedural rationality*"), understood as teleological –or prospective. Its purpose consists not in choosing either a state production by "*human design*" or by "*human action*" (F. Hayek, 1967) but in *the "deliberated design for and by human action*", without any exclusive regard to its expected final result (H.A. Simon, 1981, chap.5).

6. THIRD HEURISTICS: ECONOMICS OF THE MEMORIZING INFORMATION SYSTEM (KNOW HOW)

This is a change of style which alters the way an economics of information is thought : Would it be as meaningful as just another dimension of that economics of the immaterial which defines the economics of information ? Can anyone describe the economics of the nervous system without any reference to the economics of the living system ? While some doubts exist and if the organizational information-system is considered as a top concern, then we might derive a new, different and sensible approach to an economics of organization – an organization that will no longer be understood as a tangible machine, or a structure, producing goods and services, but as an immaterial-elaborating process for organizational behaviours defined as decisions of an organization. At this point, a metaphor might be helpful : Defining electricity, as well as information, is a very confusing job. However, the economics of a production and distribution system for electricity can be easily worked out. Can we pay attention to the economics of any information system too ? Comparisons made with production and information functions may, certainly, be too simplistic, as we have seen. But, can anyone question the functions of an organizational information system –no matter how the organization is considered, either at the macro or the micro-level of some social-economics ?

7. THE CONTEXTUALIZING FUNCTION

With such question we are to give an opportunity to economics science and to organization sciences, in a broader sense, to pay attention to the key function of any information system : its memorizing information function through which it is not destroyed when consumed and grows when shared, some paradoxical features that some classical and contemporaneous economics must tackle even if posterior beliefs are to be reconsidered. Conspicuously, the meaning of the human-memorizing metaphor will clearly shed a light on the proceeding – memory can not be reduced to either a warehouse or a shop even if comparisons with libraries, files and databases –or knowledge-bases- are useful tools for working out basic representations. What is at stake is the complex memorizing-function of information, rather than the warehousing one, which is constantly and variably connected whether a living organism, a social organization, a machine –an electronic one or not- and their conjunctions as part and parcels of any "context" are considered. This is just the "difference" generated in a prior in-formed context which clears the information and makes it intelligible (G. Bateson) –a contextualising information - and then an activation of the memorizing function. The richer and the more multifaceted these in-formed and memorized information are, the higher the "value" of information occurring at a given time. And vice-versa, the value –and then the economics- of a piece of information can not be analysed if the various memorized contexts, within which that information may appear, are ignored; without any contextual marks, information ceases to be and loses any value considered by an agent –or any teleological system. However, this great worth can only be understood within a teleological reference-system –just the one that will give a permanent guidance to interconnections. A sentence such as "*His name begins with a Z - You're right, it's Frizell*" is not an astonishing one for a human being, even if it confuses the classical computer-engineer logician. The staggering effectiveness of human memorizing heuristics is so familiar that the design and management of organizations' information memorizing systems are frequently forgotten. Whether referring to technological or prospective observation, to scientific research or human adventure, the capacity to memorize, using several components, is undoubtedly the core argument that must be considered by an economics of memorizing; in this field: the harsh technological and economic upheavals (giant data-bases, hyper-media, alarm-systems, browsing and searching systems), we have been faced with for fifteen years, have conspicuously contributed to drawing the attention of economists who were searching for concepts and bench-marks to assess and compare these capacities of memorizing-systems. (H. A. Simon gave the first insight in the fifties and had a crack at assessing human memorizing-abilities - i.e. H.A. Simon, 1969-81, chapter 3).

8. THE DELIBERATION FUNCTION

The memorizing concept, intertwined with one's information system, not only reveals this "contextualising" component in assessment, but its pooling element too –which may be called the deliberation component; as soon as the attention is not exclusively drawn to modelling communication and computational functions of the information systems –a basic argument used by N.I.T. economics- it focuses on modelling the complex function of memorizing, and much of it is devoted to the initial empirical observation – a consumed and memorized item of information cannot be destroyed, and a shared and memorized item of information grows. Then, the accompanying virtual- interactive access, shared by players involved in complex decision processes –multi-criteria and multi-players- eases the exercise of "deliberations" which are no less "intelligent" yet not always formalized. The regulation of crossroads operations may be a good example which briefly portrays this argument : the autonomous make-up of behaviour by every agent may be considered as a source of disputes and jamming within the organization, which leads to devising a meta-level of control - traffic lights- supposed to be intelligent, but that denies any behavioural autonomy to players of that organization : "*with green light they go, with red light they stop*!". However, those actors may also be considered as capable of independently making their own individual behaviour without causing any disputes and jamming, as soon as they have rich and teleological representations about the context within which they act, and as soon as they have enough time to process information to work out their next behavioural act. The crossroad-with-roundabout device compelling vehicles to slow down and then to have the required time to perceive the context and to process this information clearly portrays this procedure –having collective tacit-deliberation capacities, authorized by a shared access to the memorizing system of an organization, its players imagine a situation where they can individually work out collective behaviour that is intelligent and that can avoid those jamming towards which an other organizational arrangement, an anarchic-like one, might have led. Thus, the invention of the "*memory-based organization*" as an alternative to the "*control-based organization*" opened up perspectives for some new economic organizations, renewing the classical argument about the "*Market and Hierarchies*" dialectics (O. Williamson, 1975).

This reflection leads to question, once again, conditions within which economic agents and players of every organization are able to effectively work out their decisions: given both the endogenous aspect of the practice of human-reason (i.e., "*bounded rationality*") which allows to devise behavioural heuristics which are outstandingly efficient and effective, and the physiological limits of human players' memorizing and processing abilities (ability open to prosthetic extension by N.I.T., which is sometimes very impressive), the question is about the organization forms that fit these contexts. The issue is no longer to define optimal allocations for resources which are presumed as scarce, *"the only information presumed to be strictly useful and needed for the expected efficiency of an action* !", but consists rather in defining "inventive" cognitive navigation modes in an informational universe that is affluent, memorized and self-memorizing. This plausible shift of issue calls for a reversion of our economic conceptions of information systems so as to free them up from a "*cost-saving*" approach and to enlarge them with a *"value adding*" one –in other words, information systems that are not only operational but strategic as well.

9. INFORMATION SYSTEMS AND INTELLIGENT ORGANIZATION

This is a proposal which calls for a return to the organization complexity within which the information system grows. M. Catinat recalled in this volume the interest of the recursive conception of a "strategic system of information" as developed by H. Tardieu & Guthmann B. (1991). The so-called "*yield management systems*" coupled with booking systems (e.g. as for air companies) perfectly illustrate this conception. The implementation of an operational information-system which gives a preference to a short-run tariff policy and maximizes the "filling" of every flight resolutely induces a long-run strategy that will give a preference to new uses increasing the value of existing facilities and, as a result, to develop new facilities for exploiting the resulting competitive advantage ; this recursive interaction between the operational information system and the strategic information system transforms the economic representation we can have for each; with the constant transformation and enlargement of information –or representations- derived as such, the conditions for new organizational decision-modes are created –decisions whose results can hardly be forecast, but whose procedures can be assessed in a plausible way. The economic calculus of yesteryear is replaced with a socio-economic engineering (or an "*organizational economics calculus*", O. Favereau (1994), that is more systemic than analytic but yet relevant for modern economics.

10. THE SYSTEMIC MODELLING OF THE INFORMING ORGANIZATION

This can tackle economics of organizational information systems in the same way it did it for information centered systems (the police, health service, libraries, etc.), and this will lead to a renewal of the set of problems of N.I.T. economics (whether it is computer economics or telecommunication economics); instead of tackling it within the usual frameworks of either the manufacturing obsession with-productivity or the retail network marketing (i.e., " *market shares ?, markets of what ?* "), it must be able to develop modeling procedures for the behaviour of organizational systems within which these N.I.T. can possibly intervene. Then, the virtually-energetic performances of computer technologies are no longer the core of the analysis (e.g., a cost decrease in microprocessors, optical fibers, or CD Roms). The core is made up with the foreseeable performances, many of which are intangible (e.g., collective-decision "quality", cognitive equilibrating, cultural open-mindedness,...), with social organizations concerned with their interventions relative to their plans (from States to small businesses by multinational companies). The methods of this "*new socio-economic engineering*", based on designs of action, rather than on an analysis of things, are not coming for a while yet, but the experience that economics of information systems, information and organization has attempted to muster for a half-century (H.A. Simon presented his doctoral dissertation in 1943) allows us, today, to assert that such a project is as reasoned as it is reasonable.

11. THE ECONOMICS OF INFORMATION CALLS FOR NEW EPISTEMOLOGICAL MEDITATIONS

Initially, some could question the legitimacy of economics of information, a new-comer in the field of economics and political science. That was a usual effect deriving from a naive figure of speech, claiming that nothing can escape the hold of a discipline which aims at being simultaneously the queen of soft-sciences and the princess of hard-sciences. Between economics of education and economics of telecommunications, wasn't a cell for economics of information missing –a cell which could be easily filled in with an ad-hoc seminar? The interest of this exercise, whatever its prior motivations, is to cause an epistemic reflection, combining the status of both information and economics. In an attempt to identify the information concept, we can understand it through its intelligible complexity and irreducibility to a finite model. Whenever we strive to model an economics of information which assumes this concept in its complexity, we are led to widely enlarge the paradigmatic field within which it was originally inscribed (Theil, Machlup, Marchak, Alchian, Hurwicz, Arrow, Porat, J. Voge,...). In addition to this, a paradigmatic transformation might be needed for it not to be confined in its own language made up of a material energetics conspicuously unfitted to the conceptual, or "representational", feature of items and plans under its attention. P. Valery proposed to work out an "*energetics of knowledge*" and the modern way suggests, more and more frankly, considerations such as an "*economics of the immaterial*". In such a framework favoring the expression of interpersonal communication, social organization or collective-action decision, all of these best described as "unutterable"- an economics (or in a more appropriate manner, an "evolving socio-economics") of informing and learning organization may grow and irrigate a new engineering relevant for economic policies. Nonetheless, such a work implies an epistemological meditation which might be still unfamiliar as the beliefs on which the various tenants of neo-positivism-realism rely on, are deeply-rooted in the western cultures. One of the merits of a collective reflection on the economics of information will, possibly, be an epistemological return to the origins that will benefit both the economics and engineering of complex systems.

References

Atlan, H. (1972) "L'organisation biologique et la théorie de l'information", éd. Hermann, Paris.

Bartoli, J.A. et Le Moigne, J.L. (1994) "Qualitative reasoning and complex symbol processing", in "Mathematics and Computers in simulation" (IMACS), 36, pp. 129-136.

Bartoli, J.A. et Le Moigne, J.L. (1996) "Intelligence de l'Organisation et Systèmes d'Information stratégiques", éditions Economica, Paris.

Bateson, G. (1972) "Steps to an ecology of mind", Chandler Pub. Cy, N.Y..

Bougnoux, D. (1991) : "La communication par la bande. Introduction aux sciences de l'information et de la communication", Editions La Découverte, Paris.

Brillouin, L. (1962) "Science and Information Theory", Academic Press, N.Y., 1956, 2de ed..

Dobzhansky, Th. (1966) "L'homme en évolution" (1961, traduction française 1966), Editions Flammarion, Paris.

Favereau O. (1994) « Règle, organisaiton et apprentissage collectif : un paradigme non standard pour trois théories hétérodoxes », in Orléan A., Analyse économique des conventions, PUF, coll. Economie, Paris, p.113-137.

Feldman, M.S. et March, J.G. (1981) Information in Organisation as Signal and Symbol". Administrative Science Quaterly, 26, pp. 171-186.

Grize, J.B. (1989) "Logique naturelle et représentations sociales" in D. Jodelet (Ed.) : "Les représentations sociales", PUF, Paris, pp. 152-168.

Grize, J.B., Borel, M.J., Mieville, D. (1983) "Essai de logique naturelle", Ed. Peter-Lang, Berne.

Hanson, N.R. (1958) "Patterns of Discovery. A inquiry into the conceptual foundations of science", Cambridge University Press, Londres, U.K., 241 pages.

Hayek, F.A. (1967) "The results of human action, but not of human design", in "Studies in philosophy, politics and economics".

Kuhn, T.S. (1962) "The structure of the scientific revolutions", the University of Chicago Press, 1962-1970.

Larkins, J.H. et Simon, H.A. (1987) "Why a diagram is (sometimes) worth in thousand words", Cognitive Science, vol. 11, p. 65-99.

Le Moigne, J.L. et Pascot, D. (Ed.) (1980) : "Les processus collectifs de mémorisation", Editions de La Librairie de l'Université, Aix-en-Provence.

Le Moigne, J.L. (1988) "Communication, Information et Culture : le plus étrange des problèmes", in T.I.S., vol. 1, n° 2, pp. 11-36.

Le Moigne, J.L. (1989) "Natural and Artificial Computing and Reasoning in Economic Affairs" in "Theory and Decision", vol. 27, n° 1-2, pp. 107-117.

Le Moigne, J.L. (1990) : "Intelligence artificielle et raisonnement économique", in "Monde en Développement", T. 18, n° 72, pp. 11-18.

Le Moigne, J.L. (1990) : "La Modélisation des Systèmes Complexes", Ed. Dunod, second edition 1999, 178 pages.

Le Moigne, J.L. (1994) : "La théorie du Système Général, théorie de la Modélisation", 4e édition complétée, Editions PUF, Paris, 330 pages.

Le Moigne, J.L. (1994) : "L'Information forme l'organisation qui la forme", in Sciences et Société, n° 33, oct., p. 15-24.

Le Moigne, J.L. (1995) "On theorizing the Complexity of Economic Systems", The Journal of Socio Economics, JAI Press, Fall.

Lundvall, B.A. (1995) : "The Learning Economy. Challenges to Economic Theory and Policy". Conférence EAEPE, Copenhague, Nov..

Marschak, J.(1991) : "Economics of Information Systems". The Journal of American Statistical Association, March, vol. 66, n° 333, pp. 192-219.

Marschak, J. (1972) "Optimal Systems for Information and Decision" in A.V. Balabrishnan (Ed.). "Techniques of Optimization". Academic Press, N.Y., pp. 355-379.

Marschak, J. (1992) "Economics of Organizational Systems". Working Paper n° 193 de Western Management Science Institute", UCLA, Los Angeles, Sept. (Repris en Diskussionsschrift n° 23, Lehrstuhl für Oekonometrie, University of Heidelberg).

Morin, E. (1977) "La Méthode", tome 1 : "La nature de la nature" - English translation : "Method" Peter Lang Pub. NY., 1992- ; tome 2 : "La vie de la vie" (1980) ; tome 3 : "La connaissance de la connaissance" (1986). Editions du Seuil (Collection Point), Paris.

Morin, E. (1985) "La stratégie de relance", in Revue Internationale de Systémique, vol. 9, n° 2.

Morris, C. (1946) "Signs, Language and Behavior", J. Wiley, N.Y..

Peirce, C.S. (1984) "Textes anti cartésiens", présentation et traduction de J. Chenu (1878-1879), Editions Aubier, Paris, 318 pages.

Piaget, J. (Ed.) (1967) "Logique et connaissance scientifique", Editions Gallimard, Encyclopédie de la Pléiade, Paris.

Quastler, H. (1956) : "The emergence of biological order", Yale University Press.

Shannon, C.E. et Weaver, W. (1949) : "The mathematical theory of communication", University of Illinois Press, Chicago.

Simon, H.A. (1990) "The sciences of the artificial", 1969, Second Edition, augmented, 1981. The MIT Press, Cambridge, Mass., 1981. Traduction française : "Science des systèmes, sciences de l'artificiel", Editions Dunod, Paris.

Tardieu, H. et Guthmann, B. (1991) : "Le triangle stratégique : stratégie, structure et technologie de l'information", Editions d'organisation, Paris.

Varela, F.J. (1979) "Principles of Biological Autonomy", North Holland Pub. Cy, N.Y..

Valery, P. (1992) Cahiers 1894-1914. Edition intégrale annotée sous la direction de N. Celeyrette-Pietri et Y. Robinson-Valéry. Editions Gallimard, Paris, vol. I, 1987 ; vol. II, 1988 ; vol. III, 1990; vol. IV, 1992.

Voge, J. (1983) "The political economics of complexity", in "Information Economics and Policy", vol. 1, n° 2, pp. 97-144.

Von Foerster, H. (1984) "On self-organizing systems and their environments", 1959, in H. von Foerster : "Observing systems", Intersystems Publications, Seaside, Cal., 1981, 1984.

Williamson O. (1975) "Market and Hierarchies" : analysis and anti-trust implications, London, Mac Millan.

Chapter 2

WHAT ECONOMICS BORROWS FROM THE STATISTICAL THEORY OF INFORMATION?*

Pierre Garrouste

Professor Lumiere University, Lyon I

INTRODUCTION

Information is one of the main notions in economics. The economics of information as a research program shows that this notion is essential. As an example, Stiglitz says that "the research program in which I have been engaged over the past two decades have set out to construct a number of such simple models, evaluating how market processes work in gathering, in transmitting, and processing a variety of different kinds of information, in a variety of different market contexts." (Stiglitz, 1994, p.26). However, in economics, the notion of information is polysemic and adding an epithet to it often solves this problem. In game theory, as an example, one can distinguish the following situations :

Information category	Meaning
perfect	Each information set is a singleton
certain	Nature does not move after any players move
symmetric	No players has information different from other players when he moves, or at the end nodes
complete	Nature does not move first, or her initial move is observed by every player

Source : Rasmusen (1994, p.45)

* I thank Pierre-Jean Benghozi, Robert Delorme, Pascal Petit, Jean-Louis Rullière, and Bernard Walliser for their helpful comments.

P. Petit (ed.), Economics and Information, 33–48.

After the Second World War, a "theory of communication" or more exactly a "statistical theory of information" (STI) emerges[1]. Shannon (1948) and Shannon and Weaver (1949) set up this theory[2]. In fact the Shannon and Weaver's book is entitled The Mathematical Theory of Communication. This subtlety is important because of the fact that it is linked with the problem of the significance of the information (see below).

Shannon is a Bell Laboratory communication engineer and is a member of the Cybernetics Group[3]. In 1946, Shannon presents before this group, a communication entitled "Recently Developed Method of Estimating the Amount of Redundancy in Printed English". In this communication, he analyzes the statistical frequency of combinations of letters and shows that redundancy allows a melioration of the efficiency of the circulation of information. However the significance of the information is for him irrelevant[4]. The notion of information proposed by the STI has a precise meaning that permits to get a quantitative measure of it[5].

As soon as it is exposed, this theory is confronted to reaction coming from authors among whose some economists. Indeed, Savage and von Neumann are pertaining this group. "Savage studied the Shannon's paper, followed the theorems and proofs. He enjoyed Shannon's work, saw it as posing and neatly solving some consequential intellectual puzzles of a mathematical kind. Wiener had emphasized in particular the concept of 'information', or 'information-theoretic entropy", which has been introduced by him and independently by Shannon. Savage was not interested in putting this concept on a pedestal; it was solutions to problems that mattered to him, not the idea of 'information'". (Heims, 1993, 97). Few times after Boulding (1955) estimates that the theory of information identifies the information and the cost or the time needed to acquire it, but is not concerned with its value. We find the same reluctance in Arrow

---

1 In fact, this theory is heterogeneous. Lancry (1982) shows that one better has to say theories of information. Indeed while Shannon can be considered as the inventor of this theory, Fisher proposes, in the 20s, a statistical theory of information.

2 Brillouin (1959), Theil (1967), Atlan (1972), Lancry (1982), Le Moigne (1986) present the emergence and the content of this theory.

3 The Cybernetics Group or Macy Group is created on March 1946 and founded by the Josiah Macy Jr. Foundation. See Heims (1993).

4 « In Shannon's analysis of printed English the statistical frequency of letter combinations is fundamental but the "meaning" of a message is taken to be irrelevant" (Heims, 1993, p.76). or "From the engineering point of view it is irrelevant whether the messages have any meaning whatsoever. (Heims, 1993, p. 111).

5 We will see below that this problem constitutes of the main divergent point between the STI and the "economic theory of information" or "economics of information".

(1974) who considers that the Shannon formula is a useful measure of the cost of acquisition of information but gives no weight to the value of information.

The problems that the STI implies are due to its very object. Indeed Shannon analyzes the efficiency of the circulation of a message through a channel between a transmitter and a receiver[6]. More precisely he tries to determine "the minimal average number of binary symbols by letter to be coded from an N letters alphabet." (Atlan, 1972, p. 29). In this way the meaning of information transmitted by the message has no place.

Beyond those limits, which I will see below how they have been solved, Economics made many borrowings to STI. Those borrowings 1) concern many different domains of economics, 2) are of different scope, that is to say that they vary from the simple analogy to the use of formal results of the STI, 3) concern different periods of the development of the STI.

In fact the borrowings of economics from the STI either were applications and improvements of Shannon's results (section I), or were introducing the observer into the systems analyzed by the STI and then put to the fore the complexity of social and economic systems (section II).

1. THE BORROWINGS FROM THE STI

In this section I will distinguish the part of the economic literature that tries to apply directly the STI formal results, from the economic contributions that, although inspired directly or indirectly by Shannon's theory, shows the limits of its application in economics and then develops an "economics of information".

The application of the STI results.

The STI starts from the definition of the informative content of a given message. Let a given set of symbols with each a constant probability x_i to be present in a message, the quantity of information contented in average in the message is given by the Shannon's formula:

$$H(x)=\sum_{i=1}^{n} x_i \log\frac{1}{x_i}$$

The quantity of information given by the Shannon's formula can be applied to a set of messages that use the same alphabet, that is to say with the same number of distinct symbols, and the same distribution of probabilities among those symbols. The transmission of strings of symbols needs then to be an ergodic stationary stochastic process. In other words, the regime of the probabilities for the symbols to appear is constant with time, and the messages cannot be divided into independent processes.

The maximal quantity of information that can circulate trough a channel is given by the following formula :

---

[6] Shannon himself shows the limits of the application of his theory (Shannon, 1956).

$$C = \max(H(x) - H_y(x))$$

where $H_y(x)$ is the quantity of information that is lost during the transmission of a message x compared to the received message y. In fact this quantity of information is due to the fact, first that a maximal quantity of information can circulate from a transmitter to a receiver, second that the quantity of information received is necessarily less than the quantity of information emitted. We will see below that this inequality is abandoned by those who introduce the idea that "noise" can produce "order".

This measure of the quantity of information, thanks to some particular hypothesis, can be applied to a wide range of set of probable events. In other words, it is possible to assume that reality is emitting some messages to an observer, those messages concerning the set of the possible states of the world. The quantity of information can then be conceived as a measure of the disorder of that system or of our ignorance of the states of the world. The greater is the number of the states of the world, the closer are the probabilities associated to those states, and the more important is the uncertainty. The quantity of information is maximum when the events are equally probable. This possibility to generalize the analysis of the transmission of a message between a transmitter and a receiver to the knowledge of reality by means of the assumption that the world emits messages that we can pick up is essential inasmuch as it permits to apply the results of the STI to economics, and, as an example, to economic prediction.

Theil's works (1967) illustrate such a way. The quantity of information contained into a message represents, according to him, the expected informational content of this message. It measures the uncertainty link to the realization of a set of events.

The gain, in terms of information, of a message is given by the difference between the quantities of information of two messages. Indeed, let E be an event with a probability a priori x to be realized. Let y be the probability a posteriori of E after a message concerning E, if h(x) = -log x and h(y) = -logy, then the expression h(x)-h(y) = log(y/x) represents the gain of information of a forecast, that is to say a message of E. In other words, if the difference h(x)-h(y) is positive, the probability x induces a growth of the probability y that E is realized.

More generally, let $x_1, x_2, \ldots, x_n$, the probabilities a priori of a set of n events and $y_1, y_2, \ldots, y_n$, the probabilities a posteriori of those n events, then,

$$I(y / x) = \sum_{i=1}^{n} y_i \log \frac{y_i}{x_i}$$

This expression represents the gain of information of the forecast link to the distribution of probabilities a priori. Theil proposes two interpretations: I(y/x) can constitutes the content of information of the forecast, but can also correspond to the inaccuracy of the prediction[7]. In this way, Theil defines the informative gain that results from the relation between the predictions of the entrepreneur that concerns some economic values and the realization of those values.

Theil (1967) proposes some applications of the STI to the models of regression[8], the inequality of outcomes, and the concentration in the industry. In this last case the concentration is given by:

$$H(y) = -\sum_{i=1}^{n} y_i \log y_i$$

Where y_i represents the market shares of firm i. The more important is the entropy, the less is the degree of concentration.

In the same way, Zajdenweber (1972) using some data from INSEE measures the industrial concentration by means of the Theil's index, showing how it can be based on an axiomatisation.

Finally one can agree with the Lancry's point of view which considers that it "is clear that at the international level, H.Theil has been a great contributor to the economic development of the theory of information. His Economics and Information Theory is and is going to stay a fundamental book in this domain." (Lancry, 1982, p.74).

Thionet's works, that Lancry assimilates to Theil's ones, show, in fact, a different aspect of the possibility of applying STI to economics. Thionet (1959) revisits the pool theory, and shows that it is possible to identify the variance of the estimation on a sample, a mean and the quantity of information.

Another kind of application of STI in economics concerns econometrics. This introduction is of two types: the Onicescu and Botez' attempt (1978) to set

---

7 "First, let x_1, .., x_n be the probabilities of E_1,..., E_n before the forecast is made, and let this forecast change these probabilities to y_1, ..., y_n ; the $I(y/x)$ is the information content of that forecast. Second, let x_1, .., x_n be predictions of the allocation fractions of E_1,..., E_n and y_1,..., y_n the corresponding realized fractions, then $I(y/x)$ is the information inaccuracy of the forecasts. In the former case the forecast is considered more valuable when the posterior probabilities y_i differ more from the prior probabilities x_i. In the latter case the forecast is considered more valuable when the posterior probabilities y_i are closer to the prior probabilities x_i." (Theil, 1967, p. 48).

8 "It is quite interesting to compare the average conditional entropies with the correlation coefficients in regression analysis. Actually, the objective of analysis of this section and its predecessor is largely the same as that of regression analysis, because in both cases we are interested in 'explaining' the behavior of some dependent variable (here : production plan revisions) in terms of certain independent variables (surprises on orders received and the appraisal of inventories)." (Theil, 1967, p.58).

up an "informational econometrics", and the application of STI to determine the choice of an econometric model.

According to Onicescu and Botez, the relations between exogenous and endogenous values, considered as random variables, follow the general expression $Pr\{Y\in A/X=\alpha\}$, A be a measurable domain in the space R^n of the values of Y. Then the relation Y=f(X) between the endogenous variables of Y and the exogenous variables of X is replaced by a formulation that follows the properties of the informational statistics (Onicescu and Botez, 1978, p.306).

The second contribution of the STI concerns the determination of the best model. Lancry (1982). "Then what is called the true values of the parameters are only pseudo-true values which are obtained by means of a minimization of the informational distance between the reality and the retained model. Thanks to the estimators of the maximum likelihood, one estimates the law that is closer to the true unknown law, (Lancry, 1982, p.103).

The STI equally contributed to the achievement of results in game theory, particularly in evolutionary game theory. Indeed, the stability of equilibrium can be defined by means of the relative entropy measure that appraises the distance between the distributions of probabilities in the frame of a game with mixed strategies. The formula $H_x(y)$ measures the entropy of the distribution x relatively to the distribution y. "If a strategy x earns a higher payoff against a strategy y in the domain of entropy function H_x, the evolutionary selection, modeled by replicator dynamics, induces a reduction in the relative entropy $H_x(y)$ at the population y and hence moves into lower contour sets of H_x." (Weibull, 1993, p.28). In fact, those works are inspired by the Kullback's ones (1959) that defines the quantity of information by means of the selection between two laws of probabilities. He then measures the distance between distributions of probabilities, and finally $H_x(y)$ and the Theil's I(y/x) are identical.

The STI and the economics of information.

Lancry considers that the economics of information "is also link to the Shannonian conception but we will not find the same formalisms than those used in Theil's works." (Lancry, 1982, p.77). However, if the initial works due to Marschak and Arrow end up to similar results than Shannon's ones -a point of view which is questionable- they become progressively far from the initial Shannon's own conceptions.

In fact, the notion of information that the economists are used to employ different from the Shannon's one. As an example (Hirshleifer 1973) after defining uncertainty as a measure of the dispersion of the individuals subjective probabilities on the states of the world, considers the information as the set of events that are able to modify those distributions of probabilities. And he compares this definition with an alternative one used by the "statistical theory of communication" that shows that a dispersed distribution of probabilities is considered as less informative that a concentrated one. (Hirshleifer, 1973, p.31). He adds that the STI (or STC) uses the notion of information as a negative measure of uncertainty. The economics of information considers an information as a means to reduce uncertainty, that is to say the dispersion of the beliefs concerning the possible states of the world. At the opposite, the STI conceives an information as a quantity that measures the surprise we have when a state of the world is realized. If the probability of an event is important, that is to say that the other events have little chance to be realized, the quantity of information contained in this event is low, while when all the events are equally probable, the quantity of information is maximal et then the uncertainty is also maximal. In fact uncertainty and "expected information" are dual notions (Theil, 1967). Uncertainty is appraised before the message, and the information is what the message allows to reveal[9]. Finally, according to the STI low uncertainty and few information are equivalent whereas according to the economics of information, those two notions are antithetical: information reduces uncertainty.

From this point of view, as we will see below, the difference between the two conceptions is rooted first in the fact that for the STI the information is only existing by means of the quantity that measures it, whereas according to the economics of information, it is not measured per se, it is a qualitative variable, but it is appraised by means of the effects it can have on the behaviors whose effects are measurable.

The point of departure of the economics of information is to consider that a decision-maker determines his action according to signals of information, as an example the prices. It exists, in fact, two types of information, the primary and the future information:

- The first one is link to the knowledge of 1) the set X of the states of the world, 2) the distribution of probabilities p_i on this set, 3) the set A of the possible actions, and 4) the utility functions u(A,X) of the possible actions.

- The second is constituted of the set of the messages that the decision-maker can receive from his environment before taking his decision. This set Y of messages gives a partial description of the set X. Y can then be conceived as creating a partition on X. The relation between the two sets constitutes a "structure of information". If X is, as an example, the set of the firms of an economy; the set Y of the information on the profits of those firms permits to partition X into sub-sets defined from the grouping of the elements of Y. A function of information is such as it creates a functional relation between the elements of Y and the elements of X.

The problem is then to maximize the expected utility of the realized action, the individual being able to modify his function of action and his function of

[9] This distinction is not identical to the one established between information a priori and information a posteriori in the theories of information and of uncertainty in economics. Indeed for the STI the distinction is link to the difference of the quantity of information before and after the message, whereas according to the economics of information and uncertainty it is rooted on the difference between "terminal act" and "informational act". (Hirshleifer and Riley, 1979).

information, this last possibility being identical to an attempt to find the optimal structure of information[10].

This presentation shows that the economics of information is different from the STI inasmuch as it introduces, not only a distribution of probabilities on the set of the world, as the STI does, but also a utility function, while the Shannon's analysis defines the information only according to the distribution of probabilities of a set of signals. The Arrow's critics (1984) concerning the lack of value of the information is then justified. In other words the demand for information is not taken into account by the STI. Indeed (Arrow 1974) writes that the canals of information can be abandoned or created, and that their capacities and the types of signals that are transmitted are subject to choices which lay on an evaluation, in terms of benefits and costs. If we assume that an adequate coding of a message permits a reduction of the error on the knowledge of the state of the world, then we can assimilate the Shannonian conception of information to the sole supply of information (Arrow, 1984, Lancry, 1982). Against such a limitation, Arrow proposes a definition of an information which is considered as any signal that is able to modify the distribution of probabilities, that is to say the individuals' beliefs, on the state of the world. In other world the acquisition of information is linked to the difference between the distribution of probabilities a priori and a posteriori, difference that results of the reception by an individual of a message coming from his environment. Arrow adds :

"This definition of information is qualitative, and so it will remain for the purposes of this volume. The quantitative definition which appears in information theory is probably of only limited value for economic analysis, for reasons pointed out by Marschak; different bit of information, equal from the viewpoint of information theory, will usually have very different benefits or costs. Thus let A and B be any two statements about the world, for neither of which is its truth or falsity known a priori. Then a signal that A is true convey exactly as much information, in the sense of Shannon, as the statement that B is true. But the value of knowing whether or not A is true may be vastly greater than the value of knowing B's truth-value; or it may be that the resources needed to ascertain the truth-value of A are much greater than those for B. In either case, the information-theoretic equivalence of the two possible signals conceals their vast economic difference." (Arrow, 1974, p.38).

The economics of information, however, borrows some results from the STI. (Laffont 1991) shows, as an example, that the theorem of the maximal capacity of a canal of information can be applied to the problem of the revelation of the quality by the prices. Indeed, if the number m of the variables that describe the quality of goods is different from the number n that describes the relative prices, that is if $m \neq n$, then if $m<n$, there exist some totally revelator equilibria, if $m=n$, then there are some robust counter-examples of non existence, and if $m>n$, there

---

10 If we find an optimal struture of information, we can compare two structures of information only by comparing the sharpness of their associated partitions. (Laffont, 1991).

are some equilibria with noise if the price functions are very discontinuous. (Laffont, 1991, p.156). According to Lesourne, "for those who were interested in the Shannon's theory, its results are easily understandable: the prices, as canals of information, have a maximal capacity, they can then generally transmit only information that have a lower variety than this capacity." (Lesourne, 1991, p.109).

Until now I have supposed that the STI is not an evolving theory. Such an assumption is too strong and it is not difficult to see that the STI is right now very different if compared to the Shannon's one. Indeed first it takes into account some of its critics, second it takes to the fore such important ideas as complexity or self-organized processes.

2. THE STI, SELF-ORGANIZATION, COMPLEXITY AND ECONOMIC ANALYSIS

In this section I will analyze the consequences on economics of the evolutions of the STI models. Indeed, the von Foerster's (1960) as well as the Atlan's (1972) contributions are selected because they modify dramatically the initial STI conceptions, and they open the door to the analysis of complex systems, which are usually considered as specifying the economic phenomena.

The main characteristics of those models are the following :

- First they study systems where the number of elements as well as the relations between them are extremely important.
- Second they are based on the fact that "noise" is able to produce order.
- Third those systems are self organized[11].
- Fourth, break down, bifurcations, and punctuated equilibria possibly appear.

I will not analyze all those models[12] that are very different (Atlan, 1972, Le Moigne, 1986, Garrouste and Héraud, 1992), but only those that are based on the STI main principles.

In this way two authors need to be analyzed, Atlan and von Foerster, inasmuch as they inspired many developments in economics. Before looking at the application of those two kinds of models, I will first show how they are rooted in the STI main conceptions.

Self organization and the STI main principles.

Let x and y be two events, the quantity of information of the event y given x is :

---

[11] According to Walliser self-organization is the « capacity of a system to make emerging from local processes a global structure which is neither imposed by a superior authority nor deliberately elaborated by the basic elements." (Walliser, 1988, p.254).

[12] I will not present some important and interesting models such as Mesarovic and alii (1980), Beer (1959), Le Moigne (1986), Prigogine and Stengers (1970), Maturana (1970) and Varela (1979). For a detailed presentation of the integration of self-organization models in economics, see Paulré (1997).

$$H(y/x) = -\sum_{ij} p(i)p(j/i)\log_2 p(j/i)$$

where p(i) and p(j) are the probabilities of x and y and p(j/i) the conditional probability of y given x. H(y/x) measures the reduction of uncertainty that the event x induces in the set of the two elements. If H(y/x) = H(x)+H(y), the two events are independent. At the opposite, if H(y/x) = H(x) = H(y), it is self sufficient to know one of the two events in order to know the other. The relation between the technical and service characteristics of a product (Metcalfe, Saviotti, 1984) can be analyzed on this way.

When a message is circulating from a transmitter to a receiver, the quantity of information, given the emitted message, is a measure of the ambiguity of this message. In other words, there is an uncertainty on the output message even if the input one is known. Indeed if the information given by x is not sufficient to know y then there is an ambiguity which is measured by H(y/x).

The "equivocation" is the opposite situation where the output message is known and where the uncertainty is concerning the input message. The equivocation is then measured by H(x/y).

Before a message is transmitted, it needs to be coded. Indeed it is the very problem Shannon tries to solve in the article he presents before the Macy group. He thinks that the redundancy is able to reduce both the quantity of information and the negative effect of noise.

According to Atlan the noise has an ambivalent effect. On the one hand it has a negative effect because it reduces the quantity of information, but on the other hand, it can produce information.

Indeed, let two substructures 1 and 2 receiving a message x. The quantity of information transmitted by those two elements are respectively $H(y_1)$ and $H(y_2)$. If H is the quantity of information transmitted by both the substructures, two extreme cases are possible :

$H = H(y_1)+H(y_2)$

$H = H(y_1) = H(y_2)$

In the first case, the two elements are independent that is to say that there is no constraint between them. In the second case the constraints are so important that the information coming from one element is sufficient to know all about the second. Such an analysis can be applied to an organization if each substructure is an individual or a group of individuals exchanging information.

If there is some noise in the canal linking the substructures, then the quantity of information transmitted becomes:

$$H = H(y_1) + H(y_2 / y_1) - H(y_1 / x)$$

In this expression, $-H(y_1/x)$ measures the loss of information due to a perturbation coming from the environment, but $H(y_2/y_1)$ measures the gain of information that the noise introduces in the transmission of the information inside the two substructures.

When the number of elements as well as the relations between them are much more important, some properties are emerging.

THE ATLAN'S MODEL (1972).

In this kind of models, the noise has "two opposite effects : on the one hand it implies a growth of the total quantity of information of the system, by means of the growth of the autonomy of the parts of this system; on the other hand, it diminishes this quantity of information by the accumulation of errors in the structures of the parts." (Atlan, 1972, pp.264-65). The quantity of information that we perceive from a system is given by the following formula:

$$H = H_{\max}(1 - R)$$

H_{max} be the maximum quantity of information transmitted by the system and R be its redundancy.

The idea is that a system, transforms progressively, due to some random environmental factors, the redundancy into complexity and then H is growing up. When there is no more redundancy the quantity of information is diminishing until the death of the system. This double process can be expressed by the derivation of H:

$$\frac{dH}{dt} = -H_{\max}\frac{dR}{dt} + (1 - R)\frac{dH_{\max}}{dt}$$

The first term of the right side of the equation that expresses the diminution of the redundancy is positive because it measures the effects of the ambiguity-autonomy (that is the creation of order from noise); the second is negative because it is the result of the destructive ambiguity. (Atlan, 1972).

Applied to the firm such an approach permits to put to the fore the following phenomena:

- A firm at the very beginning of its creation possesses a capacity of redundancy that allows it to correct the errors of transmission between its elements
- Due to a process of learning it looses progressively what permits it to learn that is to say its redundancy
- The destruction of the redundancy of the firm is generating both variety and specificity
- The lost of redundancy generates the disappearance of the coherence of the firm.

Those propositions are acceptable because of an analogy between the theory of information and the thermodynamics. The first proposition is equivalent to the principle of the conservation of energy. In other word there is no creation of energy but only some transformation of a kind of energy into another kind of energy. The second proposition is the same as the second principle that establishes a hierarchy in the quality of the different types of energy: the redundancy is progressively transformed in an irreversible way into complexity.

Such a conception permits to measure the complexity of a system. According to Atlan the complexity c is:

$$c = H_{\max} - H_0$$
$$with$$
$$\frac{dH_{\max}}{dt} = 0$$

Even if Atlan modifies considerably this initial model, it seems difficult to apply it as it is to social and economic phenomena[13]. Indeed the fact that the complexity is defined as a quantity of information and the assumption that there is an initial stock of redundancy which is necessarily decreasing are strong hypothesis.

It is why the von Foerster's model is interesting to present.

THE VON FOERSTER'S MODEL.

This model (Foerster, 1960), at the opposite of the Atlan's one defined a self-organized system as a system which the degree of order is increasing, that is:

$$\frac{dR}{dt} > 0$$

If we differentiate $R = (1- H)/H_{max}$, then:

$$\frac{dR}{dt} = -\frac{(H_{\max}(dH/_{dt}) - H(dH_{\max}/_{dt})}{H^2_{\max}}$$

If we consider that the system is such that $H_{max} \neq 0$ the conditions for this system to be self-organized are given by:

---

[13] Walliser pertinently makes the remark that this transcription is not assure because the strengths that are functioning in the two cases are not the same. One touches the limits of the analogies physics-biology-economics.

$$H(^{dH_{\max}}/_{dt}) > H_{\max}(^{dH}/_{dt})$$

Two extreme cases can be identified. The first where H_{max} is constant, the second where H is.

In the first case the condition for self-organization is : $dH/dt < 0$. In other words the increasing of the order is equivalent to a decreasing of the quantity of information. That means that the constraints inside the system are growing due to the action of the internal demon.

In the second case the condition is : $dH_{max}/dt > 0$. The maximum quantity of information of the system is increasing without any modification of the quantity of information of the system. According to von Foerster, there is something like an external demon that is filtering and arranging the new elements of the system in order to avoiding any augmentation of its entropy.

When H_{max} and H are evolving together the two demons need to "work" together.

Due to its very object, those STI models cannot let the economists indifferent. The applicability of their results depends however on the kind of models selected. Indeed if one mobilizes or not such phenomena as the creation of order out of noise (or disorder) that we find in Atlan's or von Foerster's models, the cost of the application is not the same. I will rapidly present different possibilities of application of those models and show their limits.

The interest of those models, as compared to STI initial ones, is their attempt to reintroduce the significance of the information. Atlan (1979), MacKay (1969) or Pask (1990) try to solve this problem which limits the capacity to deal with the demand for information. The Atlan's solution is to consider that the significance of an information is to be found in the reaction of the receiver of this information. Implicitly he assumes a univocal relation between a message and an action. Mac Kay critics this solution as behavioral and defines the significance if a message as a selective function in the set of the receptive states of the "conditional readiness" for a finalized action. (MacKay, 1969, p.24). In other words, the individuals set up some structures of response that are activated by means of the messages they receive. Such a conception is not without relations with the Hayekian conception of the way rules are built up. The significance of an information is a function of the response it activates into the set of the repertoires of response of the communicant systems.

Those models of self-organization allow to explain, the functioning of an economy (Lesourne, 1991), the dynamics of a network (Garrouste, Gonzales, 1995), the individual as well collective learning processes (Ancori, 1992), the organizational learning (Langlois, Garrouste, 1997), and more recently the first elements of an axiomatization of a complex economy (Delorme, 1997).

Those applications take into account, from an endogenous point of view, the process of creation of information, whereas the economics of information analyzes the creation of new canals of information. The idea of a creation of order out of disorder, that the famous von Foerster's magnets illustrate, permits to take into account the fact that new information can be generated by means of some perturbations coming from the environment of a system.

As an example the learning process inside the firm, the constitution of routines, the changes of those routines can be conceived as the results of the endogenous functioning of the firm, inasmuch as the firm is modeled by means of both the Atlan's and the von Foerster's ways. "Clearly, however, our intuitive notion of 'highly organized' encompasses both Atlan's notion of complexity as high H –or, more appropriate, H_{max}- and von Foerster notion of orderliness as redundancy. In other words, self-organization means both increased complexity (or variety) and increased redundancy." (Langlois, Garrouste, 1997, p.297).

CONCLUSION

At the beginning, the limits of the STI are due to its object. Indeed the theory developed by Shannon, analyzes the modification in the quantity of information contained into a message circulating between a transmitter and a receiver through a canal. It appraises the efficiency of the canal of transmission and the coding problems. Those limits did not prevent the economists from using the STI results to analyze the economic prevision, the industrial concentration, or the proposed applications in econometrics. The economics of information is also in debt with the STI, even if it progressively evolves away from the basic postulates of STI. Some recent works, rooted into the STI, try to introduce self-organization and complexity in their models, and it is tempting to propose some applications of those models in economics.

While the appraisal of the first borrows from STI is relatively easy to do, the appraisal of more recent models, based on self-organization is much more difficult to do because of this "recentness".

References

Ancori B. (1992), "Apprentissage auto-organisationnel et problématique du choix individuel", in Ancori, B. (ed.) Apprendre, se souvenir, décider ; une nouvelle rationalité de l'organisation, Paris, éditions du CNRS.

Arrow K. (1974), The limits of organization, New York, London, W.W. Norton & Company.

Atlan H. (1972), L'organisation biologique et la théorie de l'information, Paris, Hermann.

- (1979), Entre le cristal et la fumée; essai sur l'organisation du vivant, Paris, Seuil.
- (1986), A tort et à raison; intercritique de la science et du mythe, Paris, Seuil.

Beer S. (1959), Cybernetics and management, London, The English Universities Press.

Boulding K. (1955), "Notes on the Information Concept", Explorations, 6, p.103-112.

Brillouin L. (1959), La science et la théorie de l'information, Paris, Masson.

Delorme R. (1997), "Evolution et complexité : l'apport de la complexité de second ordre à l'économie évolutionnaire", Economie Appliquée, Tome L, n°3, p.95-120.

Foerster H. von (1960), "On self-organizing systems and their environments", in Yovits, M.C. and Cameron, S. (eds) Self-organizing Systems, New York, Pergamon Press.

Garrouste P. et Gonzales S. (1995), "Information, processus d'apprentissage, et évolution d'un réseau : le cas du GBM, in Economies et Sociétés, série Dynamique technologique et organisation, 2, 9 , p.119-138.

Garrouste P. et Heraud J.A. (1992), "Auto-organisation et création technologique", in Ancori, B. (ed.) Apprendre, se souvenir, décider ; une nouvelle rationalité de l' organisation, Paris, éditions du CNRS.

Heims S.J. (1993), Constructing a Social Science for Postwar America ; The Cybernetics Group, 1946-1953, Cambridge, MIT Press.

Hirshleifer J. (1973), "Where are we in the theory of information?", American Economic Review, May, p.31-39.

Hirshleifer J. et Riley J. (1979), "The analytics of uncertainty and information : An expository Survey", Journal of Economic Literature, 17; p.1375-1421.

Kullback S. (1959), Information and Statistics, New York, Wiley.

Laffont G. (1991), Economie de l'incertain et de l'information, Cours de Théorie économique, vol.2, Paris, Economica.

Lancry P.J. (1982), Théorie de l'information et économie, Paris, Economica.

Langlois R. et Garrouste P. (1997), "Cognition, Redundancy and Learning in Organizations", Economics of Innovation and New Technology, 4 :287-299.

Lesourne J. (1991), Economie de l'ordre et du désordre, Paris : Economica.

Le Moigne J.L. (1986) (éd), Intelligence des mécanismes, mécanismes de l'intelligence, Paris, Fayard.

Maturana H. (1970), "The neurophysiology of cognition", in Garvin, P. (ed.) Cognition : A multiple View, New York, Spartan Books.

MacKay D.M. (1969), Information, Mechanism, and Meaning, Cambridge, MIT Press.

Mesarovic M.D., Macko D. et Takahara Y. (1980), Théorie des systèmes hiérarchiques à niveaux multiples, Paris, Economica.

Onicescu O. et Botez M. (1978), "Essai d'économétrie informationnelle", Economie Appliquée, 3, 4, p.305-318.

Paulre B. (1997), "Evolutionnisme contemporain et auto-organisation", Economie Appliquée, tome L, p. 121-150.

Prigogine I. et Stengers I. (1979), La nouvelle alliance, métamorphose de la science, Paris, Gallimard.

Rasmusen E. (1994), Games and Information, an Introduction to Game Theory, Cambridge, Basil Blackwell.

Shannon C.E. (1956), "The Bandwagon", IEEE trans. on Information Theory, 2.

Shannon C.E. et Weaver W. (1949), The Mathematical Theory of Communication, Chicago, University of Illinois Press.

Stiglitz J.E. (1994), Whither Socialism, Cambridge, the MIT Press.
- (1985), "Information and Economic Analysis, A Perspective", Economic Journal, 95, p.21-41.

Theil H. (1967), Economics and Information Theory, Amsterdam : North-Holland.

Thionet P. (1959), "Les pertes d'information en théorie des sondages", INSEE, Etude Théorique, n°7.

Thionet P. (1963), Application de la notion shannonienne à la des tableaux statistiques", Cahier de comptabilité nationale, 8, p. 362-365.

Varela F. (1979), Principles of Biological Autonomy, New York, Elsevier.

Walliser B. (1988), "Systémique et économie", Revue Internationale de Systémique, 2, 3, p. 245-260.

Weibull (1993), "Single-population dynamics : the basic model", miméo.

Zadjenweber D. (1972), "Une application de la théorie de l'information à l'économie : la mesure de la concentration industrielle", Revue d'Economie Politique, 3, p.490-510.

Chapter 3

STRUCTURE AND ROLE OF INFORMATION AND BELIEFS IN GAME THEORY

Bernard Walliser

Professor Ecole Nationale des Ponts et Chaussées
CERAS, Paris

In economic theory, especially in competitive equilibrium, an agent adapts his behaviour to an environment considered as exogenous, essentially the price system and some physical factors. In game theory, eventually applied to imperfect competition, a player faces a strategic environment formed of other players, whose actions have interrelated consequences with his own moves. In both cases, the perception by an actor of his environment was successively taken into account by means of information about his past, expectations about his future and beliefs about its structure. Hence, besides the preferences of the individual classically considered, his beliefs are introduced as another kind of mental states, and together are the cornerstones of his mental deliberation.

This study is an essential part of the « cognitivist paradigm », which is interested in the players'knowledge and coordination and lies on cognitive science, especially epistemic logics. But it has also tight links with the « evolutionist paradigm », which is concerned with the player's learning and networks and lies on system dynamics, especially stochastic processes. These paradigms are firmly related in « cognitive economics » since the players' beliefs are duly revised through time, while their bounded rationality is compensated by the work of time. Moreover, the models are tested by experimental psychology, which applies to belief operations the methods of cognitive psychology, and confronts game experiments with game simulations.

After a brief recall of information taxonomies in game theory (§1), four problems related to beliefs are successively treated. The individual belief structure, endowed with set-theoretic or probabilistic uncertainty (§2), applies to the value of information, often negative in a game (§3). The collective knowledge hierarchy, culminating in common knowledge (§4), justifies some equilibria by sophisticated players' reasoning (§5). The individual belief revision, taking place in different contexts of change (§6), allows a strategic use of information when it is diffused among players (§7). The collective belief revision, which is a strong incentive for some consensus (§8), justifies some equilibria by the convergence of learning processes (§9).

P. Petit (ed.), Economics and Information, 49–59.

1. INFORMATION TAXONOMY

In a game, the modeller considers two types of actors, endowed with contrasted modes of behaviour :

- a passive one, Nature, taking states generated by a mechanical and often stochastic rule ;
- active ones, the players, taking actions resulting from a rational deliberation process.

Player's rationality combines three main characteristics : opportunities, preferences and beliefs, in two complementary ways. Cognitive rationality deals with the dynamic adjustment of beliefs to information gathered all along the play. Instrumental rationality deals with the consistency of the actions with opportunities and preferences, given instantaneous beliefs.

In such a game, the modeller distinguishes two essential types of information :

- structural information, which concerns the structure of the game and is fixed all along, is composed, about Nature, of the state generating rule and, about players, of their exogenous characteristics (opportunities, preferences, prior beliefs) and of their forms of rationality (cognitive and instrumental) ;
- factual information, which summarises the play of the game and evolves with its progress, is either « retrospective » and deals with the states and actions having occured in the past, or « prospective » and deals with the states and actions expected by players for the future.

Each player is himself affected with some uncertainty on these elements :

- « structural uncertainty » concerns, besides the rationality of other players, their exogenous characteristics (« incomplete information ») ; it is treated by considering that other's characteristics are summarised in a « type », considered as a state selected by Nature ;
- « retrospective uncertainty » deals with the past actions of the other players as well as the past states (« imperfect information ») ; it is treated dynamically by considering that the game tree nodes not discriminated by the player are gathered in an information set ;
- « prospective uncertainty » deals with the future actions of other players and eventually Nature playing sequentially (« strategic information ») ; it is treated by considering the mental process by which the player simulates the other's deliberation process.

In a first step, each player uses its retrospective factual information in order to reduce his structural uncertainty, especially by revealing progressively the other's type through the implemented actions. In a second step, each player rests on his structural information in order to reduce his prospective uncertainty, by expecting the other's action from the other's assumed type combined with his own action. Hence, the action of each player depending on the other's one (through his preferences), each player is engaged in a hierarchy of crossed expectations on the actions (« I expect that you expect that I expect… »).That hierarchy is itself grounded on a hierarchy of crossed beliefs on the types and forms of rationality (« I know that you know that I know… »).

2. INDIVIDUAL KNOWLEDGE STRUCTURE

The player's uncertainty is « semantically » formalised by considering that he faces a set of « possible worlds », each world reflecting a possible occurrence of the game elements affected by uncertainty. Uncertainty is « set-theoretic » when the player is unable to discriminate between worlds in a set of worlds (or « event ») ; for instance, he considers all nodes in an information set without being able to weight them. Uncertainty is « probabilistic » when the player is able to define a probability distribution on the whole set of worlds ; for instance, he is frequently endowed with a prior probability distribution on the other's types. Finally, the events or distributions considered by the player may be conditional to the « real world », known only by the modeller, and define an accessibility relation from each conceivable world.

For each player, it is possible to consider a hierarchical belief structure about himself (« I know that I know that… ») alternating set-theoretic as well as probabilistic levels. In a bi-probabilistic structure, a player has a probabilistic « uncertainty » on a stochastic phenomenon at first level, and a probabilistic « ambiguity » on his first level evaluation at the second level. In a family of probabilities, a player is uncertain between possible probability distributions, hence affects an interval of probability and not a precise probability to any event. In a distribution of events, a player has a weighted evaluation of alternative events, which is equivalent to a Dempter-Shafer belief function, a non-linear generalisation of a probability distribution.

The player's belief is « syntactically » formalised by considering that he faces basic propositions, and is endowed with a knowledge operator stating whether he knows or not each given proposition. A correspondence rule allows to build a bridge between the syntactic and the semantic form, propositions between translated into events, and the knowledge operator linked to the accessibility relation. In a set-theoretic framework, a player knows a proposition in a given world if and only if the corresponding event is true in all worlds which are accessible from this given world. In a probabilistic framework, a player knows a proposition with probability α in a given world if and only if the corresponding event has probability α according to the corresponding accessibility distribution.

If the (deterministic) accessibility relation defines a partition on the set of worlds, the associated belief operator obeys to some strong properties. Besides logical omniscience always satisfied (a player knows all consequences of what he knows), they concern truth (what a player believes is true), positive introspection (a player knows what he knows) and negative introspection (a player knows what he does not know). However, the accessibility relation may be less constrained and leads to weaker properties, reflecting various forms of bounded cognitive rationality. For instance, weakening logical omniscience reflects player's limited capacities for computing information, and weakening truth induces the difference between « knowledge » (always true) and « belief » (eventually false).

3. INDIVIDUAL VALUE OF INFORMATION

In a « Bayesian game », a player's belief is defined by a two-fold « information structure » on the possible worlds, a partitional set-theoretic structure (private information) and a prior probability distribution (public information). A player's strategy is defined as the retained action conditionally on each possible world, knowing that he has to apply the same action in two worlds he is unable to discriminate. The player's expected utility in a given world, for fixed strategies of the other players, is the expected utility (according to his prior) he obtains for all worlds accessible from it. A Bayesian equilibrium is nothing else than a Nash equilibrium of the extended game, i.e. a profile of strategies such that each one is a best response to others' equilibrium strategies.

Since the possible worlds are restricted to states of Nature (eventually including players' types), the private information structure of each player reflects the message-event he got in each possible world. The information structures can now be ordered according to the information content of the associated message, a structure being finer than another if the accessibility domain of the first is included in that of the second for each world. The extreme structures correspond to total uncertainty (in each world, all other worlds are accessible) and to certainty (in each world, only this world is accessible). Finally, the ex ante value of information induced by an information structure finer than another is nothing else than the difference of expected utility obtained by the player for some choice based on each structure.

When restricting to individual choice under probabilistic uncertainty, the fundamental result states, for a partitional information structure, that the ex ante value of information for the decision-maker is always positive. It means that, if the decision-maker receives some message (considered as true) conditional on the real world which appears, his average utility on all possible messages is always increasing. However, this result fails when the information structure is no more partitional, for instance when positive introspection is no more satisfied or obviously when the message may be wrong. Conversely, the result holds for a probabilistic information structure, where the message is itself probabilistic and leads to a finer probability distribution on worlds (« probabilistic mixture »).

When considering a true game framework, the fundamental result is no longer valid, even for partitional information structures, and the ex ante value of information may be negative for some player. Quite naturally, when a player learns the type of the other (for instance the production cost of a firm), such a message may be favourable for the first one and unfavourable for the second one. More subtly, when both players learn some unknown state of Nature (for instance some mutually insured contingency), such a message may be unfavourable to both players who prefer not to know. Even more, it is impossible for some player to come back to a better situation by ignoring the message, since each player knows that the other has the information and acts in a consequent way.

4. COLLECTIVE KNOWLEDGE HIERARCHY

Syntactically, considering all individual knowledge operators, it is possible to define different degrees of knowledge diffusion, according to the distribution of (crossed) knowledge among players. A proposition is said to be « implicit knowledge » if no player knows it on his own, but gathering in a single knowledge all local knowledge would lead by modeller's deduction to the given proposition. A proposition is said to be « shared knowledge at order k » if each player knows it, knows that the others know it, and so on at successive levels till the k-level of crossed knowledge. A proposition is said to be « common knowledge » if it is shared knowledge at order ∞, such a hierarchical definition resting on the knowledge of an infinite number of propositions.

The common knowledge operator obeys itself to some of the properties previously introduced on individual knowledge operators, if these last do, for instance positive introspection. The common knowledge operator may be defined in a circular way too, i.e. a proposition is common knowledge if it is shared knowledge that it is true and that it is common knowledge. The circular definition implies the hierarchical one, but the converse is not true ; in fact, the circular notion appears as a formal fixed point while the hierarchical notion is constructive. The common knowledge of some event is finally implied by the fact that it is a public event ; it follows from the observation of occurrence of the event by all players, under the others' look.

In semantics, in a set-theoretic framework, the notions of shared and common knowledge have as counterpart a collective accessibility relation which can be deduced from the individual ones. Specifically, if the players have partitional information structures on the possible worlds space, the partition characterising common knowledge is the finest partition among all partitions coarser than the individual ones. To ensure that, it is necessary that the individual accessibility relations are themselves common knowledge, a condition satisfied in an informal way, but difficult to fulfil properly in a more formal way. Conversely, if the players have only bounded cognitive rationality, they may not be able to achieve common knowledge of some event, and are limited for instance to shared knowledge at fixed level k.

Always in semantics, in a probabilistic framework, the counterpart is less obvious when the players are syntactically endowed with a probabilistic belief hierarchy on physical states, submitted to consistency conditions. It is nevertheless possible to define a unique probability distribution on a possible worlds space where each world represents a hierarchy of physical and mental states, especially the common knowledge world. It can be shown that a probabilistic belief hierarchy summarises the player's knowledge, in the sense that the knowledge of the hierarchy gives no further information to the hierarchy itself. Conversely, such a hierarchy allows to define a weak form of common knowledge, where each player knows the other's probability distribution only with probability 1-ε at each level.

5. COGNITIVE JUSTIFICATION OF EQUILIBRIA

In game theory, the usual notions of equilibria are defined as stationary states of the game, i.e. states which stay unchanged in the absence of perturbations of the physical environment of the game. More precisely, in a Nash equilibrium, the players' strategies are characterised by the fact that no one has an interest to deviate unilaterally from it, once it has been established. However, the process allowing to reach some equilibrium is not expressed, except if one introduces a fictitious device, the Nash regulator, which computes an equilibrium state and suggests it to the players. The players are induced to accept that suggestion if the other players accept it too, but they may have a doubt about the others' attitude especially in case of multiple equilibria.

By contrast, the « cognitive justification » of equilibria tries to ground the equilibrium notions only on the mental reasoning of the players, i. e. to consider them as « belief equilibria » in the players' minds. Technically, in addition to the states of Nature and the exogenous players' characteristics, the endogenous players' strategies are introduced in the possible worlds space. The players are always assumed to be Bayesian rational, i.e. they maximise their expected utility with regard to the possible worlds, although the worlds are no more exogenous but partially endogenous. It is even assumed that it is common knowledge that the players are Bayesian rational ; according to some further assumptions on the players' beliefs, different equilibrium notions are sorted out.

In statics, with the assumption that it is common knowledge that the players play independently, one obtains a « rationalisable equilibrium », a far weaker notion than Nash equilibrium. It states that each player's equilibrium strategy is a best response to the other players' expected strategies, the last assessed as best responses to expected strategies of others, and so on till looping at same level. It is harder to obtain the Nash equilibrium itself, and it is in fact necessary to state that the players have a shared knowledge of their respective conjectures, a conjecture being an other's expected strategy. Moreover, if there are many rationalisable or Nash equilibria, it is necessary to select one through « conventions » which are common knowledge, even if their origin is again not explicitly given.

In dynamics, common knowledge of rationality seems enough to define a « subgame perfect equilibrium », a stronger notion than Nash equilibrium, computed mentally by a backward induction procedure. Each player at an end node of the game tree chooses his best response, then each player at a node before optimises conditionally on what the next will do and so on till the initial node. However, one faces the « backward induction paradox » which states that a player reasoning by backward induction may encounter a situation in contradiction with his prior assumptions and revise them accordingly. Hence, cognitive assumptions concerning the player's belief structure and revision have to be made precise, and lead to dynamic equilibrium notions which are generally weaker than perfect equilibrium.

6. INDIVIDUAL BELIEF CHANGE

In syntax, the belief change process assumes that the actor is endowed with some initial belief and receives some message about his environment, these two sources of information being eventually contradictory. A « homogeneity principle » states that the player looks for a final belief which is logically consistent and of same structure than the initial belief (message adopting generally a simpler structure). A « priority principle » assumes, especially in case of contradiction, that the message is considered as true while the initial belief may be false (rather than dealing with both elements on an equal foot). An « economy principle » postulates that, if initial belief may not be modified, it is unchanged, and if it must be modified, the modification adopted is a « minimal » one in a technical sense.

The change rules have to be adapted to the change context, each context being defined by the nature of the message involved, even if the third one can be reduced to the first. Revising happens when the message makes more precise or contradicts the initial belief about the real system considered as unchanged, for instance the probability distribution of the states of Nature. Updating happens when the message gives some information about the transformation or the end state of the real system treated as evolving, for instance about the consequences of some action of a player. Focusing happens when the message gives an indication about a specific object extracted at random from a system of objects, for instance about the type of a given player (through his action).

In semantics, if the initial belief is set-theoretic as well as the message, the final belief is obtained by keeping the worlds of the message which are the nearest from the initial belief for some distance. This procedure consists, in syntax, to add the propositions of the message to those of the initial belief, and in case of contradiction, to abandon the less « epistemically entrenched » ones till restoring consistency. If the initial belief is probabilistic and the message set-theoretic, the final belief is obtained by selecting the same worlds than before, and allocating to these new worlds the weights of the old worlds. This « generalised Bayes rule » can be applied whether or not the prior probability distribution contradicts or not the message and can be reduced to the usual Bayes rule only under drastic further conditions.

The belief change methods can be extended, for a given initial belief, to probabilistic messages expressing the probability of possible worlds, associated to each observed signal (Jeffrey rule). Similarly, they are extended, for a given set-theoretic message, to initial beliefs weaker than probability distributions, especially to Dempster-Shafer belief functions (Dempster rule, Fagin-Halpern rule). All methods are finally reconsidered when they are used iteratively, for a sequence of messages, and are submitted to additional dynamical properties, according to the context of change. The essential ones are « commutativity » (final belief is not dependant on the order of arrival of two messages) and « idempotence » (final belief does not change again if the same message is repeated).

7. STRATEGIC USE OF INFORMATION

In game theory, a player may receive some further information, concerned with states of Nature, with other's implemented actions or with felt utility, through a more or less independent and voluntary process. Pure experimentation refers to the possibility for a player to acquire directly an exogenous information, at some cost, through an « information action » which highlights an « operational action ». Passive experimentation corresponds to a situation where information is just a by-product of the spontaneous play of the game, and is acquired at zero cost, but in a sequence imposed by the play. Active experimentation happens in a configuration where the player deviates voluntarily from his normal action in order to test his opponent, at the expense of some local loss of utility.

In the last case, the player faces a strategic trade-off between exploration of some new information to improve long-term utility and exploitation of its past information to optimise short-term utility. Of course, exploration will be dominant at the beginning of the game in order not to be locked in a wrong action, and exploitation will be dominant at the end of the game and even exclusive after some period. The optimal compromise between exploration and exploitation can be computed in some cases, especially for a single decision-maker against Nature, affected by an unknown probability law revealed through experience. But a non-optimal compromise is more often built from the start in some specific behaviour rules, allowing a player to deviate stochastically from myopic best utility actions.

A further strategic aspect of information arises when a player is aware that the action he will implement may allow an opponent to reveal the private information he possesses and has influenced his choice. If the revealed information is favourable to him, he tries to make it as clear and univoque as possible, especially when the present action is a signal for the future actions he intends to implement. If the revealed information is unfavourable to him, he tries to hide it by a voluntarily deviated move, however trading off between the induced cost of revealed information and intrinsic benefit of action. In the second case, he may even go further and try to induce the other to reveal a false information, which goes in the way of his own interest, even if he knows that the other is aware of such a trick.

This especially happens in signalling games where one player has a private information on a state of nature (eventually his own type), sends a message to another player who responds after reception by a final action. According to the players' relative interests, the equilibrium is revealing (the first player sends a different message for each state), not revealing (the first player sends the same message whatever the state) or mixed. A player may even bluff by letting believe that his information about the state of Nature is different from the true one, for instance for a poker player about the cards he holds. He may also build a reputation for himself by letting believe that he is of another type than he really is, for instance for a manager about his soft or hard type in business.

8. COLLECTIVE BELIEF ADJUSTEMENT

Consider an event for which two players have same prior probability but different information partitions, reflecting different experiences, in which case their posterior probability on the event differs too. In a sequential communication process, at each period, the players announce their last evaluation of the event, then take into account the other's evaluation to revise their own. The central result asserts that the process has to converge towards a common evaluation, i.e. they cannot « agree to disagree » as soon as their respective evaluations become common knowledge. It works as if each of them revealed (at least implicitly) the private information hold by the other, leading to the same final evaluations, even if their final information structures till differ.

More generally, consider two players who hold asymmetric beliefs and choose actions obeying to the « sure thing principle » (if they choose the same action on two disjoint events, they choose it on their union). In a sequential communication process, at each period, the players choose and implement the ongoing action, then revise their beliefs after observing the other's action. The « agreement theorem » states that the actions have to converge towards final actions justified by symmetric beliefs (and are identical when the behaviour functions are the same). For that result, which rests on stronger assumptions that the preceding one, the observed actions allow to reveal the underlying beliefs, and these beliefs tend to converge through common experience.

A first illustration is given by the « three hats problem », where three players have to find out the (blue or red) colour of the hat they wear, knowing that they observe others' hat but not their own. Beginning with an external announce which builds a common knowledge (for instance, « there is at least a red hat » if all hats are red), at successive periods, each player says if he knows his hat's colour. In this game, after three periods at most (after three periods exactly if all hats are red), the players know the colour of their hat by a perfect process of crossed reasoning. The reason is that the number of possible worlds (the possible distributions of colours) is finite k and reduces at each period, hence any event which is k-shared knowledge becomes common knowledge.

A second illustration concerns the « two generals problem », where two generals have to coordinate on whether to attack or not, each conjoint action being adapted to some context observed by the first general. If the context is favourable, the first general sends to the second a message of attack which has probability ε to be lost ; if the second receives it, he sends a counter-message which has some probability to be lost, and so on. In this game, the generals will never attack since they are never completely sure that the information is perfectly synchronised, a necessary condition to be incited to attack. The reason is that the number of possible worlds (the number of back and go for messages) is infinite and an event which is k-shared knowledge will never become common knowledge.

9. DYNAMIC JUSTIFICATION OF EQUILIBRIA

The cognitive justification of equilibria assumes hyper-rational players able to simulate quite perfectly the opponents' behaviour, in some « inductive process », where choices are taken at the start and further implemented. A contrasted point of view substitutes to the mental work involved by crossed expectations at successive levels the concrete work involved by sequential temporality on successive periods. The dynamic justification of equilibria assumes that players have bounded cognitive or instrumental rationality, in some « evolutionist process » where choices are taken and implemented at each period. But when rationality is weakened, many models become available, even if they are built on variations about some common principles, and admit as prototypes two contrasted forms of learning.

The confrontation principle makes precise how the players meet, each one being eventually faced with only a sample of others, or being related with a neighbourhood of players on a network. The information principle details the information the players gather, under the form of implemented actions or felt utilities, in some neighbourhood eventually limited to themselves. The evaluation principle sets out how players summarise information in some indexes associated to each action (past performance) or to the global process (aspiration level). The decision principle exhibits how players choose their action by exploiting at best the former indexes and by exploring new information through stochastic deviations.

In epistemic learning, each player chooses his best response to the other's expected action, the expectation being obtained by some belief about the other's behaviour revised through time. Especially, in fictitious play, each player attributes a probability to the opponent's future action equal to the frequency of the past observation of that action, under the assumption that his behaviour is stationary. The resulting dynamic process eventually converges towards a « self-confirming equilibrium », a weaker notion than Nash equilibrium, where nobody has an interest to deviate according to his information. The selection of an equilibrium is no more a problem since the trajectory of the system (eventually a stochastic one) is completely defined by the initial conditions and revising rules.

In behavioural learning, each player chooses an action by reinforcement of those which provided a high utility in the past et inhibition of those which provided a low utility in the past. Especially, in the CPR rule, each player computes an index of the cumulated utility obtained with each action in the past, and chooses an action with a probability proportional to its index. The resulting dynamic process eventually converges toward some equilibrium notion which is not clearly identified, but reduces frequently to a pure strategy Nash equilibrium (contrary to a mixed strategy one). The selection of an equilibrium is again automatically achieved, since the system converges to some punctual, cyclical or strange attractor conditional on the initial conditions and reinforcement rules.

CONCLUSION

In the last twenty years, game theory has succeeded in putting on the foreground players' beliefs, as the essential explaining factor (with players' preferences) of their behaviours and interactions. First, since beliefs are duly formalised and their properties exhibited, it is possible to study systematically how information is treated in player's deliberation and how it acts on the decision efficiency. Second, since beliefs allow to simulate the other's behaviour through crossed expectations and knowledge, it is possible to study how players coordinate on some equilibrium by their interactive reasoning. Third, since beliefs are revised in the light of past observations of actions and resulting payoffs, it is possible to study how players converge to some equilibrium by their correlated learning.

But in the next years, game theory has still to alleviate some weaknesses in the beliefs' approach, by intensifying his links with other social sciences concerned and by proceeding to empirical experiments. First, beliefs are considered as a stock of independent pieces of information of equal weight, rather than structural mental models with internal links and heterogenous credibility. Second, information and beliefs are semantically interpreted in a univocal and identical way for all players, rather than affected by some polysemy and divergent meanings from one to the other. Third, information is considered as directly meaningful and stored in a cumulative way, rather than submitted to a filtering process and giving rise to discontinuous restructuration.

Chapter 4

INFORMATION AND PRICES

Alan Kirman

Professor Aix-Marseille III University
EHESS GREQAM, Marseille

INTRODUCTION

In the modern world a large amount of resources is devoted to producing, collecting and transmitting information. The volume of information passing through various channels seems to be expanding exponentially. Yet, in standard economic models, the amount of information required to achieve an efficient allocation of resources is minimal. The resources in the world economy have certainly not been growing at the rate of the information available. How then should one explain this apparent paradox ? In standard models, information is only transmitted through prices to anonymous and passive agents. In reality, agents communicate with each other and pass information in a number of ways. They trade with each other, they influence each others' expectations, they infer information from each others' actions and they set and modify prices individually. Without taking into account this direct interaction between agents one has a very incomplete picture of the role of information and prices in the economy. This chapter takes a look at how we can capture the nature and importance of this direct interaction between agents. However, first let me briefly analyse the role of information in most economic models.

If we consider the Walrasian model, perfected by Arrow and Debreu, as "the benchmark model" of modern economics, it is clear that, in that model, prices have a very particular informational role. In the perfectly competitive world it is the price system that coordinates the activity of all the agents. Contrary to statements often made, the only information that an individual requires, in this model, is the current vector of prices of all commodities (goods or services). He knows his own endowments and has preferences (in the case of the consumer) or technological possibilities (in the case of the producer). Each individual acting independently makes his own choices within the constraints determined by current prices and an equilibrium is a situation in which these choices are compatible (aggregate supply is equal to aggregate demand). Such an equilibrium exists under appropriate assumptions on the characteristics of the economic agents and what is more, the "first welfare theorem" of economics tells us that the allocation of resources in such an equilibrium will be "efficient"

P. Petit (ed.), Economics and Information, 61–81.

in the sense of Pareto[1]. As stated such an observation might seem rather arid, but it should be remembered that it lies at the heart of recommendations for a more extensive use of the market system and for privatisation.

Before proceeding to examine these theoretical results critically and to consider prices and information in alternative settings, it is worth noting an important result due to Jordan (1982). What he shows is that if one is interested in designing a mechanism to achieve an efficient allocation of resources in an economy, then the competitive mechanism uses less information than any other mechanism[2]. What is more, there is no other mechanism that uses so little information ! To explain this result, consider the following very simple case. In a simple barter economy there are n individuals each owning a bundle of l goods. We wish to design a mechanism to allocate these goods efficiently[3], which at equilibrium uses as little information as possible. A mechanism is understood as associating with each economy a set of messages or a message, then these messages induce actions by the agents in the economy which lead to an efficient outcome. In figure 1 the top arrow indicates which outcomes in P are associated with each economy, and these are the efficient allocations (or net trades) for that economy. The bottom two arrows associate messages with each economy and outcomes with messages.

Figure 1

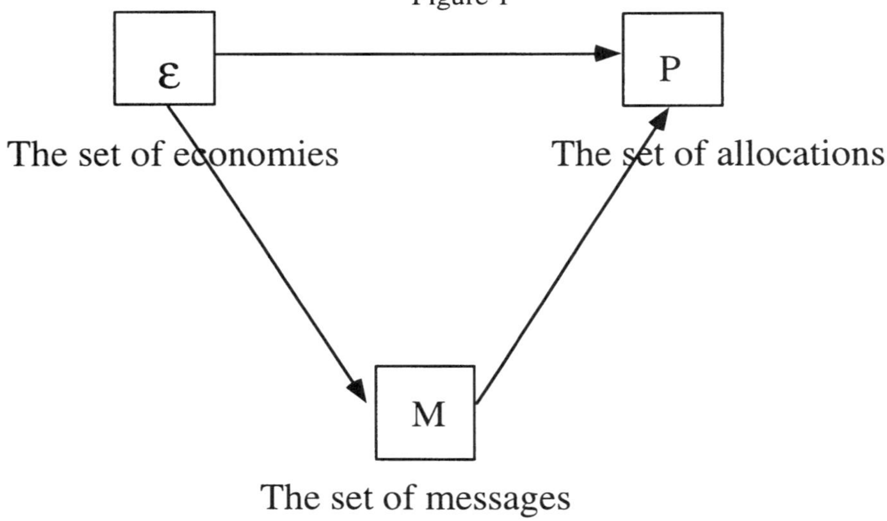

[1] A full account of these results and the assumptions necessary to obtain them may be found in any standard text on microeconomics or equilibrium theory (see e.g. Mas Colell et al. (1995) or Hildenbrand and Kirman (1988).

[2] For an account of the theory of informationally efficient mechanisms see e.g. Hurwicz (1969, 1977, 1986).

[3] In what follows whenever "efficient" is used is should be understood as meaning "Pareto efficient", unless the contrary is indicated.

How would the competitive mechanism fit into this scheme ? With each economy the messages that will be required are, the vector of prices and the vector of trades each agent wishes to make. For each economy then we need a vector of (l-1) prices (the last one can be dropped since we can normalise prices) and for each of the n individuals a vector of "excess demand" or "net trades". Since each individual satisfies Walras' law (what he purchases must have the same value as what he sells) we only need to know (l-1) of these quantities. Furthermore since we are considering the functioning of the mechanism at an equilibrium, all aggregate excess demands or net trades must be zero for each commodity, therefore we can drop one of the individuals. Thus we have 1 x (l-1) + (n-1) x (l-1) "pieces of information", i.e. the messages we use must contain n (l-1) pieces of information or put more technically "the dimension of the message space" of this mechanism is n (l-1).

As I have said earlier, the remarkable fact is that any other mechanism satisfying certain minimal requirements can only achieve an economically efficient outcome by using more information than this. In other words, the use of a price mechanism limits dramatically the amount of information required to achieve a desirable result.

To take another example, suppose in the same context of a simple economy that I wish to design a mechanism to achieve not only efficient allocations but also ones which are fair, i.e. allocations in which no individual would prefer to have somebody else's bundle of goods. This would seem to be an informationally much more complex problem than the previous one since it would seem to be the case that everybody must know everyone else's bundles. Thus instead of observing prices each agent would apparently need to know all the other agents' holdings of goods. In fact, it is easy to show that the dimension of the message space required is only nl instead of n (l-1). If each agent is instructed to choose the best bundle he can get, not given his own income as in the previous example but given average income then the result will be efficient and fair, furthermore no other mechanism can do as well in achieving these results (see Calsamiglia and Kirman (1993)).

Thus the use of prices would seem to require a remarkably small information content in achieving efficiency and one could argue that the market mechanism not only achieves efficiency it is also very parsimonious in the amount of its informational requirements. However this is illusory and to see this it suffices to recall that so little information is needed for the economy to function *at equilibrium.*

Yet if one is to claim any realism for the adjustment mechanism one has to know not only how informationally demanding the mechanism is at equilibrium but also how much information it requires to get there. This is the problem of stability. Equilibria are of interest if they can be attained through a reasonable adjustment process. It is often claimed that the "tatonnement" process is reasonable, yet, as we know from the results of Sonnenschein Mantel and Debreu the equilibria of economies are not necessarily stable with this type of adjustment. This is unfortunate since the "tatonnement" process requires little more information than the Walrasian mechanism at equilibrium. Yet the lack of stability is of great importance. If equilibria are not stable then their intrinsic interest becomes very limited indeed. If we cannot be sure that an economy will arrive at an equilibrium why should we devote so much time to studying these states?

One suggestion would be that the problem lies with the adjustment process rather than with the standard or General Equilibrium model. If a more general adjustment rule were to be specified, perhaps the equilibria of the economy could be shown to be stable. Yet, what became immediately clear after the innovative work of Smale (1976) was that stability could only be achieved at the price of an enormous increase in the amount of information[4].

Smale's Global Newton Method is an extension of standard for finding the equilibria of an aggregate excess demand function. However, as already mentioned, it uses a great deal of information. Without entering into technical details let me just mention that what is needed is a knowledge of all the partial derivatives of the aggregate excess demand function and this greatly increases the size of the messages necessary to make the mechanism function. Although the process leads to equilibria from a large set of starting prices it still does not guarantee convergence from any arbitrary starting point. An additional problem is with the economic content of the process. While the original "tatonnement" process has a very natural interpretation, despite valiant efforts by some economists this is not the case for the Newton Methods.

What is worse is that the informational content of the Newton Method cannot be avoided if one hopes to find a process which will converge globally, that is from any prices to an equilibrium. This is what Saari and Simon (1978) showed. Furthermore, all the alternative adjustment processes that have been constructed to date have no natural economic interpretation. There have been many efforts to construct globally and universally stable price adjustment processes since and in a certain sense Kamiya (1990), Flaschel (1991) and Herings (1996) succeeded. Yet if one looks closely at these results there is always some feature which is open to objection.

All of this seems, to me at least, to suggest that there is no hope of finding an economically interpretable adjustment process which will converge from any price vector independent of the economy. In fact Saari and Simon's result might be thought of as saying that such a process would require an infinite amount of information.

The unfortunate conclusion of all this is that the informational requirements of an adjustment process that would work for all economies seem simply to be too extreme. Should one then be satisfied with adjustment processes that are

---

[4] For a full account of the problems outlined here see Flaschel (1991).

specific to the particular economy in question ? This is hardly reassuring for those who argue for the plausibility of the equilibrium notion. This would be a far cry from the standard argument that the competitive market mechanism has universally desirable properties. Alternatively one could argue that, in real markets, it is something like the tatonnement process that is at work and that economies are not, in general, stable in this sense. However, if one accepts this position then one has to focus on the disequilibrium dynamics of economies. In this case much more has to be analysed if one is to understand the transmission of information as the economy evolves over time.

1. THE EFFICIENT MARKETS HYPOTHESIS

From the rather abstract General Equilibrium model let me now turn to the analysis of financial markets without forgetting that most of the models in this area have the General Equilibrium model as their origin. In particular, consider the much vaunted efficiency property of prices in financial markets. The argument here is that if all individuals have private information, the prices in an efficient financial market will incorporate all that information.

In principle no agent can gain from his private information, since the prices of the assets are sufficient statistics for all the information available. This raises a theoretical question. If the assertion is correct, nobody has any incentive to even look at his own information, since he will believe that it can tell him no more than the prices. However, in this case any price system could be an equilibrium even if it were, in fact, totally in contradiction with the price system obtaining, since nobody would ever realise that there was any contradiction.

Considerable doubt has been cast on the empirical validity of the efficient markets hypothesis. The price of an asset is supposed to reflect the discounted sum of the stream of earnings that that asset will yield over time. Yet it has been observed that asset prices have higher volatility than the underlying dividend process. This "excess volatility" puzzle has generated a large literature. There are those who argue that there is indeed excess volatility (see e.g. Le Roy and Porter (1981), Shiller (1981), Blanchard and Watson (1982) and for a recent comprehensive analysis, Lo and MacKinlay (1999)). Others have suggested that it may be the testing procedure that is at fault (for a discussion see Campbell and Shiller (1987), West (1987, 1988) for example) and that prices do, in fact, contain all pertinent information.

All of this summarises what might be thought of as the central position in economics, which is that prices are the basic and informationally efficient signals through which an efficient allocation of resources can be obtained.

What I would like to suggest in what follows is that the arguments used to justify the efficient markets hypothesis are illusory as were the claims made for the informational parsimony of the General Equilibrium model. Indeed the very fact that we observe, in reality, increasing amount of resources being devoted to informational acquisition and processing implies that the standard general equilibrium model and the standard models of financial markets are failing to capture important aspects of reality.

To turn now to financial markets, a number of points are worth mentioning. A standard argument about the evolution of prices of a financial asset is that if it were predictable then agents could make money. Hence the only evolution possible is one of a series of random shocks, hence the notion that stock market prices must evolve as a random walk, an idea which dates back to Lechatelier. This argument is, of course, open to an obvious objection. If there is predictable structure present in price series it can only be exploited if agents are able to or learn to, perceive it. Thus as Brock and LeBaron (1992) have shown, technical trading rules do have some predictive value in stock markets. Of course, once this is understood their predictive power should disappear. One thing is clear from these remarks. Prediction is based on observed prices and this prediction determines people's actions. These actions, in turn, determine prices. This means that prices can become correlated to some external phenomenon such as "sunspots" (see Cass and Shell (1983)) because agents believe them to be so linked. Alternatively the system may exhibit endogenous fluctuations (see Guesnerie and Woodford (1992)). Thus prices here incorporate the predictions of individuals as well as engendering these predictions. Any change in the information of agents, which leads them to change their predictions, will, in turn, naturally change prices.

A second observation is that the structure of financial markets and the way in which information is passed may, of itself, influence the evolution of prices. To take as a simple example the foreign exchange market, traders who have very short horizons, deal on the basis of orders from individuals or institutions with longer horizons. The traders essentially have to "close their positions" at the end of the day. Their trades will be influenced by these requirements and will in turn influence the bids and asks they make. This may in turn influence the transactions longer-term agents wish to make. Such a process may not necessarily be either stationary or stable. Indeed the very organisation of the market may influence the way in which prices evolve and may explain why prices do not remain firmly linked to fundamentals (for a detailed account of this market see for example Zaher (1994) and Guillaume et al. (1994)). Thus the simple fact that agents do not have the same horizons may lead to bubbles in financial markets. This would, in part, help to explain why in experiments where all the fundamentals are perfectly known bubbles may still appear. Individuals faced with assets yielding announced dividends over a certain fixed number of periods and with a terminal redemption value should be able to calculate the price without any difficulty. Nevertheless, the price observed frequently deviated from the theoretical value. This must either have been because of the myopia of the agents or the fact that on observing current price movements they hoped to obtain a windfall profit before the market unwound in the final periods.

2. HERD BEHAVIOUR

This brings me to another point. If agents act sequentially they may well infer information from the acts of others. This may lead to "herd behaviour" and a literature has now developed explaining how such behaviour may lead to price bubbles in financial markets (see Banerjee (1992), Sharfstein and Stein (1990), Bikhchandani et al. (1992), Welch (1992), Hirshleifer (1992), Kirman (1993, 1994)). Thus as trading develops, individuals may influence other individuals' expectations and fluctuations may occur as a result, or individuals watching others may abandon their own information in favour of that conveyed by the actions of others and an "informational cascade" may result.

Consider a very simple stylised example, due to Banerjee (1992). Agents receive private signals, but also observe the choices made by others. There are two restaurants, A and B and one restaurant, A, is, in fact "better" than the other. Individuals receive two sorts of signals as to which of the two is better. They receive a public signal which is not very reliable and which, say, has 55% probability of being right and a private, independently drawn, signal, which has 95% probability of being correct. Given that restaurant A is actually better suppose, not unreasonably, that 95 out of the 100 potential clients of the two restaurants receive a private signal to that effect and 5 get a signal indicating restaurant B as being superior. However the public signal recommends B. Now, suppose that one of the 5, who received a signal indicating B, chooses first. The second client, observing the first, realises that the latter must have received a B signal. He is aware that all private signals are equally reliable and that his own signal, if it indicated A, is cancelled out. He will therefore have to follow the public signal and enter restaurant B. Thus, whatever the private signal of the second agent, he will enter restaurant B. The third client is now in the same situation as the second and will enter restaurant B. Thus all the clients will end up in B, and this is an inferior outcome. In the particular example there is a five percent probability of this happening, but Banerjee's result is to show that such a result will always occur, with positive probability.

A criticism that is frequently made of such models is that they depend, in an essential way, on the sequential nature of the decision taking process. This, it is argued, is not a common feature of actual markets. Yet, in financial markets, for example as I have mentioned, in addition to any information acquired from a private source, a trader observes what other participants are doing, or at least, proposing to do. Consider the market for foreign exchange. Traders try to anticipate the direction of the movement of market prices and they gain a great deal of information from various sources including other traders. Each such piece of information modifies their individual information set. However, since there is no central equilibrium price, this information cannot be incorporated and become public through the price. It can only be inferred from the observable actions of the individuals. What is observed and made public on financial markets is the price at which the last transaction was made. Thus, the deal made by one individual, based on some private piece of information may give rise to a whole sequence of actions by others and may, as a result, lead to significant moves in prices.

Thus when agents change their actions, in the light of the information they obtain from observing others, the so-called "information cascade" that I have mentioned, may arise. In such a situation individuals progressively attach more importance to the information they infer from the actions of others. They gradually abandon their private information. Thus, as the number of people involved grows, the cascade reinforces itself. Whilst quite fragile to start with, cascades later become almost immune to relevant, private, information. Hence, as more and more individuals act in this way, a trader would have to have almost unbounded confidence in his own information not to conform, particularly if such cascades lead to self-fulfilling outcomes. There is a significant loss of efficiency here. The private information, acquired by all the early agents, would be of use to their later counterparts, but, if they choose to follow what others do, this information is not made available. In this way, possibly relevant private information about fundamentals, for example, may never be used and prices might no longer be related to these fundamentals.

Thus what this work shows, is that the information obtained by observing the actions of others can outweigh the information obtained by the individuals themselves and lead to inefficient outcomes. Although all the information necessary to arrive at a socially efficient outcome was available at the outset of the process some of it was lost as individuals followed the actions of others rather than rely on their own source. Thus interaction generates a result other than that which would have been obtained had individuals only observed signals and not behaviour. The efficient markets hypothesis breaks down because of the way in which transactions happen in the market and because of the way in which the information about transactions is made available.

This serves to illustrate the idea that the relationship between prices and information is far from simple.

One important idea which sheds light on the way information may be transmitted is that individuals may not only observe what others do but may try to imitate what seems to be successful behaviour. If success depends on the number of people who behave in a similar way the problem becomes complicated. The result of this may be what Keynes referred to as the "beauty contest" phenomenon. If, as is the case in financial markets, the number of people following a particular forecast has a direct impact on the price of an asset, then individuals have to take this into account when making their choice. Think of the candidates in the contest as different forecasts or visions of the way in which the economy works and then think of the economic agents as choosing amongst them. Suppose that the situation is completely symmetric and that if everybody chose a particular view the associated forecast would turn out to be correct. In this case it is not at all clear which view would be chosen. Mutual agreement to choose any one of the candidates would be a Nash equilibrium since no individual would have any incentive to deviate. This would even be true, in a one shot setting, even if the views, when collectively held, had differing forecasting abilities but these were not known a priori. However, in a situation, which evolves over time, the track record of the different views will become known. If, furthermore, the profitability of an opinion increases with the number of people who hold it then one might expect the population to "herd" on that view. However, if this happens then one might wonder why views eventually fall from favour.

In an example I gave in Kirman (1999), there are two important features which prevent the system from getting blocked on one vision forever. No model or representation of the economy is perfect even if all agents believe it. All forecasts contain errors. The error may be due to a mistake about a variable that is being predicted or may be due to their mis-specification of the way in which the market functions or may simply be due to some unforeseen shock. When the IMF makes a prediction it does so on the basis of some conceptual model of an economy, which involves various "fundamentals". However, even if everyone believed the IMF it is unlikely that their forecast would be perfectly accurate.

Secondly agents will not shift with certainty to the currently most profitable view, but their probability of doing so will increase with the relative profitability of the view in question. This may be for a number of reasons, the most simple of which is that individuals do not revise their policies at every point in time.

Now the basic idea should be clear. As one vision becomes successful people will shift to following the associated forecast, reinforcing its success. Despite this, since it is not perfect, its prediction will sometimes be wide of the mark. If this happens to coincide with a random, rather unlikely, more accurate forecast by one of the rival views there will be a drift away from the prevailing view towards the view that, by chance, has just made a more accurate forecast. This will undermine the accuracy of the prediction and this, in turn, will reinforce the drift of its followers elsewhere. The coincidence of an inaccurate forecast by the popular view and a more accurate prediction by a neglected alternative is unlikely, but over time, given the nature of the model, it will certainly occur. Thus, the population will drift to one view, will stay with it for a while and then will move on to another.

This might suggest that there would be no distinction between various possible views even if they have different capacities to forecast. In the simple model I refer to this is not quite true. Although there will be an inevitable drift from one view to another the time spent by the population following an intrinsically "better" view will be higher and the time taken to pass from a good view to a bad one will be longer than in the other direction. In other words if one vision of the way in which the world functions proves more accurate, or put alternatively is more accurate than another it will dominate for longer periods of time.

This idea is admittedly very simple but it serves to illustrate the basic point. In the market for a financial asset people's focus of attention will switch from one vision to another but, unlike the models of technological choice suggested by Arthur (1988), David (1986) and others, no irreversible "lock-in" will occur.

Thus, a fundamental feature of financial markets is a constant switching between periods of dominance of fundamental economic factors and periods in which extrapolation takes over. In the latter case, bubbles are generated and crises occur when, as inevitably happens, the bubble bursts. The crisis will be worse if the fundamentals for some reason start to decline and the return to them will be sharper and more painful than it would be, had they remained at their earlier level. Thus, there are periods when information from fundamentals is no longer captured in prices and then an abrupt change when fundamentals are again taken fully into account.

3. NETWORKS

Throughout what I have said so far I have assumed that such information as is available is available to everyone in the market. Yet one of the most obvious stylized facts is that agents do not observe all such information. In particular, they trade and communicate with a limited number of other agents. Two questions arise here. How does the network structure of the interactions influence outcomes and how does the network become established ?

In the previous discussion nothing specific was said about particular interactions or relationships. Consider now an example in which individuals may have different views but may also be able to choose between several individuals with whom to trade. Suppose also that they only trade with those individuals to whom they are "linked" in some sense. In other words they are part of a network, which does not include all possible partners. This sort of idea requires the specification of a graph-like structure on the agents to determine who is linked to whom. What determines the nature of this graph ? It might for example depend on geographical distance as in locational models (see Gabszewicz and Thisse (1986) for example), closeness in characteristics (see Gilles, Haller and Ruys (1993)) or the potential gains from bilateral trade. Individuals, firms or banks may be more likely to trade with their counterparts, which are close in some sense, which produce goods of particular interest to them or where they see chances of high profits. They will thus establish " links " with those traders. The problem is, of course, highly complex since many individuals do not trade directly with others but do so through intermediaries. This does not change the underlying nature of the problem and simply means that there are more links in the network. What is plausible is that the more heavily linked an intermediary is with a certain group the more likely somebody who trades with that individual is to be influenced by changes in that group. In the context of the model discussed above, for example, the cumulated wealth an individual has obtained from trading with an individual will determine how strongly linked he will be to that individual and the group with whom the latter trades.

My preferred approach is to consider the network itself as random[5]. People do not necessarily have fixed links but may use the existing links with a certain probability. I may be less likely to invest in a fund, which places a great deal of its resources in countries with which I am not familiar for example. Agents will be constrained in their choices by the network but they may not even be aware of some of the links in which they are indirectly involved. Their attention is more likely to be drawn to a certain link the more important that link is in channelling their investments.

Note however, that if the network, or the set of links used, is a particular realisation of a random drawing the outcome will, itself, be random. In many applications of graph theory to economics individuals have been portrayed as situated on a lattice. Thus, in the basic Markov random field model, interaction is probabilistic but between neighbours in the lattice, and the lattice structure is given exogenously. However, the stochastic graph approach allows for more complicated neighbourhood structures, e.g. by permitting agents, who are not "near" in terms of some underlying characteristics to have a positive probability of communicating.

In the stochastic graph approach, the basic idea is to consider a set of agents A and to attach probabilities to the links between them. Let p_{ab} denote the probability that individual a "communicates" with agent b. In graph terms, this is the probability that an arc exists between nodes a and b. The graph is taken to be undirected, i.e. the existence of the arc ab implies the existence of ba and thus one-way communication is ruled out.[6]

In the case of a finite set A this is easy to envisage. The resulting stochastic graph can be denoted.

$$\Gamma(p_{ab})$$

If there is no obvious underlying structure which is thought of as affecting the probability that agents communicate, then, one could consider $p_{ab} = p$ that is the probability of interaction is the same regardless of "who" or "where" the individuals are. Thus global interaction is a special case of this model.

---

[5]This was introduced by Kirman (1985) and developed by Kirman, Oddou and Weber (1986), Durlauf (2000) and Ioannides (1990).

[6]This, of course, excludes a whole class of interesting economic models in which the direction of communication is important. Much of production involves transactions which are neccessarily in one direction from inputs to outputs, for example. This can be taken care of by specifying wheher the link is active and then specifying the nature of the transaction. More difficult to handle is, for example, the transmission of information from a central source which is clearly best handled by considering the links as directed. Evstigneev (1994) has modelled some economic equilibrium problems using directed graphs but, as he indicates, the task is made difficult by the fact that some of the mathematical tools, which make the undirected case tractable, are not available for directed graphs.

An economist interested in how trading relationships are established would argue that the possibility of mutually profitable trade increases with increasing difference in characteristics whether these be differences in tastes, endowments or abilities. Identical agents have no trading possibilities. Hence one might well expect transactions to involve complementary partners. In financial markets where the links are both between individuals and between individuals and assets the situation is more complicated. Be this as it may the network that governs transactions is important. It is also important for agents who are not linked directly since reactions may feed in a chain-like way from one agent to another. The spread of a financial panic, for example, will depend on the connectivity of the graph. Hence, one wants to know how closely connected the graph is since this will determine the speed of transmission.

An answer to this sort of question is available. Stochastic graphs become surprisingly highly connected as the number of agents increases, provided that the probability that any two individuals are connected does not go to zero too fast. To understand what is meant by this, consider a result of Bollobas which states that, if the probability p_n that any two agents know each other, in a group with n agents is such that $\lim_{n\to\infty} p_n = 0$ and $p_n \geq \frac{1}{\sqrt{n}}$ then, as n becomes large, it becomes certain that the diameter of the graph will be 2. In other words, it is sure that any two individuals will have a "common friend" if the graph is large enough, even though the probability that any two agents know each other goes to zero as n goes to infinity. Thus, as was observed in Kirman et al. (1986), one should say on encountering someone with whom one has a common friend, "it's a large world". This somewhat surprising result suggests that, as sociologists have long observed empirically, relational networks are likely to be much more connected than one might imagine. The reservation about this result is that it is highly unlikely that individuals will have equal probability of meeting each other. However recent work (see Watts (1999), has shown that the addition of very few links can radically change the average connectivity of a network and in the end it is this rather than the worst distances in a network which is important.

Let me repeat how important this is in economic models, in particular in financial markets, since the degree of connectedness determines how fast information diffuses and how quickly an epidemic of opinion or behaviour will occur. Thus the aggregate consequences of a local change will be very much linked to the structure and degree of connectivity of the network through which information flows.

More generally consider the state of an individual as being described, at least in part by the composition of his portfolio of assets. Now the dynamic evolution of the states of the individuals who are influenced by each other through a graph-like structure is of interest since the stable configurations of states, if there are any, will depend on the graph in question. Some of the results from other disciplines (see Weisbuch [1990]) can be evoked in the context of economic models.

A problem which is present in many economic situations but which has received little attention is the existence of multiple networks. Economic agents are usually linked to others in different ways for different purposes. They may be linked through social, commercial or professional groupings and the interaction through all of these may jointly determine their choices. For example, firms are linked with other firms either because they have direct relations with them or because they invest in funds, which in turn invest in those firms, or they may hold shares in firms or banks, which invest in those firms. All of these links are possible routes for economic or financial "contagion" and what is interesting is that such contagion may be more or less important depending on the network structure even if the underlying information is the same.

The simplest example is that in which agents in a market react to price signals but also to the actions taken by certain other individuals. In this case, interaction restricted by a network generates a non-uniform aggregate phenomenon.

Since I have emphasised the importance of the structure and organisation of interaction the natural question to pose is, how does this structure emerge ? This is closely related to the general problem of self-organisation and here, as there, (see Kauffman (1996)) the evolution of stochastic graphs plays a central role. If one wants to proceed to a theory of endogenous network formation, a first step might be to find out which organisations of individuals, institutions or countries are stable. Thus one would look for "rest-points" of a dynamic process of network evolution. Such rest points would be arrangements, or networks, which would not be subject to endogenous pressures to change them. One might then want to see if these are the rest-points, if any, of a dynamic model of evolving networks. This is the natural question for the problem that we are faced with in this paper. If networks are important in determining the spread of information then where do these networks come from?

Thus, the most interesting challenge in this area, is to study the evolution of the network itself. As is well known, the evolution of the links between individuals, particles or molecules is at the heart of the idea of self-organisation. Durlauf (1990) makes a step in this direction when he starts with a given geographical network, but allows agents to choose where to place themselves in the network. This recalls an older model of neighbourhood preferences due to Schelling.

The obvious way in which to proceed is to specify models in which the links between agents are reinforced over time by the gain derived from those links. Thus longstanding economic relationships would be derived endogenously from the agents' experience. Instead of thinking of learning only at the individual level, the economy as a whole could be considered as learning and the graph representing the communication in the economy as evolving

In the simple model that I discussed above one can think of the graph that links traders to views. The links that agents have to certain views are modified in the light of their experience. This is not the only sort of graph that is needed to explain the transmission of information but it gives an idea as to how links evolve.

In a recent paper, Weisbuch et al (2000) examine the formation of links on a particular market and conclude that agents in that market fall into two groups, those who are continually searching for information about new prices and those who trade systematically with the same partners. This illustrates an old problem in the literature on communication in markets. The trade-off between "exploration" and "exploitation". There are those who explore in the hope of finding new information and those who have learned to be satisfied with the information they have obtained from trading with their current trading partner. There is an interesting analogy with the evolution of certain social insects here. Those who search for information provide some sort of control over the process as a whole since their influence generates information for those who do not search for it. However, the latter do not waste valuable resources and time searching.

4. PRICE SETTING AND THE ORGANISATION OF TRADES

To go back to the general equilibrium model for a moment, it is worth observing that two significant problems remain untreated. Firstly, who sets the prices? The fiction of an "auctioneer" is not an adequate description for many markets and the basic problem of where prices come from is only treated, and this is significant, in what are described as models of "imperfect competition". If the economic agents set prices themselves then we clearly have to dispense with the fiction that they take them as given and this, in turn, is not consistent with the mechanism concept through which informational efficiency is obtained. Although the idea that prices adjust in some systematic way in response to excess demand is commonplace, since the latter part of the 19th century little attention has been paid to the way in which this is done.

Of course, there is a literature in which individuals meet, bargain, trade and then continue to circulate in the market until all profitable opportunities are exhausted. Work of Fisher (1983), and of Rubinstein and Wolinsky (1990) is very much in this spirit. Under certain conditions such meeting and bargaining processes will converge to the competitive outcome. However, prices now play a very different role, they are the results of bargains between individuals and are not anonymous signals observed by individuals in isolation. Only as this process continues over time can the prices be thought of as giving an indication of the terms of trade available in the market.

There is a further literature which recognises explicitly that different prices may exist for the same good on a market (see for example Diamond (1989)) and then looks at what might be an equilibrium in such a market in which individuals search, at a cost, to find the lowest price. A number of authors have shown that price dispersion may persist. Here one can take the view that the market signal is now the distribution of prices rather than the price itself but these models can, at least, allow for the sellers to set their prices. What is also worth remarking is that as Diamond has shown the equilibrium in such a market may be the monopoly price rather than the competitive price. In the face of transaction costs firms will try to cream off the surplus arising from their local monopoly and the result will be that the monopoly price will prevail. What is clear from this is that in such situations we are far from the situation forecast in the perfectly competitive framework.

Consider a further example that of understanding inflation i.e. the evolution of prices over time. For this, it is important to understand how individuals set prices and in particular what information they use in doing so. There is a plethora of models with different explanations for the way in which people set prices, (staggered price setting, see Ball and Mankiw (1994); implicit contracts, see Rosen (1988); imperfect competition in product and labour markets, see McDonald and Solow (1981) ; costly price setting see Sheshinski and Weiss (1983) ; among others. These explanations contribute to an understanding as to why prices are "sticky" and many of them depend on considerations of the information that is available to agents. Blinder (1991) and a number of subsequent authors also asked individuals directly how they set prices and used this to develop additional arguments for "price stickiness".

A particularly interesting suggestion originally due to Lucas concerns what happens when there is imperfect information about inflation which influences price setting and, this in turn, feeds back into inflation. This is particularly important in episodes of hyperinflation (see for example Heyman and Leijonhufvud (1995) on hyperinflations in general and Rostowski (1994) on the recent Serbian hyperinflation) and when inflation is too high sellers either cease to trade or index on a foreign currency. In such situations the information necessary to make rational decisions in the domestic context is no longer available and it is this that leads agents to withdraw from the market by withholding goods or transferring their capital elsewhere or to continue to transact while pinning their beliefs to some external variable, which remains predictable. Once the link between prices and information is broken, individuals have nothing on which to base their purchasing decisions and the relevant market collapses.

In less extreme situations there are many examples of the ways in which the prices set by one seller influence the other sellers in the market. Once one allows in an imperfectly competitive setting strategic behaviour the outcome will depend crucially on the rules used by the sellers. Margaret Slade's elegant analysis of a local gasoline price war illustrates the evolution of prices and the transmission of information in such a setting.

A second problem that is, in general, not addressed in the standard model is how the trades necessary to clear the markets are organised. In the absence of any central authority how do those with excess supply at the competitive price find and trade with those with excess demands ? With the exception of very special markets such as that for gold, the Walrasian auctioneer who equilibrates the market after receiving bids and offers from all agents cannot be invoked as a reasonably realistic description. What this suggests is that market organisation is important and that the prices obtaining in a market and their informational content may well be dependent on that outcome.

Let me give a simple example of how this may occur. Consider an individual who wishes to sell one or many goods (the classical example is that of the sale of government bonds). He has a choice of different mechanisms to do this. Which one should he choose if he wishes to maximise his revenue ? A number of authors (see, for example, Riley and Samuelson (1981), Milgrom and Weber (1982), or McAfee and McMillan (1987)), have shown that in the absence of transaction costs an auction with reserve price is the optimal selling institution in the sense that it achieves the highest yield to the seller. Once costs are introduced the situation becomes more complicated. As De Vroey (1987) has shown, posted prices may be preferable if the costs of implementing auctions are too high.

The point here is that the relationship between prices and market mechanism is important. Since different mechanisms can yield different prices for the same good the informational content of prices has to be re-evaluated. Furthermore the price achieved will be dependent on the information available in the market. If individuals' evaluations of goods are the same neither the prices nor the optimal mechanism will be the same as in the case where values are private, particularly if they are not drawn from some known distribution. Maskin and Riley (1989) demonstrate how by using a clever pricing schedule a monopolist who has several units to sell can achieve a better yield than by using an auction if his clients have downward-sloping curves. Thus mechanism, information and price are intimately related.

CONCLUSION

There are, of course, many other aspects of the relationship between prices and information, which merit consideration, for example the price of information itself (see for example La Valle (1968)). However the point of this chapter has been to indicate a number of particular aspects, which help to show why the "naive" view of the efficiency of markets and of the price mechanism in particular may be misleading.

One has, in fact, to take into account the direct interaction between individuals, in particular in financial markets. Several aspects of this interaction are important. Economic agents observe each other and infer information from each other's actions. They are influenced by the expectations of others and have a tendency to mimic what they consider to be profitable behaviour. Even in the most extensive markets, they interact with only a limited number of other agents.

Taking all of these aspects into account makes the analysis of economic phenomena more complicated but more realistic. The traditional relationship between micro behaviour and macro outcomes has to be rethought. However, this rethinking brings with it the advantage that we can analyse such phenomena as "epidemics of opinion", "herding behaviour" and "bubbles" which are intrinsically aggregate in nature and cannot be attributed to the decisions of some representative individual.

We are then led to study economies as complex interactive systems, which coordinate the interaction between heterogeneous agents who have access to different types and amounts of information. The system evolves as the agents learn from others through aggregate and local signals. Such systems, which are frequently studied in physics and other sciences, will not necessarily have equilibria in the traditional economic sense. Nevertheless their analysis should provide us with the tools necessary to obtain a better understanding of the way in which information is transmitted and the use to which it is put in markets.

REFERENCES

Arthur B. (1988) "Competing Technologies, Increasing Returns and "Lock-in" by Small Historical Events", *Economic Journal,* march.

Ball L. and G. Mankiw (1994), "A sticky-price manifesto", NBER working paper no. 4677.

Banerjee A. (1992), "A simple model of herd behaviour", *Quarterly Journal of Economics*, 108, pp. 797-817.

Bikhchandani S., Hirschleifer D. and Welch I. (1992), "A theory of fads, fashion, custom and cultural change as informational cascades", *Journal of Political Economy*, 100, pp. 992-1026.

Blanchard O.J. and M. Watson (1982), "Bubbles, Rational Expectations, and Financial Markets", in: P. Wach (ed.), *Crises in the Economic and Financial Structure*, Lexington MA, Lexington Books.

Blinder A. (1991), "Why are prices sticky ?", Preliminary results from an interview study, NBER working paper n° 3646.

Brock W. and B Lebaron (1992), "Simple Technical Trading Rules and the Stochastic Properties of Stock Returns", *Journal of Finance*, 47, pp. 1731-1764.

Calsamiglia X. and A. Kirman (1993), "A unique informationally efficient and decentralized mechanism with fair outcomes, *Econometrica*, 61, 5 (September), pp. 1147-72.

Campbell J. Y. and R. J. Shiller (1987), "Cointegration and Tests of Present Value Models", *Journal of Political Economy*, 95, pp. 1062-1088.

Cass D. and K. Shell (1983), "Do sunspots matter ?", *Journal of Political Economy*, 91, pp. 193-227.

David P. (1986) "Understanding the Economics of QWERTY : The Necessity of History", in W.N. Parker , ed., *History and the Modern Economist*, Basil Blackwell, Oxford

De Vroey M. (1987), "La possibilité d'une économie décentralisée. Esquisse d'une alternative à la théorie de l'équilibre général », *Revue Economique*, 38 (4), pp. 773-805, juillet.

Diamond P. (1989), "Search theory", in *The New Palgrave : A Dictionary of Economics,* (J. Eatwell, M. Milgate and P. Newman eds.), Macmillan, London, pp. 273-79.

Durlauf S. (1990), "Locally Interacting Systems, Coordination Failure, and the Behaviour of Aggregate Activity", *Working Paper*, Stanford University.

Durlauf S. (2000), "A framework for the study of individual behavior and social interactions", mimeo, Department of economics, University of Wisconsin.

Fisher F.M. (1983), *Disequilibrium Foundations of Equilibrium Economics*, Cambridge University Press.

Flaschel P. (1991). "Stability – Independent of economic Structure ?" , *Structural Change and Economic Dynamics,* Vol.2, No. 1, pp.9-35, June 1991.

Gabszewicz J. and Thysse J. (1986), "On the nature of Competition with Differentiated Products", *Economic Journal* , 96 (381), pp.160-72 march.

Gilles R.P., Haller H. and Ruys P. (1993), "Modelling of Economies with Relational Constraints on Coalition Formation". Virginia Polytechnic Institute and State University, Working Paper in Economies, E 93-13, August.

Guesnerie R. and Wood A. (1992), "Endogeneous Fluctuations", in J.J. Laffont ed, Advances in economic theory, Sixth World Congress, vol. 2, Econometric Society, Monographs, n° 21, Cambridge, New York and Melbourne, Cambridge University Press, pp. 289-412.

Guillaume D.M. et al. (1994), "From the bird's eye to the microscope: a survey of new stylised facts of the intra-daily foreign exchange markets", O and A Research Group Discussion Paper, Olsen and Associates, Zurich, Switzerland.

Herings P. J.J. (1996), "Equilibrium existence Results for Economies with Prices Rigidities" *Economic Theory*, January, pp. 63-80.

Heyman D and A Leijonhufvud (1995), *High Inflations*, Clarendon Press, Oxford.

Hildenbrand W. and A. Kirman (1988), *Equilibrium Analysis*, North Holland Publishing Co.

Hirshleifer J. (1992), "Selection, Mutation and the Preservation of Diversity in Evolutionary Games", *Revista Espagnola de Economia*, 9(2), pp. 251-73.

Hurwicz L. (1969), "Optimality and Informational Efficiency in Resource Allocation Processes," in *Mathematical Methods in the Social Sciences*, edited by Kenneth J. Arrow, Samuel Karlin, and Patrick Suppes, Stanford University Press, 1960: also in Readings in Welfare Economics, edited by K. J. Arrow and T. Scitovsky Irwin, 1969.

Hurwicz L. (1977), "On the Dimensional Requirements of Informationally Decentralized Pareto-Satisfactory Processes," in *Studies in Resource Allocation Processes,* edited by K.J. Arrow and L. Hurwicz, New York: Cambridge University Press.

Hurwicz L. (1986), "On Informational Decentralization and Efficiency in Resource Allocation Mechanisms" in Studies in Mathematical Economics, edited by S. Reiter, MAA Studies in Mathematics, vol. 25, The Mathematical Association of America, 1986.

Ioannides Y.M. (1990), "Trading Uncertainty and Market Form ", *International Economic Review*, vol. 31, 3, August, pp. 619-38.

Jordan J.S. (1982), "The competitive allocation process is informationally efficient uniquely", *Journal of Economic Theory*, 28, pp. 1-18.

Kamiya K. (1989), A globally stable price adjustment process, Osaka : Mimeo

Kirman A. P. (1985), "Organisation et communication dans les marchés", *Economie Appliquée*, 38 (3/4), pp. 597-609.

Kirman, A.P. (1993), "Ants, rationality and recruitment", *Quarterly Journal of Economics,* CVIII, 137-56.

Kirman A. (1999), "On the Transitory Nature of Gurus", mimeo, GREQAM, Marseille.

Kirman A.P., C. Oddou and S. Weber(1986). "Stochastic communication and coalition formation", *Econometrica*, January, pp. 129-138.

La Valle I.(1968), "On cash equivalents and information evaluation under uncertainty, Part I : basic theory", *Journal of the American Statistical Association*, 63, 252-276.

Le Roy S.F. and R.D. Porter (1981), "The present value relation: tests based on implied variance bounds", *Econometrica*, 49, 555-74.

Lo A, and A. MacKinlay (1999), *A Non-Random Walk down Wall Street*, Princeton University Press, Princeton, N.J.

Mc Donald I. and Solow R. (1981), "Wage Bargaining and Employment", *American Economic Review*, 71(5), pp. 896-908, December.

Mas-Colell A., M.D. Whinston and J.R.Green (1995), *Microeconomic theory*, Oxford University Press, Oxford.

Maskin E. and J. Riley (1989), "Optimal multi-unit auctions", in F. Hahn (ed.), *The Economics of Missing Markets, Information and Games*, Oxford University Press, New York.

McAfee R.P. and J. McMillan (1987), "Auctions and bidding", *Journal of Economic Literature*, 25, pp. 699-738.

Milgrom P. and R. Weber (1982), "A theory of auctions and competitive bidding", *Econometrica*, 50, 1089-1122.

Riley J. and W. Samuelson (1981), "Optimal auctions", *American Economic Review*, 71, pp. 381-392.

Rosen S. (1985), "Implicit contracts: a survey", *Journal of Economic Literature*, 23, pp. 1144-1175.

Rostowski J. (1994), "The Yugoslav hyperinflation and stabilization of 1992-1994", C.E.P. Discussion Paper n° 213, L.S.E.

Rubinstein A. and A. Wolinsky (1990), "Decentralized trading, strategic behaviour and the Walrasian outcome", *Review of Economic Studies*, 57, pp. 63-78.

Saari D. and C.P. Simon. (1978). " Effective Price Mechanisms ", *Econometrica*, 46, 1097-1125

Sharfstein D.S. and J.C. Stein (1990), "Herd behavior and investment", *American Economic Review*, 465-79.

Sheshinski E. and Weiss Y. (1983), "Optimum Pricing Policy under Stochastic Inflation", *Review of Economic Studies*, 50(3), July, pp. 513-29.

Shiller R.J. (1981), "Do stock prices move by too much to be justified by subsequent changes in dividends ?", *American Economic Review*, 71, pp. 421-36

Smale S. (1976). " Exchange Processes with Price Adjustment ", *Journal of Mathematical Economics*, 3, pp. 211-226.

Watts D. (1999), *Small Worlds*, Princeton University Press, Princeton.

Weisbuch G., Kirman A., and Herreiner D. (2000), "Market Organisation and Trading Relationships" , *Economic Journal*, 110 pp. 411-436

Weisbuch G. (1990), *Complex Systems Dynamics,* Redwood City (CA) : Addison Wesley

Welch I. (1992), "Sequential Sales, Learning and Cascades", *Journal of Finance* 47 (2), pp. 695-752, June.

West K.D. (1987), "A specification test for speculative bubbles", *Quarterly Journal of Economics*, 102, pp. 553-80.

West K.D. (1988), "Bubbles, fads, and stock price volatility tests : A partial evaluation", *Journal of Finance*, 43, pp. 639-655.

Zaher S. (1994), "Market makers: a study of the effects of global market integration in the currency trading industry", mimeo, C.L. Carson School of Management. University of Minnesota.

Chapter 5

THE SELF CENTRED LOGIC OF FINANCIAL MARKETS

André Orléan

Director of Research
CNRS CEPREMAP, Paris

Today, in whichever direction the economist looks, whether to companies, households, technological innovation or economic policy, he sees the same hold exerted by financial realities. To propose a clear analysis of this financial logic has become an absolute challenge for anyone who wants to understand how contemporary economies work. The central thesis developed in this text suggests that financial evaluation is the product of logic of opinion. One cannot imagine a point of view more opposed to that professed by academic thought. For the latter, stock exchange prices are objectively the expression of "real values", in other words companies' profitability. Opinion has nothing to do with it, just the most accurate calculation of companies' long-term gains. For us, *a contrario*, organised financial markets are structures whose primary goal is to create consensus within the financial community and to allow for shared beliefs to emerge in a place where, without them, an infinite variety of idiosyncratic ways of deciphering the future would exist[1]. With regard to this conception, finance is considered to be more an autonomous power of evaluation than the reflection of the real values, which exist before it.

The idea of the autonomy of finance is firmly rejected by traditional economic theory for whom stock exchange prices have an objective basis, that is to say companies' ability to make profits or, what is still called their "fundamental value". According to this approach, referred to as "fundamentalist", the function of the market is to reveal this value publicly by putting the available information to best use. When stock exchange prices faithfully reflect the fundamental value, the market is then said to be "efficient"[2]. Thus, to a fundamentalist theorist, finance is the reflection of the real economy. It does not possess any autonomy. Its function is to evaluate the future potentialities of the productive economy to guide investment choices by directing them towards expanding sectors. We

[1] This first part relies on the analyses, which I developed in André Orléan (1999)

[2] Financial efficiency is by nature informational since it designates the supposed ability of the market to make adequate use all of the information, which it has at its disposal. An efficient stock exchange provides capitalism with the functional equivalent of a planner since the reading of share prices alone allows investors to know the future profitability of various companies. It is this property, which, in the view of a liberal economist, justifies the existence of financial markets.

P. Petit (ed.), Economics and Information, 83–92.

disagree with this far too reductionist vision of the economy/finance relationship for at least two reasons.

On the one hand, we reject it because the estimation of the fundamental value does not at all derive from calculation. In fact, on what basis might we calculate the profits of a company in five, ten or thirty years in the future ? The future is, by nature, opaque and subject to radical uncertainty, which prevents us from giving this estimation any scientific basis whatsoever. It is never more than an opinion, a pure gamble expressing personal convictions, grounded on a basis, which is always fragile[3]. On the other, observation of stock exchange prices leads to keeping one's distance in relation to the fundamentalist approach. In fact, the very strong price variations in shares, from day to day or from hour to hour, cannot be explained by the modifications of a real economy whose evolution is slow and of weak amplitude with regard to stock exchange volatility.

Therefore one cannot claim that finance is the simple reflection of real values. For us, the market is a place where norms of evaluation are constructed, where a particular vision of the future is invented. Prices reflect nothing more than the beliefs of financial opinion. Financial power and its autonomy are measured in relation to its ability to impose its judgement and evaluations on the economy. Consequently this analysis breaks with the concept of information put forward by the orthodox theory of finance. In our perspective, one cannot determine in an objective way, free from the beliefs of the investors, -what the relevant information is and what its impact is a priori on the public evaluation. Only current opinions on stock markets will select, at a given time, which signals should be considered as relevant -and they also impose their meaning. Thus, highly paradoxically, " they can bear radically different opinions on the same state of affairs"[4]. Objective information does not exist but only contingent interpretations, transmitted by the conventions, which forge financial opinion. Advancing in the explanation of this thesis calls for a rethinking of the role of financial markets and the way in which they form the opinion of investors. Such a task cannot be fulfilled in the restricted framework of this chapter[5]. We shall therefore attempt in what follows to present only the fundamental conceptual

---

[3] If such a calculation is envisaged by orthodox financial theory, it is always at the price of excessive simplifications. It supposes that the world is stationary and that an exhaustive list of events likely to occur is known. Keynes JM. was one of the first economists to call this modelling of uncertainty into question. In chapter 12 of *General Theory* devoted to "The State of Long-Term Expectation", he insists on "The outstanding fact is the extreme precariousness of the basis of knowledge on which our estimates of prospective yield have to be made" (1973), p.149). In other words, even in the case where investors were solely interested in the fundamental value, the estimation of the latter is never more than a particular opinion lacking an objective framework allowing calculation.

[4] Pierre Balley (1987) p187.

[5] The present text constitutes a brief exposition of some of the theses developed in A. Orléan (1999).

relations, leaving aside a more complete analysis. The line of argument therefore will not follow the pattern of traditional scientific exposition and will proceed more by means of affirmations than by demonstrations, though it allows for an overall view of our approach to finance and its coherence. The theoretical framework, which is presented here, is built around three fundamental concepts: liquidity, self-referentiality, and convention. They are presented successively in the three following sections. Let us begin with liquidity.

1. LIQUIDITY

In response to the question "Why do organised financial markets exist?» we saw that orthodox theory's answer was: "To give the best possible estimation of companies' value and, in doing so, to allow for an efficient allocation of productive capital". In our opinion, this answer is erroneous. Stock markets were invented to respond to a much more pragmatic, immediate and urgent need: to make property deeds easily negotiable at all times so as to diminish the risks related to productive investment. In order to understand this let us recall that shares, insofar as they are ownership rights over a company, represent a physical capital immobilised in the form of machines and factories, which generate profits progressively over years, following the development of the production process. In doing this, holding a share gives you a right over the coming flow of anticipated dividends. It is only a promise of money. There follows a risk for the owner who, faced with unforeseen expenses, can end up with great difficulties due to being unable to immediately transform his shares into money. It is to eliminate this risk that organised financial markets were created. They allow, at any moment, to negotiate shares, which nonetheless represent fixed and immobilised capital. Stock markets are institutional creations invented to respond to a specific demand of creditors: to transform ownership rights into liquid form[6].

Contrarily to the "theory of reflection", this conception of finance brings to light a complex and contradictory relationship between the real economy and financial markets. The latter, far from being simple extensions of relationships between production and exchange, appear as the expression of a will to bypass the constraints which production time cause to weigh on the process of evaluating capital. Whereas in the view of the partisans of stock exchange efficiency, the lack of connection between financial evaluation and the world of production is thought of as an accident, as the transitory product of the irrationality of the speculating masses, we are of the opinion that this lack of connection is inscribed into the very definition of the project pursued by market finance. Financial liquidity shows itself to be, *from its origins*, a transgression of real economy. It introduces a radical gap between the time of production and the time of finance. While the valorisation of productive capital is a long-term

[6] For a more precise analysis of liquidity and how it can be measured, we refer the reader to our book, Orléan A. (1999)

process, since it requires the irreversible immobilisation of capital, liquidity produces constant opportunities for re-evaluation and therefore for profit. With regard to the necessities of production, this frequent re-evaluation of share prices, by the minute or by the hour, which the stock markets impose, makes no sense. There is nothing in the nature of productive capital, which corresponds to this liquidity. It creates *ex nihilo* an artificial world of price and contracts whose finality is to allow for an easing of the risk borne by owners.
This artificiality of the stock exchange world is often emphasised by analysts, for example when they underline the extreme disproportion between the circulation of finance and the circulation of goods[7]. However, for lack of an adequate theory, it appears as a pathologic phenomenon while it should be seen as a transgression, willed and programmed by the financial community. The new regulation, which it is imposing, has the characteristics of organising property transactions on the basis of public evaluations, that is to say market prices. In doing this, it distinguishes itself strongly from other forms of organisation of capital within which the transmission and the control of property are negotiated outside the market between major shareholders, as is the case when banking power or shareholders' pacts dominate. This stock exchange finance centred on liquidity is at the very heart of contemporary capitalism. It has undergone unprecedented development and has given rise to a new type of shareholder power, represented by the American pension funds, creating new norms and practices, which have led to the emergence of an original macroeconomics. But it goes further than this: through company management, pension schemes and the structuring role that capitalisation in the formation of pensions has come to play[8], is introducing a project, which aims at a radical mutation of the social contract in France and in Europa. It is this point of view, which justifies a renewed analysis of market finance as a power leading to a deep social transformation. In order to understand it, it is relevant to analyse its central device: public evaluation. We shall do so using the concept of self-referentiality.

2. SPECULATIVE SELF-REFERENTIALITY

Having abandoned the fundamentalist perspective and the hypothesis of efficiency, is it still possible to propose a scientific analysis of stock prices ? This is an essential question. Is saying that price has the dimension of an opinion are we not recognising its fundamental lack of determination ? Are we not then necessarily forced to abandon all scientific rigour ? We would like to show that this is not the case. The notion of "financial convention" will allow us to propose an analysis which acknowledges the inter-subjective dimension of price but which does so by objectifying its principles of formation. The

[7] A ratio of 1 to 50, even of 1 to 60 is often cited.

[8] Or that it seeks to play

rapprochement with the Kuhnian notion of paradigm is, from this the point of view, enlightening. It is a question of constructing a method, which integrates the role which collective beliefs play while avoiding the pitfalls of relativism[9]. At the stock exchange, to earn money, it is essential to foresee how the market is going to evolve: this is, stated in an extremely concentrated manner, the starting point of our reflection. This very simple idea distances us from the fundamentalist analysis, which, for its part, considers that what is important to make a profit, is to guess the fundamental value of the companies as accurately as possible. Yet, on the market, what counts are the prices such as they are determined at every moment and not as what they should be. It is the prices, and the prices alone, which condition the gains and losses of the investors. As a practitioner in the field writes: "The quality of the reasoning matters little if it is to be contradicted by the stock exchange, that is to say by the collective opinion which predominates there. No more than a politician, the broker or the analyst cannot be right in practice against the majority opinion of his electors; it is the market which votes"[10]. There follows a singular structure which differs from the fundamentalist model in that the norm it establishes is an endogenous variable, namely market opinion, and not an objective reality external to the market, that is to say fundamental value. For each person who has observed a new public information, the task is not to analyse the effects of this information on the fundamental value, but to foresee how the market will react. If one anticipates a rise in share value, one buys; in the opposite case, one sells. Contrarily to the fundamentalist model, this analysis tells us that the anticipations of the agents are not turned to the real economy, but to the anticipations of the other dealers. This rule of behaviour leads to a disconnection between finance and real economy to the extent that what dominates on the market is not he real content of information with regard to fundamental facts, but the way in which collective opinion is supposed to interpret it. This gives rise to a singular rationality, fundamentally mimetic in nature in that it seeks to imitate the market, however erratic it may be. If I think that tomorrow share prices will rise on the stock exchange, then it is in my best interest to buy shares, even if I think, with regard to fundamental values, this rise is aberrant. Imitation is perfectly rational behaviour at an individual level even if, collectively, it leads to highly harmful situations for the economy, as is the case when speculative bubbles appear, that is to say durable differences between stock exchange prices and fundamental values.

We find ourselves before a complex and innovative vision, which breaks with traditional models of evaluation. To analyse this structure, Keynes proposed a simple and enlightening illustration. He compares "professional

---

9 For Kuhn, scientific statements depend on collective representations which, at a given moment, the scientific community shares, while remaining relevant descriptions of the surrounding physical world.

10 see Balley P., (1987, p.187)

investment to those newspaper competitions in which the competitors have to pick (the prettiest photograph) from a hundred photographs, the prize being awarded to the competitor whose choice most nearly corresponds to the average preferences of the competitors as a whole[11]". In this game, as in the previous analysis, it matters little what one thinks is really the nicest photograph. What counts is to determine how the others analyse this problem to be as close as possible to what they are thinking. One attempts to anticipate collective opinion. However, if one supposes that the participants in the game are all rational, it results that each other person's opinion is also determined based on the idea that they themselves make of the group opinion. As Keynes writes, "each competitor has to pick, not (the photograph) that he himself finds the prettiest, but (the one) which he thinks likeliest to catch the fancy of other competitors, all of whom are looking at the problem from the same point of view"[12]. One is therefore confronted with a "specular" structure since, as in a game of mirrors reflecting each other, each person is attempting to penetrate the minds of the other participants, while these other participants, are doing exactly the same thing. Such a logic is called "self-referential".

Its properties make it remarkable, but there is one quite particular one, without equivalent in the fundamentalist model and which plays a central role where the financial question is concerned, that is to say the self-validation of beliefs: if everyone believes that the other participants prefer photograph A, it results that each rationally will make the choice of photograph A, which will have the consequence of effectively making this photograph the preferred photograph of the group. This property clarifies an essential dimension of self-referentiality: the photograph selected isn't the prettiest one, but the one which in the participants view is seen as most likely to receive the votes of the group. For this reason, the object of analysis that self-referential rationality gives itself is not individual opinions, but the opinion of the group, considered as a collective entity endowed with autonomous judgement. It is in this way that where finance is concerned, statements of the type "the market believes that..." or "the market thinks that..." are often heard. In this exercise, self-referential rationality gives the past experiences of group, experiences which have shaped its representations and beliefs, an important role to play. For example, if one considers "the Keynesian beauty contest" once again, it seems that the collective choice of the group under consideration will vary strongly according to whether on the previous day, this same group, having had to attribute the prize for best film, will have chosen a film in black and white or in colours. Although this is a fact manifestly without relevance for whoever is trying to really determine what

---

11 Keynes, op. cit., p. 156. To simplify, I considered that the nicest face was being looked for where Keynes gives the choice as "the six prettiest faces".

12 This quote from Keynes has been slightly transformed to take account of the fact that each person is looking for the nicest photograph and not the six prettiest faces as in the text of *General Theory*. Cf. previous note.

the nicest photograph is, it is not at all the same from the point of view of self-referential rationality. In fact, the past choice of black and white or colour imposes itself in everyone's view as a remarkable salience. Thus, a great number of participants will be tempted to see this as a criterion likely to be retained by the others participants as characterising the aesthetic judgement of the group. In these conditions, the selected photograph will verify this criterion, which will validate *ex post* the relevance of self-referential reasoning. In this example, as in financial practice, it is always a question of copying salient behaviours, that is to say those that are considered to be likely to be copied by the others: such is the principal key of self-referential rationality. As we will see, a characteristic of this self-referential process is to allow for more or less durable consensus to emerge to structure the beliefs and the expectations of the group.

3. FINANCIAL CONVENTION

Applied to financial markets, self-referential analysis describes an active and anxious community, questioning all the hypotheses and all the rumours, to determine those likely to obtain consent of the market. This process of exploration degenerates frequently in sporadic mimetic polarisations when a given event is selected simultaneously by a great number of actors because of its supposed saliency, happening independently of its real information content[13]. Strong and sudden variations in price follow, unconnected with fundamental values. This is a cognitive mechanism, which contributes powerfully to the excessive volatility which stock exchange prices undergo. This process of the mimetic exploration of hypotheses can however stabilise durably when an interpretation draws the general adhesion of the market. In these conditions, a model of evaluation recognised by all as legitimate emerges: this is called a convention. It is in this way that the self-referential group provisionally overcomes its lack of objective reference: as long as the convention is accepted, the specular dynamic is notably simplified since in that instance, to foresee what others are going to do, all one has to do is to refer to what is foreseen by the convention. Through the game of the self-validation of beliefs, there follows a relative stability of the convention, which, for the agents, becomes like second nature.

With the concept of convention, after those of liquidity and self-referentiality, our theoretical analysis of finance as an autonomous power of

---

[13] One finds the same self-referential logic when one looks into the workings of the media. The constraint of competition, that is to say that of audience ratings, leads those in the media not to seek out relevant information with regard to "fundamental" criteria, but in fact information likely to attract the interest of the public such as the media anticipate this to be. In the case of finance, as in the case of the media, one finds, for example, the same excessive valorisation of speed, and this occurs independently or almost so of the content of the information revealed. The most important thing is always to be first. The congruence of these two logics of opinion plays an important role in the constitution of what we will call a "general opinion".

evaluation comes to an end. It shows us the market's ability to organise itself around the collective adhesion to certain beliefs about the future of the economy. The most recent example of such a convention is given to us by what we can call the "Internet convention", that is to say the model of evaluation, which dominated the international stock markets during recent years until the crash in April 2000. This convention fully illustrates our thesis of the autonomy of self-referential finance. To see this, let us consider the way in which, in 1999, it conjointly evaluated the toy company Toys "R" Us which belongs to the "old economy" and its brand new electronic competitor eToys[14]. The former is old and well known, its sales are 400 times larger than the latter and it makes big profits while eToys only loses money. However, in 1999, its capitalisation was half a time smaller[15]! Why? Because it was supposed that the exceptional growth of electronic commerce would uniquely benefit the company eToys. If all objectives and fundamental criteria (size, reputation, seniority, sales and profits) can be swept away in this way in the name of a vision of what the future will be, which by nature is very uncertain, then very clearly everything is possible where the evaluation of the market is concerned. It follows that, to make the level of share prices intelligible, one has to start from the conventions that the market gives itself through the game of mimetic consensus. *In fine*, it is always the stock exchange, which imposes its vision.

CONCLUSION

The theoretical approach of market finance developed in this chapter presents three main characteristics, which differentiate it from more orthodox approaches. On the one hand, organised financial markets are the result of, a project to bypass some of the constraints set on the economy of production. The purpose is to build a collective mode to monitor commitments, which reduces the individual risks of investors, which we called liquidity. On the other, the logic of evaluation is self-referential: what counts for investors is not a fundamental value but how the opinion of the majority evolves. A large propensity towards mimetic behaviours follows which often degenerates into tense contagious crises. Imitation and contagion are well documented, easily understandable for those sharing a self-referential view of the stock market, but are difficult to understand in a fundamentalist framework[16]. Finally, self-referentiality is stabilised when a convention, which durably structures

---

[14] see Robert Shiller (2000), p.176

[15] This is a very banal situation which one finds, for example, in the comparison between Amazon.com and Barnes & Nobles for book sales. And this was occurring at the very moment when the companies of the old economy were also starting to develop sites for electronic commerce.

[16] Mimetic behaviour in finance is analysed extensively in A. Orlean and Y. Tadjeddine (2000) pp.80-97.

individual expectations, emerges. In our approach, such convention plays the role devoted to equilibrium in the standard orthodox approach.

These characteristics build a theoretical vision in which finance appears as an autonomous power of evaluation. What is the effect of this autonomy of the economy ? It depends on the room left to stock markets. When their place is minor, as was the case in France between 1962 and 1978, the Paris stock market went through 16 years of stagnation without it affecting economic growth in any way. Over this period real GDP doubled while the stock market index lost 75% in real terms. On the contrary, when the room left is fundamental, as it is today, financial conventions have great impact. One has been able to measure it for instance with the Internet bubble and its effects on the development of the new technologies.

Finally, our analysis leads us to take some distance with the "objective" concept of prices as defended by the marginalist theory of value. The self-referential theory tells us that the fundamentals of the economy (e.g. resources, technologies and consumer preferences) are insufficient to understand the movement of prices. One has also to account for how economic agents are figuring and analysing their economic environment. The cognitive dimension becomes absolutely essential. The economist must therefore take interest in individual representations and analyse the collective process through which common belief emerges.

REFERENCES

Balley P. (1987), *La Bourse : mythes et réalités,* Paris, Presses Universitaires de France.

Keynes J.M. (1973), *The General Theory of Employment, Interest and Money,* Macmillan, Cambridge University Press for the Royal Economic Society.

Orléan A. (1999), *Le pouvoir de finance,* Paris, Odile Jacob.

Orléan A. and Tadjeddine Y. (2000), *Imitative expectations and Informational paradox* in F. Gardes et G. Prat eds, "Prices expectations in goods and financial markets" Edward Elgar, 2000.

Shiller R. (2000), *Irrational Exuberance*, Princeton University Press.

Chapter 6

THEORY OF INFORMATION : FROM BOUNDED RATIONALITY TO INTERPRETIVE REASON

Olivier Favereau
Professor Paris X-University
FORUM Nanterre

INTRODUCTION

In the current terms of dominant economic theory, which I would qualify as Extended Standard Theory (as opposed to Standard Theory, represented by models of general equilibrium), the place of information is absolutely central. It is defined as *a variation of subjective probabilities in a theory of rational decision*, a variation with which it is always logically possible (or even actually feasible) to associate a marginal willingness to pay: if information circulates then it is as a merchandise that it does so. The passage to a hypothesis of bounded rationality will allow us to gain access to a more general notion of information, admitting the latter definition as a limited case. Information will be defined as *every source of meaning in a general theory of human action*; it is not always susceptible to receiving a price, for although it circulates it is as an intermediary (in the sense used by Michel Callon, 1991, p. 197 : "Everything which passes from one actor to the other and which constitutes the form and the matter of relations which arise between them") and an intermediary only has the form of merchandise in highly particular, that is to say, decontextualised situations!

The paper will be divided into three parts, each devoted to one aspect of the change which the notion of information has undergone and introducing the hypothesis of bounded rationality into Extended Standard Theory : the first will deal with the *dynamic* aspect, the second with the *structural* aspect, the third with the *collective* aspect. So as to clearly mark the conversion to cognitive realism, each part will be centred on one of the three heuristics which Daniel Kahneman, Paul Slovic and Amos Tversky (1982) developed, synthesising a decade of work in experimental psychology. These are, respectively, the heuristics of availability, representativeness, and contextualisation (i.e. anchorage and adjustment). I will attempt to show that, considered in relation to a "substantive" conception of rationality, these approaches can generally benefit from the more enviable status of the manifestation of a "procedural" rationality, according to the terms introduced by Herbert Simon in 1976.

P. Petit (ed.), Economics and Information, 93–120.

1. THE DYNAMIC ASPECT OF INFORMATION : THE INCOMPLETENESS OF EXPECTATIONS AND THE LOGIC OF LEARNING

Before developing further, it is necessary to recall that the fundamental axiom in the theory of decision is the absence of unforeseen contingencies : the list of states of nature has to be fixed and predetermined.

Hence the paradoxes in extending the theory to intertemporal choices, when there are perspectives for the acquisition of information and some consequences of the choices are irreversible (see Claude Henry's reinterpretation of the value of the option (1974), which Jean-Pierre Ponssard (1975) then links to the expected value of information, whether perfect or imperfect).

Hence, also, the failure of attempts to give axiomatic form to a criterion of temporalised rationality (Kreps and Porteus, 1979), which only confirms Karl Popper's recurrent warning (for example, 1984, §21) : learning cannot be given axiomatic form because it cannot be anticipated, for it were so, it would already be realised.

Hence, finally, the major negative result according to which the incomplete views of the future destroys the possibility of reducing incertitude to subjective probabilities, in Leonard Savage's demonstration (see Michèle Cohen and Jean-Yves Jaffray, 1980, on the situations of "total ignorance"). The contradiction between substantive rationality and learning (in the fullest sense) is therefore fundamental, which goes hand in hand with a equally fundamental criticism of the pretension of Bayesian processes to offer an acceptable representation of learning behaviour.

This brief recap of Standard Theory must, in all cases, incite us to never dissociate the exploration of the positive aspect (learning) and that of the negative aspect (incompleteness) in our undertaking to integrate bounded rationality : the *homo oeconomicus* of bounded rationality is less rational but more intelligent than the *homo oeconomicus* of unbounded rationality, if we take it as true that intelligence has something to do with a superior learning ability.

1.1 The dynamics of adaptation to the unforeseen

The essential idea is that the concrete economic agent is a lot more at ease with incompleteness that his official representative in neo-classical theory, for the simple reason that it is a basic fact of practical existence, and that, out of necessity, he had to develop efficient adjustment mechanisms. This diagnostic signifies that *the activities of understanding, memorisation and inference are already giving way to the perspective of learning processes :*

(i) *the search for a minimal dose of redundancy*: see the classic studies on organisational "slack" (Cyert and March, 1963) or the more recent one of Donald Chisholm (1989).

(ii) *the importance of mechanisms intended to economise cognitive resources*, memory, above all. Here we must mention the analyses of Andre

Leroi-Gourhan on "this unique property that man possesses of placing his memory outside of himself, in the social organism" (1965, p.34). This is the first reference to a notion which is almost totally absent from orthodox economic theory, that of *object*; it will not be the last.

(iii) *the systematic elaboration of theories or models*, to subsume single facts under headings of typical facts (see Karl Popper, 1967).

(iv) *the over-valorisation of incidents or problems* with, symmetrically, the under-valorisation of cases where the status quo is reproduced : the confirmation of the model is a more comfortable and, as such, less interesting piece of information (in the sense of attracting less attention). This property, joined with the previous one, introduces a primary characterisation of what can be called "*interpretation*" (and which is opposed to "calculus") : that is to say *elaborating models simultaneously deciding what is general (which can be dealt with by the model) and what is particular (exterior to the model).*

This brief panorama reveals an intriguing feature : these four properties seem to contradict each other in pairs, in the sense that (i) seems to deny the will to economise manifested by (ii), while the approach implied by (iv) amounts to contesting the relevance of (iii). In reality, the apparent contradiction has to be able to cancel itself out by mobilising Jean-François Richard's remark (1990, p159-60) according to which a logic of learning requires both (i) and (ii), where memorisation is concerned, as well as (iii) and (iv), where understanding and inference are concerned. All of which prepares us for the introduction of the following point, which seems, also, to completely invalidate my initial argumentation.

1.2 The Dynamics of Resistance to Change

The *homo oeconomicus* of bounded rationality, being structurally in a learning position, is going to show himself to be strongly conservative, where the methods, the tools and the knowledge gained from previous learning are concerned. The reluctance to change theory is perfectly rational, in a learning situation, for theory, seen as a way of imposing order on reality, admitting exceptions and singularities, rather than as a schema of universal explanation, excluding exceptions and singularities, is precisely what makes learning possible. Moreover, it is so costly to come up with a theory that the resistance to change is further enforced by the application of the economic calculus to cognitive resources confirming that the hypothesis of bounded rationality is more general than the hypothesis of unbounded rationality, which certainly wastes cognitive resources, supposing them to be free.

One can appreciate the error there is in treating learning as the transferral of a static knowledge : in this instance, everything stems from the dynamic, even the stasis which expresses the blocking of a dynamic. Nonetheless, one must refrain from outraged denunciation of the defence of the (cognitive) advantages acquired, this auto-braking of learning presents certain collective virtues, among which that of maintaining a high level of predictability in behaviour.

1.3 The Heuristic of Availability

Kahneman and Tversky (1982) show that "there are situations where people estimate the frequency of a class or the probability of an event by the ease with which the examples or illustrations come to mind"; they add that "similarly, one can evaluate the probability that a given business project will fail imagining the various difficulties that it could encounter" (op. cit., p.11).

The authors supply numerous experimental verifications of the existence of such a heuristic, which seems to solicit two classes of mental operations : recall in memory and the construction of scenarios. The first class relies, in an obvious manner, on the preceding developments; the second is more interesting still for my thesis, for the authors see in this the result of a mental process of a sort simulation model (op. cit., chap.14). Availability constructs and organises itself around the ability to elaborate scenarios, which first of all draws on the stock of scenarios which have made an impression on the imagination, because they have placed events of extreme utility (or lack of utility) to the forefront of the mind. The example of the clinician who, faced with a depressed patient, remembers suicide cases and neglects all the comparable patients who did not commit suicide illustrates a case of disutility. Kahneman and Tversky have no difficulty in evoking cases of utility : a lottery winner who played his birthday numbers immediately gives rise to imitators, etc. In conclusion, the heuristic of availability suggests that the *homo oeconomicus* of bounded rationality will naturally develop a propensity for excess optimism and/or pessimism.

It would be interesting to link up these two cognitive approaches to Keynesian considerations, on the one hand on the "liquidity preference", and on the other, "animal spirits", but this would be a digression in relation to my thesis according to which these two approaches, factors of irrationality in a closed world, are vectors of rationality, in an open world where the risk of error "by omission" adds itself to that of the risk of error "by action", that is to say where the worst of regrets is that of "not having tried". This is obviously a world whose future is incomplete, and within which the decisions taken influence, unpredictably, the conditions of their success or of their failure : the actions take effect on their own probability of success.

Albert Hirschman (1967) is the first to have identified, unknowingly, the impact of this phenomenon in terms of what we will have to qualify as "rationality reversal". Re-examining 11 big investments projects financed by the World Bank ten years after their application, he observed that, in all cases, costs and problems were underestimated. Had these been correctly estimated the project would not have gone ahead. The surprise comes from the fact that the error committed out of excess optimism was, in the majority of the cases, more than compensated by action taken to adapt or to transform the initial project, rendering it more financially viable than predicted ... thanks to a learning process, still less predictable. Hirschman proposed calling this fortunate connection among humans between two errors of opposite directions, one out of excess optimism, the other out of pessimism, the "principle of hiding hand".

There is no need to call on natural selection, it suffices to remark that the first error is the cause of the second. This part of the argumentation provisionally concludes on the realisation that information depends crucially, for its meaning, on the role that it can play in a dynamic learning process : can it be reduced to a model, in the form of solution or of exception, and, in this last eventuality, does it or does it not instigate a revision process of the model ? Whatever the answer, information is worth only what the learning associated to it is worth. Hence this first conclusion :

Conclusion 1 : all information does not circulate as merchandise, because it is not all exploitable.

2. THE STRUCTURAL ASPECT OF INFORMATION : THE MANAGEMENT OF ATTENTION AND HIERARCHICHAL LEVELS

The point of view of the Extended Standard Theory, according to which information is a merchandise, has just been criticised, in a way which is still classical, by arguing on the specificity of the considerations of quality which this merchandise calls for. The quality of information is linked to its semantic content and this is in relation to the highly personal characteristics of the concerned agent: as it happens the possibility (and the modality) of inscription into the learning dynamic of this agent. As a result, the space within which information circulates, when it circulates, is essentially heterogeneous and riddled with discontinuity.

The full recognition of information as a non-merchandise (and no longer only as a special merchandise) would broaden, instead of limiting, rationality's field of action. However, this broadening would not contradict what has just been said about heterogeneity, for *although the quality of merchandise is not merchandise, the quality of information is information.* This information is not only distinct from the first but it is also on a superior level of logic: we will speak of information-object and meta-information, borrowing from the terminology of the Palo-Alto school (see Watzlawick et al, 1972).

These preliminary remarks suffice to introduce the two propositions which shall constitute the second stage of my argumentation.

2.1 The Scarce Resource is Attention Rather than Information

Justification of the proposition. The question of quality (notably relevance, weight, reliability, etc.) of the information available allows the latter to escape from the rule of merchandise: no information is rationally exploitable without this information extension which follows it like its shadow and which is related to its quality. Yet this meta-information is rarely provided with the information-object, either out of ignorance, or as a strategy (in the case of a commercial relationship).

What came before can be summarised by the following, deliberately provocative formula : I can buy information, I cannot buy information on the quality of the information, for I am at minimum co-responsible, at maximum fully responsible for the production/consumption of this information of the second order. We discover, once again, the necessity to *interpret*, this more in the sense where it calls on us to show a critical spirit. By accepting the idea of an essential implication of the individual in the elaboration of meta-information, we are in the process of introducing *a new variable of control, well known to psychologists and little known to economists* (with the exception of Simon): *attention*. The omission of the variable "attention" brings the analysis back into a Bayesian universe, where only information-objects circulate, giving rise to simple perception.

Thus the splitting of information into two parts is a first access route to the notion of attention. There is a second, taken by Simon (1971, 1978), which draws directly on the limits of individual rationality. The ability to receive and to process information very quickly reaches saturation point, because, among other reasons, the human spirit functions sequentially, with the result that the most banal of situations combines both uncertainty (therefore a deficit of information) and excess information (in relation to what the human spirit can handle for a determined duration). The emphasis on attention which implies handling limited cognitive resources to maximum capacity, and therefore rationally, highlights *a property of rationality, up to that point suppressed by an optimising rationality, in other words reflexivity.*

As a further variable, attention finds its place between the two poles just identified : the double nature of information, the self-referential character of rationality.

Application of the proposition. The first stage of the argumentation emphasised the strategic role of learning. What then does the notion of attention, introduced in this second stage, contribute ? On the one hand, a clarification of cognitive mechanisms at work in all learning processes ; on the other, an enhancement of these same mechanisms.

Let us begin with the clarification.

Argyris and Schön's theory of organisational learning (1978) offers a particularly pedagogical illustration of the "attention" factor in learning, even where collective learning is concerned. For these authors, there is learning as soon as an agent confronts results and intentions, such as they follow from the "main variables" with his "theory of action". The confrontation of intentions and results will lead either to the pursuit of the current actions, or their revision – with two possible scenarios : the revision can take place without modification of the main variables or else oblige the exploration of new variables. In *all* the eventualities, learning consists in applying rules while maintaining a critical attitude towards them, sometimes for one to evaluate oneself, sometimes to evaluate them themselves. This paradoxical attitude of critical conformity, intrinsic to all learning, suggests a second characterisation of what we call "interpreting" (as opposed to "calculating") : that is to say *entering into a system of rules (in the broadest sense), by giving it meaning and relevance, while remaining exterior to this, so as to perceive it through critical judgement, as a way of reimbursing of the initial semantic credit.*

Along the way, to connect learning and interpretation, I left attention to one side. Everyone can certify from experience that learning uses up a lot of attention, directly by the effect of mental and physical fatigue associated with it, indirectly by the fact that successful learning expresses itself as the disappearance of effort and the putting in place of routines, whose great virtue is to economise attention, this scarce and precious resource.

From that point onwards, learning does not consist so much in changing routines, as the evolutionist theory supposes, as in changing attitudes in relation to routines : first of all, re-qualifying them as markers, then exploring systematic differences, finally stabilising and validating these differences by shifting the markers and progressively diminishing the attention charge. Attention and learning mutually define each other: learning is attention brought under control, attention is free learning. The philosopher Simone Weil saw studying above all as a "gymnastics of attention"(1962, p. 122).

So much for the clarification. Now for the enhancement.

The most spectacular contribution of the theory of bounded rationality is to *extend the domain of cognition beyond the cognitive*. There is in fact an "intimate connection of emotions with attention" (de Sousa, 1987, p. 238). Let us first of all consider the link between the emotions and attention : emotion sets off attention. Simon looks at the problem in a evolutionist perspective, which seems completely justified here : "What characteristics does an organism need to enable it to exercise a sensible kind of bounded rationality ? It needs some way of focusing – of avoiding distraction (or at least too much distraction) and focusing on the things that needs attention at a given time. A very strong case can be made, and has been made by physiological psychologists, that focusing attention is one of the principal functions of the processes we call emotions" (1983, pp.20-21). Let us now consider the link between attention and emotion. To this end, it is useful to introduce the classic distinction between analytic processes (which methodically explore the entirety of possible solutions) and intuitive processes (where a familiar schema is suddenly recognised) : "The searching, plodding stages of problem solving tend to be relatively free from intense emotion; they may be described as cold cognition. But sudden discovery, the "aha !" experience, tends to evoke emotion ; it is hot cognition" (Simon, 1983, p.29). The attention/emotion link evoked here is not exactly reciprocal with the previous one; it is situated more at an early stage. As it happens, attention produces an intuition, immediately accompanied by an emotion, as if, for the mind, it were necessary to greet and acknowledge the importance of its discoveries which otherwise it would be in danger of neglecting, perhaps because of the fact that they emerge from who knows where.

Nonetheless, this articulation of the emotional and the cognitive must above all not be understood as an exaltation of subjectivity. On the contrary, the methodological message of the model of bounded rationality includes the absolute necessity of no longer confining economic analysis to the universe of mental representations. What was said above on the subject of objects (see §1.1.(ii)) can henceforth be generalised. The finality of learning is incorporation into routines and there are two modalities of incorporation, both physical but one in objects, the other in bodies. The second, which can henceforth draw on the rediscovery of emotions (via attention), plays a fundamental, although implicit, role in understanding what "following a rule" means. As for the first, in placing "objective contents of thought" outside itself, it makes the critical spirit possible (Popper, 1978 ; Goody, 1986). In neither of the two cases, does the attention/emotion connection consecrate the triumph of subjectivity.

2.2 Dealing with Complexity in Bounded Rationality is Hierarchical

What precedes can be summed up in the formula: attention introduces hierarchy. What follows turns the analysis the other way round : hierarchy organises attention. In fact, although it is true that attention produces hierarchy, this production is transitory. Therefore an exteriorisation and a material expression are to be expected of this effort of attention in objects such as rules of behaviour or institutional bodies and their hierarchical phenomena, which are more common than we think.

What are we to understand by "hierarchy", abstractly, in the perspective of grouping the maximum of observations under this label ?

The answer will be borrowed from Simon. We call "hierarchy" the order in the resolution of a system of equations, when the matrix representing this system can be broken down into blocks. In terms of images, certain variables have to be determined before others, which justifies considering them as more important. The fundamental theorems have been gathered in Ando, Fisher and Simon's study (1963). They have been extended by Courtois (1977). A general presentation is offered by Simon's Compton and Gaither conferences (1981).

Simon's thesis is that "one path to the construction of a non trivial theory of complex systems is by way of a theory of hierarchy"(1981, p.229). The principal argument in favour of this thesis has it that "complex systems will evolve from simple systems much more rapidly if there are stable intermediate forms than if there are not"(1981, p.209).

The organisational efficiency of hierarchy invites us to look not with instantaneous cross-section, as is usual, but in a chronological series, because its most interesting properties are dynamic in nature : "the time required for the evolution of a complex form from simple elements depends critically on the numbers and the distribution of potential intermediate stable forms"(1981, p.202). One goes further... by going in stages.

Here are four illustrations, reorienting the theoretical gaze towards a *structure-approach* either of judgement, or of behaviour, as opposed to the *measure-approach* of Standard Theory of decision, in the sense that rationality, henceforth, consists less in making everything uniform so as to spot the best than in weighing everything up so as to separate what is important from what is secondary. It is a question of going from a logic of calculus to a process of interpretation.

The two first illustrations concern *individual* judgement or behaviour. Keynes opened a debate that nobody among the probability theorists has succeeded in closing, introducing, not without hesitation, the complementary notion of the "weight" of a probability judgement (1921, chap.6). The probability of an argument depends on the relationship between favourable and unfavourable information. Keynes then argues the case of a non probabilistic consideration of weight and concludes with this metaphor : "the weight measures the *sum* of the favourable and unfavourable evidence, the probability measures the *difference*"(1921, p.84). In total, the recourse to the "weight" of probability judgements signifies that the *homo oeconomicus* is recognised to have a specifically *critical* aptitude, beyond the standard calculating aptitude (the ability to transform his knowledge on the world into quantitative or qualitative probability judgements): the ability to reflect in relation to this knowledge so as to evaluate "credibility" (Georgescu-Roegen, 1967, pp.266-269).

Now to behaviour. Through short and long-term expectations Keynes, very finely distinguishes reversible decisions (production and employment, financial investment) admitting a close horizon of expectations, and irreversible decisions (productive investment) calling on a horizon of distant expectations, in the absence of a perfect second-hand market. Obviously this second type of decision is, in size and in importance, greater than the first.

The following two illustrations focus on *collective* judgements or behaviour. We know that a certain number of theoretical innovations of "General Theory" are to be found, without possibility of reciprocal influence, in Kalecki's studies from the thirties. Do we stand before an eminent case of multiple discovery ? Breaking with a quasi consensus among economists, including Keynesians, Patinkin (1982) chose to reply in the negative. While Keynes's theoretical innovations served his "central message" well (that is to say the balancing of underemployment), their replies in Kalecki's studies were made serve another, more banal "central message": cycles of investment. In other words, what constitutes theoretical innovation in one scientific community is not so much the chronological priority of what is said than its enunciation within a "central message", as if the attention given by the author was the necessary condition (surely insufficient!) for generating attention in the community.

Finally, to conclude, I shall deal with the question of behaviour. The judge's reflection leads to a judiciary decision, which decides in a conflict with the usual effects of attribution, or of destruction, of property rights. Dworkin (1977) proposes a particularly instructive analysis of "judgements" made in "hard cases". These can be recognised in the impossibility of deducing the solution of unequivocal rules. Should unequivocal rules be lacking, the judge will turn to rules of a higher order, the principles, which are ethical-political in nature. Their origin is undetermined, their content is to be interpreted and their application calls on the intuitive sense of an enlightened public in relation to what is appropriate, or not, in the situation. In concrete terms, the judge, by his resolution of the "hard case", seeks the best "fit" with the totality of the judiciary undertaking, seen as the deployment in time of these higher norms which are the principles.

All of these examples lead to the conclusion that there is no sense aggregating or collecting information. This field is not sufficiently uniform to give rise to calculus ; on the contrary, it is its heterogeneity which is the object of all attention : how can a heterogeneous mass of information be transformed into a dynamic structure, a source of learning ? This operation of voluntary heterogeneisation and control is called interpretation.

Following the examples, the experiments.

2.3 The Heuristic of Representativeness

The difference in relation to Bayesianism stems from the taking into account of the relative pertinence and importance of the information. According to Kahneman, Slovic and Tversky economic agents in bounded rationality use a heuristic of representativeness : "A person who follows this heuristic evaluates the probability of an uncertain event, or a sample, by the degree to which it is: (i) similar in essential properties to its parent population ; and (ii) reflects the salient features of the process by which it is generated. Our thesis is that, in many situations, an event A is judged more probable than an event B whenever A appears more representative than B." (1982, p.33). In many respects, "representative" functions as a synonym of "typical"(1982, p.86).

The following portrait serves as an example : "Bill is 34 years old. He is intelligent but unimaginative, compulsive, and generally lifeless. In school, he was strong in mathematics but weak in social studies and humanities". Having seen this portrait, eight statements are to be classified ("Bill is an architect", "Bill surfs for a hobby", etc.) in order of probability. It is no surprise to see that, among the eight, the statement "Bill is an accountant" gathers the maximum probability, while the statement "Bill plays jazz for a hobby" gathers the weakest probability. The surprise occurs when it is discovered that the composite statement "Bill is an accountant who plays jazz for a hobby" gathers an intermediary probability, which contradicts a fundamental rule in the calculus of probabilities : the conjunction of the events A and B is necessarily less probable than event A alone, or event B alone.

The experiments gave approximately the same results, whatever the public questioned and whatever way the statements were presented. The most troubling point is that after discussion and reflection, the participants easily admitted their logical mistake, while continuing to argue in terms of representativeness. Hence we have it that the rule (of judgement, not of behaviour) is willingly recognised in its abstract formulation and just as spontaneously broken in practical application. *Everything occurs as if the passage to practice added something*, which completely transforms the problem. Let us note that the semantic content of A or of B was not chosen at random by Kahneman, Slovic, and Tversky : on the one hand, there is a "relevant" or "important" item of information, matching the portrait of Bill with the type-portrait of a profession, and, on the other, there is a secondary or accessory item of information which doesn't individualise Bill to the same degree. In the end, these two items of information are not on the same level; one is lexicographically superior to the other, in so far that it is worthy of attention, the other is not (or significantly less so). It is therefore perfectly logical that the probability of A+B be superior to that of B, if B is the non relevant information and if A is the relevant information. That the probability of A, moreover, is superior to that of A+B, apart from the fact that it conforms with logic, corresponds, according to my reinterpretation, to a set of possible worlds, more general, less specified, less idiosyncratic, in the case of A than in that of A+B : it is easier, for a company, to recruit an accountant ... than a jazzman accountant !

The *homo oeconomicus* of bounded rationality only seems to be lacking from the point of view of Bayesian logic because he has to manifest a superior logic to be able to operate in a more complex universe, where information has to undergo an effort of interpretation, so as to evaluate its importance or relevance. Hence this second conclusion, at the end of this second stage of the argumentation :

Conclusion 2 : all information does not circulate as merchandise, because it is not commensurable.

3. THE COLLECTIVE ASPECT OF INFORMATION : SITUATED RATIONALITY, CO-ORDINATION AND DISTRIBUTED COGNITION

The third transformation undergone by the notion of information, by integrating the hypothesis of bounded rationality, concerns its collective aspect. The two reasons which render human cognitive workings dependent on its inscription in a collective thinking of itself as somewhat more than a collection of individuals are entitled "co-ordination" and "power". These two reasons are introduced through the following two propositions :

3.1 Boundedly Rational Actors Cannot Neglect Co-Ordination

Standard Theory is constructed on the rigorous separation of the questions of rationality and co-ordination. The shift of Extended Standard Theory towards a bilateral and contractual conception of co-ordination in the market cancels de facto this separation but without modifying the tools of analysis all the same. The theory of decision in a situation of interaction with another person is taken up in its entirety from the theory of decision in games against nature, which is highly important in the reduction of economy of organisations to an economy of opportunism (moral and anti-selection hazards). Only non Standard Theory, thanks to the hypothesis of bounded rationality, will show itself to be capable of abolishing the frontiers between the question of rationality and that of co-ordination. If the hypothesis of bounded rationality plays a role in this salient point, it is in virtue of the new idea that it expresses : *reflexivity*.

(i) *Even on a strictly individual level*, bounded rationality contains an important, even essential, part of co-ordination, on the one hand with oneself, on the other with personal objects.

Let us begin with the most surprising and the most fundamental : co-ordination with oneself, which consists in judging oneself, that is to say metaphorically looking at oneself from the outside. The hypothesis of bounded rationality implies that cognitive resources are scarce and have to be carefully managed, in the same way as other scarce resources: in other words rationally! A central point is the adoption of a learning logic. However, what does learning mean if not an action coming from oneself carried out on oneself, through time, that is to say finally a particularly delicate form of co-ordination, with oneself admittedly but in a dynamic ?

The most concrete manifestation of the requirement of co-ordination, that which is most easily identified from the exterior, bears on the innumerable objects which each individual surrounds him or herself with, out of reflex, to relax the constraint of cognitive limitations in the daily exercise of his or her tasks. These objects have a status apart: Norman (1993) baptised them "cognitive artefacts", artificial devices which improve the performances of human thought, either through direct amplification of abilities, or through the transformation of the tasks to be carried out. An example of the first type of device is the book, which relieves memory; an example of the second is the use of a checklist, which, as well as relieving memory, "introduces three new tasks: making out the list, remembering to consult the list, reading and interpreting the items on the list" (1993, p.23).

This distinction is important, because the cognitive aptitudes of the individual, from the point of view of the individual, remain unchanged, while, from the point of view of the observer who considers the individual system + cognitive artefact + task, they have augmented.

(ii) *On the inter-individual level*, it is a priori less surprising to overlap rationality and co-ordination. The hypothesis of bounded rationality calls for the overlapping of rationality and co-ordination, for the simple reason that the *homo oeconomicus* of bounded rationality can once again (see § 1.1) hope to commute his deficit of rationality into a gain of intelligence : *precisely because each person's rationality is limited, each person has to expect, in his or her interactions, to meet problems of co-ordination, and since they expect this, they prepare for it.* This argument can be extended by remarking that each person assumes, in others, the same limits as in him or herself. Let's examine rationality once more in the light of co-ordination, either through objects or rules.

Human societies have the exclusivity of "framed interactions", restrained and strictly local one-on-ones. Latour's thesis (1994) is that it is objects (not just any objects) which produce this precious, very Simonian decomposability (see § 2.2) : "While I am at the counter to buy postage stamps and I speak into the into the grill, I have neither my family, nor my colleagues, nor my superiors on my back; nor does the person at the desk, thanks be to God, tire me with talk of her mother in law or her kids' teeth" (1994, p.594). How can we denominate these co-ordinating objects which have the paradoxical property of "containing" (in the two meanings of the word) the collective ? Livet and Thevenot (1994) chose to call them "qualified objects", distinguishing "personalised objects", "common objects", and "conventional objects", according to the type of collective action which recruits them. The authors (1994, p.161) remark, in passing, that currency is the co-ordinating object par excellence, which might explain the famous impossibility of its integration into this same (Extended) Standard Theory.

These co-ordinating objects perhaps made their first appearance in economic theory under the particular figure of "focal points". Schelling (1960) shows that situations where two individuals want to meet, in the same town, without prior information or possible communication on the precise meeting place, end up finding a solution in the majority of cases: the selection of a prominent place in the sense that it strikes the imagination or attracts the gaze, because it presents "salient" characteristics. This salient nature should be linked to the meta-information, evoked in § 2.1, because of its link with the ability to channel attention.

The notion of "focal point" simultaneously illustrates a very general idea (being rational, here, is strictly equivalent to being co-ordinated) and a highly specific case (co-ordination, here, is strictly equivalent to the identification of an object of co-ordination). One ought to be able to find less spectacular and more familiar examples without difficulty, if it is true that bounded rationality succeeds. as well in matters of co-ordination in contexts as unfavourable as this. The organisation of the Central Control Post of the A line of the RER (rapid transit rail system in the Paris area) will, as it happens, be obtained almost directly and without excessive salary cost, through a physical organisation of the work stations, suggested by cognitive ergonomics, such as the information received and processed by each member of the PCC or, automatically, communicated to all the other members (Joseph, 1994; Theureau and Filippi, 1994).

After the objects, the rules follow. The *homo oeconomicus* of bounded rationality must see the paternity of *the invention of a supplementary means of co-ordination* attributed to him *: the rules* (meaning by this the normative statements stipulating the required, preferred or prohibited behaviour in determined situations).

Entering through the objects is perhaps the most direct route to begin to speak about rules. After all, a co-ordinating object is not enough, on its own, to co-ordinate. Its use must be appropriate, which amounts to saying that a co-ordinating object is nothing without its instructions, without its rules for use. Formal rules being currency, implicit and idiosyncratic rules beings "focal points" – but rules all the same. *A co-ordinating object is the part of the iceberg above the water, whose immersed part consists in rules.* Nonetheless, the most interesting link between object and rule goes in the other direction. To be convinced of this, it is necessary to consider the problem of co-ordination by rules in completely general terms.

Almost all the dimensions of bounded rationality are implied in the characterisation of the efficiency of rules, such as they result from a generation of studies, in Philosophy, Law, logic, and human and social sciences: rules are always incomplete, to the extent that they don't exhaustively fix their conditions of application. As a consequence, there is an irreducible and sometimes capital part of interpretation in the execution of a rule. Rules are the heuristics within (and at the service of) a learning process (Favereau, 1994). Rules serve less before than during or after the action : "Rules are *procedures for dealing with conflicts of interpretation*, therefore for revising the framework of action, and not the determinants of the immediate action" (Livet and Thevenot, 1994, p.144). To these general considerations, one can add that there are furthermore certain affinities between the meaning of conformity to rules and to the Simonian operation model of bounded rationality in terms of thresholds of satisfaction or of levels of aspiration : these serve as markers, can be reached in various ways, are adjustable according to the difficulty there is in reaching them, stem from non commensurable criteria, etc. In the same way that objects can make it possible to compensate the limits of our rationality, *in rules one must see the projection outside of oneself of a satisfying and trusted model of collective interaction, and for this reason, a normative charge*. Books increase our memory ability, rules increase our co-ordination ability ; the principle is not substantially different. The specificity of rules obviously resides in the fact that the course of action will concern a collection of individuals. We know, thanks to (Extended) Standard Theory, that collection transforms itself with difficulty into collective. Non Standard Theory proceeds from the conviction that this very real difficulty has been artificially inflated by the hypothesis of optimising rationality. A collective will emerge from the collection, more easily than is believed, under the effect of two couples of closely linked factors :

First of all the utility of co-operation is better perceived in bounded rationality, simply because co-ordination is judged by all to be highly probable to have faults. Human societies have fortunately developed a propensity to practice *distributed cognition :* in my relations with another, who can say if what he or she knows completes what I don't know, or if what I know is what he doesn't know ? It is impossible to answer this question without trying the experience. The risk is great, however, for he who is first to expose himself... Except if this risk taking is functional. Yet it is so, if one understands that my consent to incompleteness can serve me as a signal to signify the seriousness of my intention to co-operate with my interlocutor. An efficient signal is a costly signal to imitate and this one is intrinsically so: fraud is excluded, since one constitutes oneself as "hostage" (see Favereau, 1997, for the full explanation of an argument partially borrowed from Williamson). What is not excluded, on the contrary, is the exploitation of this good will by the interlocutor. But he or she cannot escape from suspicion except by adopting a symmetric attitude. The absence of this signal becomes the indication of non co-operative intention. The entirety of this schema could be paraphrased in terms of trust, but that tends erase the logic of the situation, to the benefit of an ad hoc psychology.

Then there is this network of *rules* which proposes schemas of interaction in a discontinuous manner in various places of the social space, schemas which, as we saw above, require a great ability of interpretation on the part the very people who wish to conform with them. Does this new manifestation of incompleteness strongly diminish the benefits hoped for from this further mode of co-ordination in rules ? After reflection, the answer is negative. The *objects of co-ordination*, which, for non Standard Theory, now populate the universe of economic agents and which have seen to it that these are no longer operative, as in (Extended) Standard Theory, caught in a sort of social no man's land, are going to remove a great part of the ambiguity specific to rules by bringing indisputable elements of identification to the situation: "The interpretive perspective on the rule shifts attention to the adjustment to circumstances. It is the taking into account of circumstances and *objects* present in the situation which can halt the prolongation through new rules of application leading to aporia" (Livet and Thevenot, 1994, p.147).

The attentive reader will have noticed the complementarity between co-ordinating objects and rules. A moment ago, it was the latter which came to the aid of the former. Now it is the inverse. *A co-ordinating object is the part of the iceberg above the water, whose immersed part consists in rules.*

In any case, this detour through the question of co-ordination leads, clearly, to a third characterisation of what "*interpreting*" means (as opposed to "calculating"), which completes the previous characterisations introduced in § 1.1 and § 2.1 : that is to say *putting us in another's place, not so much to anticipate his or her reactions from outside, as to give us every chance of communicating our intentions, unequivocally, and thereby understand, from inside, the deep meaning of his or her reactions*. This formulation (stated from the point of view of the person who takes the initiative of interaction) implies a to and fro between two opposed hypotheses : a priori, another person resembles me, but I have to envisage the possibility that he is different from me. This sort of theoretical hesitation before the other represents the normative side of the empirical realisation of incompleteness.

As a provisional conclusion to this detailed justification of the first proposition of that 3rd part, the reader is invited to keep the following idea in memory. Information is something which only has meaning in a human context. As humans live in society, the value of information will crucially depend on the situation where it is extracted, intending by "situation", like Livet and Thevenot (1994, p.147), all the significant elements (objects, rules) which are of use to the *homo oeconomicus, in his social environment*, for his rational action. Rationality is admittedly *limited* but precisely it must be *situated,* so as to identify its limits and, at the same time, envisage shifting them. I will immediately introduce the second proposition of that 3rd part.

3.2 Between Boundedly Rational Actors, There Are No Powers of Co-Ordination Without The Constitution of Powers

The transition between the two propositions results from a realisation and a question, which are closely linked. Let us begin with the realisation: we have still not completely finished with the objects/rules connection, where co-ordination in the universe of bounded rationality is concerned. In fact, an insidious question emerges from the preceding considerations on the co-ordinating power of rules : why are we so quick to obey ? Why do we so willingly conform to rules ? Why do we respect authority so naturally ? Neither fear of sanctions, nor personal gain suffice as responses.

Two factors that we have just distinguished allow us to reply : on the one hand, the neutralisation of incompleteness in relations with others through the mobilisation of the aptitude for distributed cognition, on the other, the functional complementarity of co-ordinating objects and rules. The synthesis of all these elements (which bear a familiar name: organisation !) produces a chemical reaction of formidable efficiency : limited individual knowledge, when combined, engenders a collective competence of an order so superior that its objectification grants it the status of an anonymous third, all-powerful and omnipresent, to whom trust is due, under the form of spontaneous adhesion to the rules... This adhesion will confirm the initial combination of individual knowledge and the wheel has come full circle.

In saying this, we take leave of the visible side of the problem of co-ordination and are about to deal with its hidden side: the problem of power. *If power introduces itself so naturally into the universe of bounded rationality, it is because the latter cultivates the art of shifting its limits, by exteriorising resources or finding itself allies outside itself: objects, rules. Henceforth the appropriation of the former and the mastering of the latter will allow certain people to instrumentalise the behaviour of their fellows.* It would be totally erroneous to only see this as a confirmation of risks run by leaving the secure universe of optimising rationality, for it is precisely because of its ability to manufacture coordination, that bounded rationality also, involuntarily but inevitably, manufactures this joint product of co-ordination known as power.

What role does information play in this fatality ? Like any other source of meaning in a general theory of human action, it is par excellence that which all power seeks to control, because it is by nature that which cannot be totally controlled. Information therefore concerns power on two levels : firstly, it is its most efficient vector ; secondly, it is its most formidable antidote.

Level 1 : information, in part collectively produced, contributes to producing collectives, whose principal power consists in providing their members an analytical grid to interpret information...

After having revealed the dead-ends to which, in his opinion, Marx's holistic approach to society leads, Michael Piore (1983, p. 253) writes : "The alternative to Marxism is to understand the society in terms of the nature of cognitive processes. Here the critique of liberalism is that it views information and thought, more or less as it views society, as consisting of discrete individual elements, which produce through aggregation the continuous homogeneous phenomena of social life. It fails to recognise that those discrete elements are processed in terms of some model, framework or "structure" of thought, and the same discrete "bits" lead to very different outcomes, depending upon what that interpretative framework turns out to be. Society, social groups, and institutions are part of the process through which that framework is generated. (…) Because it is so central, one must focus upon where the interpretative framework comes from and how it evolves ? This notion of cognitive processes provides the framework for much of modern anthropology and sociology as well as developmental psychology and a good deal of modern linguistics".

This long quotation has the merit of introducing, in complete generality, the idea of groups as collective cognitive structures. This is the perspective traced in the studies of Bruno Jobert and in those of Pierre Muller on public politics: this is inseparable, one the one hand, from the elaboration of a "referential", "a set of cognitive images determining the perception of the problem by the groups involved and the definition of appropriate solutions", and on the other, from the intervention of "mediators", collective actors (professionals, administrative workers, elected representatives) which will allow for the articulation of a vision of the world and a new leadership within a sector of the system (Muller, 1994 ; see also Hilgartner and Bosk, 1988, for a study of public attention as a scarce resource).

This interaction between the cognitive and the collective provides us with the access key to a renewed approach to power. It explains the mode of efficiency specific to power (level 1), before explaining its limits (level 2).

1) It is very tempting to identify the fundamental part in the reconstruction with the notion of "*routine*". A's power over B would be measured by the behaviour which A can obtain from B in a routine way. In fact, it is in the habitual, not in the exceptional, that power is recognised. Barnes (1988) proposes a theory of this type : "Social power *is* the capacity for action in a society and hence is predominantly but not wholly identifiable as that which is routinely possible therein. Social power is *possessed* by those with discretion in

the direction of social action, and hence predominantly by those with discretion in the use of routines" (1988, p. 58) [italics in the text]. It is far from absurd to speak of routines but it is insufficient to stop at this: if routines are respected by hypothesis, then theory has nothing more to explain, and if it is necessary to explain why routines are respected, that means that there are notions which are more fundamental than routines.

2) Where Barnes spoke of routines, Callon and Latour speak of *"black boxes"*, in a text from 1981, essential for my thesis. Rather than power, they consider the notion of macro-actors (institutions, organisations, social classes, states) as opposed to micro-actors (individuals, groups, families), but the distinction makes use of an original characterisation of power. According to them, there is no difference between the actors which is inherent to their nature; the difference of size is a result, that is to say something which must be dealt with as a variable, instead of being taken as a fact. A macro-actor is an actor who can say "we", thus expressing other actors in a single will. This increase in size would be severely constrained if it had to be accompanied by a permanent struggle for acknowledgement.

It is at this point that the black boxes intervene. "An actor grows with the number of relations he or she can put, as we say, in black boxes. A black box contains that which no longer needs to be reconsidered (...). The more elements one can place in black boxes – modes of thought, habits, forces and objects – the broader the construction one can raise. (…) Macro-actors, to say the least, do not have to negotiate with *equal intensity* everything " (1981, p.285). What we call power, is a handy label, in my opinion, to refer to this distribution of degrees of intensity in the negotiation on a set of actors, micro and macro. One will remark that the content of the black boxes can be linked back to the rules and objects, analysed in § 3.1, as soon as they come under the control of an economic agent. An interesting implication of this approach to power is that it invalidates the prejudice according to which macro-actors seen to be more complicated than micro-actors. One sees exactly the opposite, which, moreover, links up with the common opinion regretting the impoverishment of information in the process of going from the micro to the macro, with, however, this capital nuance that impoverishment, far from resulting from a malfunction, is an intrinsic property in the passage from micro to macro. One will find a symmetric confirmation in the fact that the inverse trajectory, from the macro to the micro, is clearly accompanied by an enhancement of the information, as can be seen in the studies on the creativity which is required for the execution of public politics (CEE, 1995) : the simple application of a rule is never a simple application. Both being dynamic, impoverishment or enhancement result from the fact that "all information is transformation" (Callon and Latour, 1981, p.300).

3) From routines to black boxes, the progress in the investigation is quite clear. It remains, however, to understand what makes the operation of simplification-routinisation, symbolised by the black boxes, possible. The solution is to be found, I believe, in the reinterpretation of the classic notion in

psycho-sociology of "role" that Simon proposed in 1963 : "A role is a social prescription of some, but not all, of premises that enter into an individual's choices of behaviours"(1963, p. 345). Popper's comparison of institutions and tools is henceforth fully justified : "Institutions, like levers, are needed if we want to achieve anything which goes beyond the strength of our muscles" (1945, p.67).

Information's ability to making a contribution to producing its own frame of analysis, through collective structures, therefore implies that it can reproduce a frame of analysis just as easily as call it into question, with the predictable effects either of consolidation or destabilisation of power games...

Level 2: Information, always susceptible of leading to a questioning of its own frame of analysis, will always be suspect from the point of view of collectives, except if an improbable trust causes the latter to privilege change over co-ordination...

Distributed cognition is to non Standard Theory what the asymmetry of information is to Extended Standard Theory : not only a discreet point of entry to the question of power but furthermore a sort of magnifying glass, which allows to see phenomena arising from this question, well beyond the perimeter which is usually attributed to it. The unequal distribution of information represents a fall, an exile from the lost paradise of Walrasian general equilibrium, that theory will try to reintegrate by means of incentive contracts, neutralising the humans shrewd tendency for opportunism. On the other hand, this inequality is stroke of luck, in the universe of bounded rationality, a universe where collective intelligence allows to go *further* than the sum of individual intelligences, and not *less far* than the sum of Walrasian behaviours. Yet co-ordination has a cost, which constitutes a new paradox in relation to the Walrasian universe : *the more co-ordination there is, the less collective learning there is*. Here is the second function of information : in distilling doubt over received solutions and instigating possible new worlds, information is an anti-power.

It is to Argyris and Schön (1978; see also Argyris, 1988), basing themselves on a long experience of intervention in the most diverse organisations, that we owe the most vigorous enunciation of *the quasi-impossibility of a collective change which would be simultaneously deep, deliberate and endogenous*. While "single loop learning", which consists in regulating the problems of lack of adjustment between results and objectives without modifying the main variables of the collective model of action, tends more to reproduce the systems of power, "double loop learning" supposes the revision of these main variables, thus destabilising the dividing line between the established powers in the organisation. Even in the particularly favourable hypothesis of consensus on the collective benefits to be taken out of the change, the members of the organisation have to leave their shelters in the form of conventional roles and recurrent interactions, to confront the risk of embarrassing situations without a schema prepared in advance. Unless they have exceptional trust in their interlocutor, which is all the more exceptional in that it had not been possible to build it, by definition, on a prior sequence of similar cases, the individuals and the groups are going to use "defensive routines", which will progressively worsen the problem. *The marked change in behaviour contradicts the expected content of change*, installing a dynamic of blockage in which the organisation will only escape from – eventually – before the imminence of a catastrophe or the decree of a superior authority. Herbert Simon (1976) had forged the concept of procedural rationality, for individual action ; we suggest extending it to collective action, since in this instance also, perhaps even more than elsewhere, it is the path which defines the destination and it is the means which justify the end.

There is an abundance of examples of changes blocked by the inability to establish cumulative reciprocal trust between the people managing and the people who carry out the work. Edward Lorenz (1990), reflecting on the decline of British shipyards shows that this decline is due to the former lack of trust between workers and management, which prevented them from co-operating to make the transition in time from a trade based organisation of work, centred on the qualified workers, to a new, better performing, system characterised by the standardisation of products, bureaucratic management methods and a less qualified workforce. Casey Ichnioski and Kathryn Shaw's recent statistical enquiry (1995) studies 36 production lines in the steel industry in the USA, all manufacturing the same product with the same technology. The authors define an ensemble of 12 management practices among the personnel (supposed to be representative of a "dynamic" Human Resources department), which are not distributed haphazardly on the 36 production lines since, according to various statistics methods, their presence by clusters suggest 4 types of management, organised in a hierarchy according to the number of practices they gather. Econometric tests establish that the progression from one type to another is accompanied by an increase in productivity, the maximum being reached by the type which cumulates the 12 practices. This result poses a problem: if these practices generate, without ambiguity, gains in productivity, why are they not systematically adopted ?

The similarity between the 36 production lines will allow them to isolate the influence of two factors hampering adoption. These are, one the one hand, the complementarity between clusters of practices, on the other, the accumulation of specific skills, all factors blocking the possibilities of change, once the line is set up. The gross figures, the econometric tests and the interviews converge on the idea that institutional innovations have a greater chance of being adopted when a new line is being set up. The probability of lines which are already established of adopting them is all the weaker for the reason that they are older and/or that their personnel (on all levels) is more experienced, except if there is a threat of closure, and this last condition is still not sufficient. The interviews suggest that a long history is a handicap, essentially as a result of the accumulation of mistrust between those managing and those carrying out the work (or trade unions). Yet "the new work practices require trust to be effective"(1995, p.51), and it is very costly to *re-establish* trust. Hence the comparative advantage of new installations.

Let us not be mistaken : the emphasis placed on trust in the efficiency of innovations had nothing to do with the naive exaltation of a sort of unfailing good will, nor with a psychological disposition inclining towards benevolence. On the contrary, it is a question of *the construction by "two" (individuals or collectives) of a collective representation, whose principal property is to open the space of possibility for all concerned, by progressively lifting the restriction of this space in exclusively non-cooperative equilibria.*

The opening of possibility characterises power, and therein resides the nub of the problem posed to power by information-innovation, or "double loop learning": the only way of inspiring trust, in such a context, for power, would be to give power... A *direct* demonstration is the exceptional impact, in laws of decentralisation, incentives in the form of power granted to municipalities, rather than in the traditional form of financial advantages (Worms, 1994). This last example is emblematic of the *divorce between Extended Standard Theory (incentives in cash to neutralise lack of trust) and non Standard Theory (incentives in power to organise trust).*

Let us conclude. The distinction between the two levels of efficiency in information (renewal, or transformation of its own frame of analysis) has brought to light that the best controlled mechanisms of co-ordination, and as a result those which are analysable in terms of power, could concern only superficial dynamics ("single loop learning"), and let the dynamics of transformation escape ("double loop learning"). *There is no pre-made co-ordination for collective learning of the higher order – it is indeed in that that one recognises it.* The required co-ordination would call on the construction of appropriate trust in the situation ; yet the very characteristics of power, which show themselves to be so efficient in producing conformity, are in contradiction with the mechanisms which produce trust. Power always favours information-reproduction over information-innovation, for lack of daring to become multiple, and at the risk of irremediably weakening itself in the long term, by blocking the collective learning of the higher order.

Fundamentally, information is clearly an anti-power. Nonetheless, it would be a shame to stay at this negative formulation. While the regulatory ideal of power is if not obedience, then at least this learning of a lower order, which renews and generalises the existing frames of interpretation, the regulatory ideal of information is disobedience, but not just any disobedience : that which envisages the possible around the real, by not considering the real as the only possibility. It is no doubt on these foundations that a theory of "meaning" appropriate to the economic discipline should be built. In the universe of bounded rationality, "meaning" is, in all senses of the term, what we are lacking, that which we can never have enough of. It would be necessary to clearly solidify these foundations by showing how the overlapping of bounded rationality and co-ordination with other people can give an ethical dimension to the cognitive (see Favereau, 1998) : to this end, it would be necessary to have a theory of identity, both individual and collective, to which there will be a brief allusion in the conclusion. A last series of experimental results can be invoked, I believe, going from this perspective.

3.3 The Heuristic of Contextualisation

Kahneman, Slovic, and Tversky (1982) have come up with a third heuristic, that of "adjustment and anchorage". I am going to give it a more synthetic label, basing myself, moreover, on their later studies (Tversky and Kahneman, 1986) on "the framing effect". The approaches of adjustment and anchorage, as with the last effect, result from the same cognitive process of "contextualisation". The context of information significantly conditions the content of the information. Various experiments will show, effectively, that by manipulating the context, one can influence the content of the information, but, in the same way as for the other heuristics, our two authors shall remain at the point of the realisation of the difference in relation to standard rationality, while I will risk the conjecture that this difference is the manifestation of a non standard rationality, at least in the context of interaction.

First of all, the approaches taken: "In many situations, people make estimates by starting from an initial value that is adjusted to yield the final answer" (1982, p.14). The point of departure chosen exerts an influence which seems out of proportion. In the first experiment, subjects are asked to estimate, for example, the percentage of African nations in the UN, after having turned a wheel before them where a number between 0 and 100 will come up, and inviting the person to first of all specify if the percentage sought is superior or inferior to the number which came up, then to evaluate what is necessary to add or to subtract from this number. The median estimations were 20 and 45 for the groups who had received, respectively, 10 and 65 as points of departure. In the second experiment, what served as a point of departure was a partial mental calculus: students have five seconds to estimate the product of eight figures written on a blackboard. The group confronted with 8x7x6x5x4x3x2x1 provided the median estimation of 2250, while the group confronted with 1x2x3x4x5x6x7x8 provided the median estimation of 512. It is clear that the subjects are artificially influenced by the ascendant or descendant character of the sequence of figures. Let us note that the correct answer is 40320.

One must recognise that all of these approaches seem to manifest a fault of rationality. My intention will not be to deny the evidence but rather to suggest that, behind this fault hides a mode of functioning of intelligence which, placed in another, less artificial, context attests to a superior form of adaptation to a universe marked by lack of fulfilment and opacity, notably concerning the behaviour of others. My hypothesis is that the *homo oeconomicus* of bounded rationality sets out to immediately detect in which context its interactions with others are situated, or, to express things differently, to extract the right frame of analysis from the information he receives to interpret it.

Kahneman, Knetsch and Thaler (1986) continued with a telephone survey among a random selection of a hundred residents of Toronto and Vancouver, between May 1984 and July 1985. The questions were on the subject of equity in prices and salaries. One series of answers is particularly revealing. This is the scenario : a company which makes modest profits, in an area affected by the recession and massive unemployment (but without inflation), and which attracts a lot of candidates for employment, decides to lower wages by 7% for the year. 62% of the people questioned judge this decision "unfair", 38% "acceptable". Now we have the scenario, identical to the previous one, except for the addition of a 12% rate of inflation and a decision to make a limited increase of wages by 5% for the year. This time, the proportions are reversed : 78% consider the decision "acceptable", 22% "unfair". The evolution of the real wage being approximately equal in the two scenarios, the effect of the formulation seems to return to the oldest fault of substantive rationality, detected and denounced by Standard Theory : *money illusion.*

But it is not money illusion which is in question : lowering the nominal wages represents a violation of the social agreement, on which the company link is based, which is more serious than increasing it insufficiently. Even if the variation in purchasing power is identical, the employer breaks a contractual promise in one case, and not in the other.

As for the authors, they account for the effect of the formulation by explaining that equity judgement requires a focal point, a point of reference, and that this is provided by the present level of nominal wages. This minimalist explanation does not do justice to the wealth of their results. If the influence of context on meaning is the bad side of the coin with regard to substantive rationality, the ability to detect or elaborate conventions, allowing to give sense to interactions, is the good side of the coin with regard to procedural rationality. In any case, this third and last conclusion is justified :

Conclusion 3 : all information does not circulate as merchandise because all information cannot be transported.

CONCLUSION

The general conclusion of this exploration of the concept of information in non Standard Theory is double :

On the one hand, starting off from a simple substitution (that some might believe to be insignificant) of the hypothesis of bounded rationality with that of optimising rationality in the traditional paradigm in the economics of methodological individualism, we have followed the trail of all paths opened by this conversion to cognitive realism and have ended up in the base camp of the comprehensive method in social sciences. The refusal of optimising rationality's simplification of the world has allowed us, after having assessed the limits of rationality, to successively integrate learning, interpretation, attention, reflexivity, hierarchy, the critical spirit, emotion, relevance, context, objects, rules, power, roles, groups, collective cognitive structures, authority, obedience and disobedience, trust, meaning... all notions which depict an infinitely less limited world than that of unbounded rationality, and which stem from an approach of understanding. *The "cognitive trend" in economic science concurs with the "interpretative trend" in social sciences,* and, as a consequence, not understanding that they are intimately linked it is to forego the most important aspect of each.

On the other hand, we owe the discovery of this theoretical and epistemological space which is common to so many human sciences to a reflection on the theory of information, as if the concept of information had, by nature, a more than fundamental role, a founding role. This can be explained technically by the fact that the standard criterion for the maximisation of the subjectively expected utility firmly maintains information in the field of syntax, that is to say in quantitative calculus, while non Standard Theory, in off-loading this constraint (which is also a handy tool), through a natural dynamic, gains access to the semantics and the pragmatics of dealing with information (at the risk of cutting itself off from quantitative calculus). This technical explanation, nonetheless, is still to be situated on the level of symptoms. Let us risk a final conjecture : if information fulfils such a decisive theoretical function, it is because it provides the key to our conception of the *homo oeconomicus*. In Standard Theory, optimising rationality makes him a *calculating machine*, which is congruent with the syntactical character of information. In non Standard Theory, bounded rationality, if one makes sure to take the totality of its analytical and epistemological consequences into account, grants him the status of a *conscience in search of meaning,* which is in accord with the semantic and/or pragmatic character of information.

This last affirmation, even if serves as a summary of this chapter, has the effect of *shifting theoretical work from a point after questions of rationality (individual and collective) to a point before questions of identity (individual and collective)*, etc.

Let us immediately apply this schema to the society described by Extended Standard Theory, where the twinning of optimising rationality with the asymmetries of information creates generalised problems of moral hazard and adverse selection. In concrete terms, this means that individuals operate in an atomised society, where all those who see their own profit in it, cheat, lie, avoid paying and fraud if there are not sufficiently strong and clever financial incentives in place to dissuade them. Moreover, this is a subject of common knowledge. To the very extent that this theory aspires to any descriptive value of real society, simple common sense indicates both that this society must go through a acute crisis of social ties, and that this theory has nothing to say about the remedies to apply. What matters to this society is exactly that which escapes from this theory.

This contradiction, which is today that of the standard approach in economics, opens the way to a non standard approach, of the very type to which this chapter was concerned with. The problems are perhaps not resolved but at least they can be formulated.

REFERENCES

Ando A., Fisher F.M. and Simon H.A. (1963), *Essays on the structure of social science models*, Harvard university press, Cambridge.

Argyris C. and Schön D. (1978), *Organizational learning: a theory of action perspective*, Addison-Wesley, Reading, p. 344.

Argyris C. (1988), "Problems in producing usable knowledge for implementing liberating alternatives" in Bell D.E and alii, eds, *Decision making*, Cambridge university press, Cambridge, pp. 540-561

Barnes B. (1988), *The nature of power*, University of Illinois Press, Chicago, p. 205.

Callon M. and Latour B. (1981), "Unscrewing the big Leviathan: how actors macro-structure reality and how sociologists help them to do so", Chap. 10 in: Knorr-Cetina K. and Cicourel A., (eds.), *Advances in social theory and methodology: toward an integration of micro- and macro-sociologies*, Routledge and Kegan, Boston, p.277-303.

Callon M. (1991), "Réseaux technico-économiques et irréversibilités", in: Robert Boyer et al ii, eds., *Les figures de l'irréversibilité en économie*, éditions de l'EHESS, Paris, p.393.

C.E.E. (1995), *Les politiques d'emploi et leurs acteurs*, Cahiers du Centre d'Etudes de l'Emploi, n° 34, PUF, Paris, p.349.

Chisholm D. (1989), *Coordination without hierarchy: informal structures in multiorganizational systems*, University of California press, Berkeley, p. 273.

Cohen M. and Jaffray J.Y. (1980), "Rational behavior under complete ignorance", *Econometrica*, July, p. 1281-1299.

Courtois P. J. (1977), *Decomposability: queueing and computer applications, ACM monograph series*, Academic Press, New York, p. 201.

Cyert R.M. and March J.G. (1963), *A behavioral theory of the firm*, Prentice-Hall, Englewoods Cliffs.

Dworkin R. (1977), *Taking rights seriously*, Harvard university press, Cambridge, p. 371

Favereau O. (1994), "Règle, organisation et apprentissage collectif : un paradigme non standard pour trois théories hétérodoxes, in Orléan A. ed., *Analyse économique des conventions*, PUF, Paris, pp. 113-137

Favereau O.(1997), "L'incomplétude n'est pas le problème, c'est la solution" in Reynaud B. ed., *Les figures du collectif*, Tome 2 of *Les limites de la rationalité*, La Découverte, paris, pp. 219-234

Favereau O. (1998), "L'économie normative de la rationalité limitée", in Brochier H. ed., *L'économie normative*, Economica, Paris, pp. 109-123

Georgescu-Roegen N. (1967), "The nature of expectation and uncertainty", chapitre 6 in: *Analytical Economics*, Harvard University Press, Cambridge, pp.241-275.

Goody J. (1986), *La logique de l'écriture: aux origines des sociétés humaines*, traduction française, Armand Colin, Paris, p.198.

Henry C. (1974), "Option values in the economics of irreplaceable assets", *Review of economic studies*, Symposium on the economics of exhaustible resources, pp. 89-104

Hilgartner S. and Bosk C.L. (1988), "The rise and fall of social problems: a public arenas model", *American Journal of Sociology*, July, p.53-78.

Hirschman A.O. (1967), Development projects observed, The Brookings Institution, Washington, 1st ed., 1967, new preface, 1995, p.197.

Ichniowski C. and Shaw K. (1995), "Old dogs and new tricks: determinants of the adoption of productivity-enhancing work practices", Brookings papers: microeconomics, pp.1-65.

Joseph I. (1994), "Attention distribuée et attention focalisée", *Sociologie du travail*, n°4, pp.563-586.

Kahneman D., Slovic P. and Tversky A. (1982), *Judgment under uncertainty: heuristics and biases*, Cambridge University Press, Cambridge, p. 555.

Kahneman D., Knetsch P. and Thaler R. (1986), "Fairness as a constraint on profit seeking", *American economic review*, September, p.111.

Keynes J.M. (1973), *A Treatise on probability* (1921), The collected writings, vol.VIII, Macmillan, Londres, p. 514.

Kreps D. and Porteus E.L. (1979), "Temporal Von Neumann-morgenstern and induced preferences", *Journal of economic theory*, february, pp. 81-109

Lakatos I. (1970), "Falsification and the methodology of scientific research programmes", in Lakatos, I. and Musgrave, A., eds.., *Criticism and the growth of knowledge*, Cambridge University press, Cambridge, pp.91-196.

Latour B. (1994), "Une sociologie sans objet ? Note théorique sur l'interobjectivité", *Sociologie du Travail*, n°4, pp.587-608.

Leroi-Gourhan A. (1965), *Le geste et la parole*, tome 2: la mémoire et les rythmes, Albin Michel, Paris, p.285.

Livet P. and Thevenot L. (1994), "Les catégories de l'action collective", chap.6 in: Orlean, A., ed., *Analyse économique des conventions*, Collection économie, PUF, Paris, p.139-168.

Lorenz E.H. (1990), "Une explication évolutionniste du déclin de la compétitivité: la construction navale en Grande-Bretagne, 1890-1970", *Travail et Emploi*, n°4, pp.66-81.

Muller P. (1994), *Les politiques publiques*, Collection Que Sais-Je, PUF, Paris, 2nd edition, p.128.

Norman D.A. (1993), "Les artefacts cognitifs", *Raisons Pratiques*, n° 4: Les objets dans l'action, pp.15-34.

Patinkin D. (1982), *Anticipations of the "General Theory" ? And other essays on Keynes*, Basil Blackwell, Oxford, p.285.

Pïore M. (1983) , "Labor market segmentation : to what paradigm does it belong ?", *American economic review*, may, pp 249-253

Ponssard J.P. (1975), *A comment on the irreversibility effect*, Working paper, Ecole polytechnique

Popper K.R. (1984), *The open society and its enemies*, vol.1: Plato, 1st edition, 1945, Routledge and Kegan, Londres, p.361.
- (1980) *The logic of scientific discovery*, Hutchinson, 1st ed., 1959, 10'th ed. , Londres, p.480.
- (1967) “La rationalité et le statut du principe de rationalité”, in: Claassen, E.M., ed., *Les fondements philosophiques des systèmes économiques: essais en l’honneur de Jacques Rueff*, Payot, Paris, pp.142-150.
- (1978) *La connaissance objective* (1972), Editions Complexe, Bruxelles, p. 170.

Richard J.F.(1990), *Les activités mentales : comprendre, raisonner, trouver des solutions*, Dunod, Paris, p. 435

Savage L.J. (1954), *The foundations of statistics*, Dover publications, New-york, 1st edition, 1954, 2nd edition, 1972, p.310.

Schelling T.C. (1960), *The strategy of conflict*, Harvard University Press, Cambridge, 1st edition, 1960, 2nd edition, 1980, p.309.

Simon H.A. (1982), “Economics and psychology” (1963), reprinted in: *Models of bounded rationality*, vol.2: behavioral economics and business organization, MIT Press, Boston, p.318-355.
- (1971), “Designing organizations for an information-rich world”, in Greenberger, M., ed., *Computers, communications and the public interest*, Johns Hopkins Press, Baltimore, pp.38-52.
- (1976), “From substantive to procedural rationality”, in Latsis, S., ed., *Method and appraisal in economics*, Cambridge University Press, Cambridge, pp.129-148.
- (1978), “Rationality as process and as product of thought”, *American Economic Review*, Mai, pp.1-16.
- (1981), *The sciences of the Artificial*, 2nd edition, The MIT press, Cambridge, p.247.
- (1983), *Reason in human affairs*, Basil Blackwell, Oxford, p.115.

Sousa (de) R. (1987), *The rationality of emotion*, The MIT Press, Cambridge, p.373.

Theureau J. and Filippi G. (1994), “Cours d’action et conception d’un système d’aide à la coordination: le cas de la régulation du trafic du RER”, *Sociologie du Travail*, n°4, p.547-562.

Turner J.C. (1987), *Rediscovering the social group: a self-categorization theory*, Basil Blackwell, Oxford, p.239.

Tversky A. and Kahneman D. (1986), “Rational choice and the framing of decisions”, *Journal of business*, October, pp.67-100.

Watzlawick P., Helmick-Beavin J. and Jackson D. (1972), *Une logique de la communication*, traduction française, Editions du Seuil, Paris, p.286.

Weil S. (1962), *La pesanteur et la grâce*, Plon, 1st ed., 1948, new ed., UGE, p. 186

Williamson O.E. (1993), “Calculativeness, trust and economic organization”, *The journal of law and economics*, April, p.453-486.

Worms J.P. (1994), “Mais si, on peut changer la société par décret !”, in: PAVE, F., ed., *L’analyse stratégique*, colloque de Cerisy: autour de Michel Crozier, Seuil, Paris, pp.255-264

Chapter 7

INFORMATION, KNOWLEDGE AND THE EVOLUTIONARY THEORY OF THE FIRM[1]

Patrick Cohendet
Université Louis Pasteur,
BETA, Strasbourg

According to Fransman (1994), there are two main approaches for conceiving the theory of the firm :

- On the one side, the traditional theories of the firm (transaction costs theory, agency theory, theory of teams, etc...) consider the firm as a « processor of information ». For these traditional approaches, the behaviour of the firm can be understood as an optimal reaction to the environmental signals that are detected by the firm. The focus is thus on the process of allocation of resources needed to cope with this adaptation to external information. As Langlois and Foss (1996) pointed out, this vision led to a contractual approach of the firm, where «*firms and other institutions are alternative bundles of contracts understood as mechanisms for creating and realigning incentives* », in order to better cope with the information that comes from the environment.

- On the other side, the firm is conceived as " a processor of knowledge " (Fransman, 1994). In this perspective, the firm is viewed as a locus of setting up, construction, selection, usage and development of knowledge. It is more sensitive to the sharing and distribution of knowledge than it is to the distribution of information. In this approach, the key role is played by the concept of competence, which relies on that of routines and rules, and refers to a view of the firm as a social institution, the main characteristic of which is to « know (well) how to do » certain things. In fact, considering the firm as a processor of knowledge leads to the recognition that the cognitive mechanisms are essential, and that routines play a major role in keeping the internal coherence of the organisation. In other terms, the governance of the firm is not focused on the resolution of informational asymmetries, but on the co-ordination of distributed pieces of knowledge and distributed learning processes. "*It is not so much the saturation of its abilities to deal with information which concerns the firm, as the risk of becoming too confined by inefficient routines*" (Cohendet et al., 1997).

[1] This contribution results from long discussions with Patrick Llerena and Luigi Marengo. It also benefited from the comments of the two discussants of the paper, Philippe Lorino and Olivier Weinstein, when I presented it at the working session of Commisariat Général du Plan.

P. Petit (ed.), Economics and Information, 121–137.

The seminal contributions of Penrose (1959) and Alchian (1951), but also in some sense of Knight (1921) and Coase (1937), have allowed the development of approaches which consider the firm as a processor of knowledge (Fransman, 1994), or as a "repository of knowledge", where cognitive processes and co-ordination mechanisms play a dominant role. Chandler (1992),also acknowledges the importance of knowledge creation and management in the development of modern organisations (see also Nonaka, 1994 ; Nonaka, Takeuchi 1995).

This contribution will focus on the evolutionary theory of the firm as a leading representative of all those theoretical approaches that view the firm as a processor of knowledge[2]. The main purpose of the article is to show that, when viewing the firm as a processor of knowledge in the evolutionary approach, one comes to reconsider the classical theoretical results that are obtained by the contractual (information based) approaches. In particular, we will revisit the two main mechanisms at the core of the conception of the firm, the co-ordination mechanisms and the incentives mechanisms. It will be shown that the co-ordination and incentive mechanisms which develop in a knowledge-based context, aim at regulating the interactions between employees who are permanently in a situation of "interpretative ambiguity" (Fransman, 1994). In general, it is impossible to generate knowledge in an unambiguous manner from a set of information retained by an agent, especially if he is in a situation of incomplete information. It is also clear that different agents will infer different, even contradictory, knowledge from the same set of information. This result is essential: it claims that there is no "tight coupling" between information and knowledge. Knowledge cannot be reduced to mere processed information. Knowledge cannot be assimilated to a stockpile resulting from the accumulation of flux of information. The evolutionary theory that views the firm as a processor of knowledge cannot thus be deduced simply from the classical theoretical results. It requires a specific analysis and assessment.

1. THE FIRM AS A PROCESSOR OF INFORMATION

For the traditional theories of the firm, from the pure neo-classical one to the transaction cost approach, the behaviour of the firm can be understood as an optimal reaction to the information that comes from the environment. The

---

[2] The evolutionary approach to the firm (Dosi, Teece, Winter, 1991 ; Teece 1988) does not really exist yet as a coherent set of propositions, but there are indeed many promising (and some of them already quite fruitful) streams of research in need of some form of unifying principles. In addition, there are other approaches which are, in different ways, complementary to the evolutionary one, as either they constitute one of the backgrounds of evolutionary theories (as in the case of the behavioural approaches to organisation theory) or are largely overlapping with them (as with the competence- and the resource-based approaches) or, finally, they are largely compatible, though different in their emphasis on core issues.

behaviour of the firm as a rational information processing signifies that the same signals will give rise through time to the same pattern of action, provided that the technical conditions (as expressed by the production function) remain unchanged. As quoted by Fransman (1994), in these approaches, "*information may be defined as data relating to states of the world and the state contingent consequences* that follow from events in the world that are naturally or socially caused. The total set of data is closed in that here is a closed set of states and consequences". Even if they provide different theoretical angles to view at the firm, the traditional theories of the firm share an essential feature: each of them aims at solving a specific informational problem. Let us consider some key examples:

- the principal/agent theory of the firm (Jensen and Meckling, 1976) focuses on incentive schemes to cope with asymmetries of information." Opportunism theories assume that individuals are self-seeking and often dishonest... In these models, incentives, monitoring and control procedures are seen as reducing the externality problems among individuals caused by cheating and shirking" (Postrel, Rumelt, 1992).

- in the theory of teams (Marschak, Radner, 1972 ; Radner, 1986), it is the unequal distribution of information among the members of the team which is at the origin of the firm. Because it is impossible to assess the real contribution of each individual member of the team to the overall performance of the group (and thus to avoid the risk of free-riding), a "monitor" (a hierarchical authority) has to be chosen.

- the Coasian approach (1937) is concerned with the costs of access to information. The existence of the firm is explained by too high costs of using the market information-price signals.

- the transaction costs approach, as developed by Williamson (1975, 1985, 1993), is by definition a « defensive » one as a response to an environment which is characterised by imperfect information and by behaviours of agents who are opportunistic. Thus, it is in a sense a « theory of frictions » to quote Favereau (1989). Its very reason of existence is to correct the market failures, when the functioning of market mechanisms in terms of information processing are too costly, transaction cost theory agrees with the principal/agent vision that information is imperfect and that the existence of potential asymmetries of information authorizes unproductive rent-seeking behaviour. Williamson shares with the principal-agent theory the same basic assumption that the firm is conceived as a nexus of bilateral contracts. Firm is conceived as an institutional mechanism creating a governance structure to solve the problem of misaligned incentives attendant on imperfect information.

- the Simonian vision of the firm (Simon, 1957) is addressing questions related to the bounded capacity of agents to acquire, process and store information. In such conditions, there is an interest for agents having bounded capacities to deal with information to create firms. Firms can be seen as institutional devices that allow agents to go collectively beyond the limits to deal with information that each one is individually facing.

- In his approach of the firm, Aoki (1986, 1988) considers the key problem of "structure of information". He shows that, when the environment is uncertain, the horizontal and flexible structure of information of the Japanese firm is more efficient that the vertical and rather fixed structure of information of the American firm.

As Coriat and Weinstein (1995) point out, all these approaches of the firm have basically reduced the coordination principles to a bundle of bilateral contracts, which are meant to achieve coordination by devising appropriate incentive schemes in order to align self interested individual action with the common organisational goals. An important consequence of this vision is the absence in it of any serious treatment of the production process as a collective activity.

In all the above approaches of the firm, the treatment of information (distribution, asymmetries, incompleteness...) is thus the focal point of the organisation. Each specific theoretical vision is related to a question of adaptation of the firm to the imperfect information signals coming from the environment. This implies that the existence and distribution of cognitive capacities are given and there is no learning process that could modify them. It must be clear that such a statement does not signify that the traditional approaches are unable to incorporate some cognitive dimensions of economic agents and their abilities to experience learning processes. Transaction costs approach is based on the hypothesis of bounded rationality that precisely admits the existence of cognitive constraints for the individuals, and the analysis of key learning processes as learning by doing is part of the traditional theory. However, the scope of such an analysis is extremely narrow. The mere reason is that in fact in such perspectives, the cognitive capabilities of agents remain unchanged throughout any decision process. Agents are not changing their representation of the world through time, they do not differ in their perception of the environment, they do not pay attention to the definition and evolution of common sets of rules, codes and languages within the boundary of the organisation.

Also, to some extent, it can be said that the traditional approaches tackle the notion of knowledge. But here again the scope of analysis is restricted to a very limited conception of knowledge. These theories conceive knowledge as a mere stock resulting from the process of accumulation/deccumulation of information (considered as a flux). Knowledge is thus viewed as "processed" information. That is a restricted conception of knowledge that does not suppose any cognitive mechanism at stake. The relationships between information and knowledge are much more complex. As Boulding mentioned (1955), "*we cannot regard knowledge as simply the accumulation of information in a stockpile, even though all messages that are received in the brain may leave some deposit here. Knowledge must by itself be regarded as a structure, a very complex and loose pattern, with its parts connected in various ways by ties of varying degrees of strength. Messages are continually shot into this structure, some of them pass right through its interstices without affecting any perceptible change in it. Sometimes, messages stick to the structure and become part of it...Occasionally, however, a message which is inconsistent with the basic pattern of the mental structure, hits the structure which is then forced to undergo a complete re-organisation*". Boulding clearly rejects the hypothesis of "tight-coupling" between information and knowledge. This essential distinction between knowledge and information is precisely the one adopted by the evolutionary theories of the firm and some related theories. This theoretical perspective, where the firm is viewed as a processor of knowledge, opens new ways to look at classical results of the theory of the firm.

2. THE EVOLUTIONARY THEORY OF THE FIRM

The evolutionary approach of the firm is characterized first in that it relies on the use of the constituent principles of any theory of evolution. It puts great emphasis on interaction between mechanisms which generate diversity and those which promote selection. To be more specific, it considers on the one hand, routines[3] as principle of permanency (or "heredity"), as the real biological genes of the firm. On the other hand, it accepts, as the principle of variation or mutation, the searching behaviour which is the basis of mechanisms generating diversity. Finally, it accepts, as filters of evolution, the mechanisms of selection which influence the genes/routines and/or the mutation/searching (the market being one selection mechanism amongst others). Within this framework of hypotheses, a large part of the theoretical debate is devoted to the permanent tension between the exploitation mechanisms of existing routines and the exploration mechanisms of new routines.

Alongside these basic principles, the evolutionary theory of the firm is characterized by the acknowledgement of the essential role played by cognitive mechanisms. These imply the development of a collective knowledge base, the definition of a set of rules, of a code and a common language. The important element of this approach is the set of cognitive processes by which agents create their representation of the world. The functioning of these processes (which over time constitute and change the behavioural routines of agents) occupies, within the evolutionary approach of the firm, the place of substantive rationality in the traditional theory. The creation of new knowledge and the development of new learning procedures are thus at the heart of the analysis. On this point of view, the evolutionary approach differentiates itself completely from those theories

---

[3] Along with Burkhart et alii (1996), we can define routine as "*an executable capability for repeated performance in some context that has been learned by an organization in response to selective pressure*".

which see the firm as a "processor of information". The mechanisms of governance which guide the evolutionary firm are not focused on information problem-solving through its transactions, but they structure the schemes for accumulating and producing new knowledge. As Langlois and Foss (1996) pointed out, the evolutionary approach suggests « *a qualitative coordination, that is helping cooperating parties to align not their incentives but their knowledge and expectations* ».

Finally, the evolutionary approach is characterised by stress put on the concept of competences. On this issue, the evolutionary theories echoe with a significant number of works that are originated from different disciplines (economic history, industrial organisation, sociology of organisation, evolutionary theory, management science, etc....). These works have seriously questioned the traditional contractual vision of the firm (Chandler, 1962, 1992 ; March and Simon, 1993 ; Penrose, 1959 ; Richardson, 1960, 1972) ; Nelson and Winter, 1982). They converge towards a common characteristic: they consider the concept of competence as the leading explanatory variable for understanding the organisation of firms, and its diversity and its persistence (Dosi and Marengo, 1994). The concept of competence, which relies on that of routines and rules, refers to a view of the firm as a social institution, the main characteristic of which is to « know (well) how to do » certain things. These competences are coherent sets of capabilities to use them in an efficient way. Some of these competences are strategic ("core competences" according to Teece (1988)) and constitute the main sources of the competitiveness of a firm. They are the results of a selection process both internal and external to the firm. The management, the construction and the combination of these competences are critical in order to understand the limits of the firm and the co-ordination as well as the incentive structure of the firm.

According to these approaches, the firm is conceived as an institution where competences are continuously built, shaped, maintained, and protected. This is a cumulative and strategic process that relies intensively on the management of knowledge : The competence-based approach is essentially depending on the ways, for a given firm, knowledge is acquired, produced, absorbed, memorised, shared and transferred. This has some important consequences in particular for the issue of co-ordination by the firm: First because knowledge of complex production processes is necessarily distributed (cf. von Hayek, 1937) and cannot be fully grasped and controlled by a single individual. A primary role of an organisation becomes that of co-ordinating this dispersed knowledge. Second, because co-ordination in this case generally involves the creation of commonly shared bodies of knowledge : sets of facts, notions, " models of the world ", rules, procedures which are – at least partly – known to all the members of the organisation involved in a given interaction. In a sense this kind of co-ordination is a pre-condition for the co-ordination of actions which is examined by most current literature and which implicitly assumes that all these mechanisms for the co-ordination of dispersed knowledge are already in place. It seems in any case most unlikely that mere incentive mechanisms could alone be sufficient to promote this kind of co-ordination. But, and perhaps even more important, this focus on knowledge issues brings about also the issue of how such knowledge is generated, maintained, replicated, and modified (and possibly also lost), i.e. the issue of learning and its nature. As repeatedly argued, (cf., for example, Nelson and Winter, 1982 ; Dosi and Egidi, 1991), innovative activities involve a kind of learning quite different from Bayesian probability updating and regression estimation: it requires agents to build new representations of the environment they operate in (and which remains largely unknown) and to develop new skills which enable them both to explore and to exploit this world of ever-expanding opportunities. Such representations are embedded in the routines, which characterise the organisation.

3. ROUTINES AS CO-ORDINATION AND GOVERNANCE MECHANISMS

The role of routines as co-ordination mechanism in the firm is one of the main orientations of the evolutionary theory. As Nelson stressed (1994) *"a firm can be understood in terms of hierarchy of practised organisational routines, which define lower order organisational skills and how these skills are co-ordinated, and higher order decision procedures for choosing what is to be done at lower level'.*

In this representation of the hierarchy of routines, the evolutionary approach pays particular attention to the tension between centralisation and decentralisation in the organisational learning process. Indeed, firms need both centralisation and decentralisation to be able to function satisfactorily in a turbulent environment. Henceforth, one of the major aims of the firm is to maintain a co-existence between these two dialogic forms. Learning processes can thus be compared to self-organisational phenomena. According to Lesourne (1991), self-organisation can be defined as *"the possibility of a system to acquire new properties, while organising or changing its own organisation"*. Therefore, self-organisation requires from the firm a certain capacity to adapt and to question. But, as Walliser (1988) suggested, the process of self-organisation also confers on a system the capacity to bring about local processes in an organisational structure. Here *"the interference of levels"* (Héraud and Garrouste, 1993) is a determining factor. The emergence of new properties comes, therefore, both from individuals and from the organisation.

Decentralisation in the acquisition of knowledge is a source of variety, experimentation and learning. However, it may be that this knowledge needs to be made available to the whole organization. When employees differ in their representation of the environment and in their cognitive capacities, a body of common knowledge must exist within the organization, which guarantees the coherence of the learning processes, in order to provide for an efficient management of competencies. In order to be able to confront a perturbed environment, the means of creating and modifying such a body of common knowledge must respect certain forms of centralization, even if it is basically maintained by decentralized learning processes. Thus, inevitably, there is a conflict between the forces which favour decentralised learning and those which favour the setting up of a shared knowledge base. The *"balance"* between these two forces depends on the characteristics of the learning processes and those of the environment in which the firms operate. By means of simulation models, Marengo (1994) has shown that, when it is necessary to adapt in a fine and flexible way to the environment, local learning processes can be more effective provided that hierarchical levels are able to co-ordinate them globally. Real decentralisation can happen much more from extended knowledge and from *"bottom-up"* flows than from simple horizontal flows of information as stated by Aoki: *"If the correct emphasis is placed on knowledge and learning, higher degrees of decentralised learning are not necessarily conducive to higher degrees of organisational learning, but only to the extent in which they can be pulled together and made coherent with the overall organisational learning process"* (Marengo, 1994).

These results are important, they suggest that each specific method of organising production implies a specific set of routines oriented towards problem-solving. However, they also suggest that the idea of routines contains another characteristic through the implementation of mechanisms of governance and authority in the context of a collective behaviour where each employees strive towards their own interest. The establishment of a routine within an organisation, its evolution, the testing of its problem-solving capacities, its reinforcement or its rejection, require a direct link between the notion of routine and the control and incentive mechanisms. The conflict-solving mechanisms and the sharing-mechanisms of the relational quasi-rente which govern relationships between individuals whose interests are not necessarily convergent. And, as Coriat and Dosi (1995) stress, governance feature of routines is strictly dependent on the given mode of organisation of production : *"The set of 'Japanese' production routines does not only embody different channels of information processing but also distributes knowledge within the organisation in ways remarkably different from the Tayloristic/ Chandlerian enterprise. And, at the same time, on the governance side, individuals incentives to perform efficiently and learn are sustained (in the Japanese firm) by company-specific rank-hierarchies, distinct from functional assignments, while in the Taylorian approach, the specific mechanism of incentive governance is twofold: on the one hand the design of a new pay system (the so called 'differential piece rate system'), on the other hand, incentives had to be matched by direct visual control upon work-practices by foremen"*.

In this conception, the new focus which is directed towards the mechanisms of governance comes from the fact that the creation and the distribution of knowledge appear as being indissociably and principally linked to the distribution of power and of conflicts of interests. Inequalities in the distribution of information are no longer so much considered to be the origin of the mechanisms of governance, but rather the stakes that the dynamics of the creation and distribution of knowledge reveals. In this context for example, setting up incentive schemes results not so much from the need to correct asymmetries of information as from the need to control learning dynamics. In fact, the existence of shared knowledge reduces, *a priori,* the risks of moral hazard and of adverse selection as the risks of asymmetries of information become less acute. One can even put forward the hypothesis that if one considers that all agents possess cognitive capacities, the divergence of preferences may lead to other effects than those generated by the strategic use of organisational asymmetries. Cohen (1984) thus showed that diversity with regard to preferences and objectives 'in a disrupted environment where learning and the creation of competencies are the main elements for success, can be a source of increased performances. In this way, he stressed that where agents pursue objectives which are specific to their unit, and which might be contradictory, the resulting performances are more higher compared to the situation where a group of members concentrate on the same objective. Such a situation can be explained by the effects of cross fertilisation in the solution-seeking process. The collective advantage of this type of diversity is also mentioned by Loasby (1989) for whom the differences in interpretation by individuals of the same group are the origin of organisational learning. The same reasoning is to be found in Schelling (1978) in the prisoner dilemma with N number of players. Whereas the traditional principal-agent theory is explained in a static context, a dynamic approach of learning in a evolutionary perspective leads to a thorough reconsideration of the setting up of incentive schemes. But, how can one orient learning towards desired directions while at the same time ensuring the "repatriation" of different experiences; how can diversity be stimulated while maintaining coherence ; how can individuals be incited to launch a process of cross-seeking, to implement new tasks and to evaluate their results and use them widely; and how can new incentive schemes be created which would make it possible to carry out, in the best conditions, processes for the creation and distribution of knowledge ?

The origin of incentive schemes from an evolutionary perspective must therefore, according to us, aim to avoid, within the firm, a number of risks which are specific to a collective learning framework. Among these risks are the following:

- the risk of a lack of incentive to explore new routines. As Nonaka (1994) stated, incentive scheme should influence an individual's commitment to create new knowledge. This commitment, which aims to avoid the risk of too great a conservatism, relies on the deep-rooted "intention" of the individual to evolve in a learning context;

- the risk of "conflicts" between individual learning and collective learning. This type of risk of a lack of incentive to combine individual and collective learning can take on many forms. Argyris and Schön (1978) noted that a major obstacle to the evolution of learning or of common knowledge stems from the gap which may exist between what individuals say ("espoused theory") and what they actually do ("theory in use", which actually controls agents' actions).

- the risk of a lack of incentive to improve an existing routine by "locking oneself in" a given practise without ever seeking to change. This refers to the risk of over-exploiting existing routines and causing practises to become inflexible ,without questioning them in the light of new experience and new information.

Remarks set out above plead for the existence of mechanisms of governance which are linked to the distribution of knowledge. A priori, this analysis seems to differentiate itself from Williamson's view for whom the analysis of forms of governance is intrinsically linked to the approach based on transaction costs. According to him, a transaction is the basic unit and a structure of governance can be assimilated itself to an institutional scheme through which the whole of a transaction is decided: *"More generally, the study of governance is concerned with the identification, explication and mitigation of all forms of contractual hazards, and the mechanisms of governance show how and why simple contracts give way to complex contracts and internal organisation as the hazards of contacting build up"* (Williamson, 1996). However, in our opinion, far from substituting Williamson's analysis, the taking into account of mechanisms of governance linked to the distribution of knowledge supplements the construction based on these transactions. It abides by a wider perspective of governance as Williamson himself explains when he writes (1996): *"Governance is the means by which order, is accomplished into a relation in which potential conflicts threaten to undo or upset opportunities to realise mutual gains"*. Williamson's analysis of transactions describes the mechanisms which govern a world of resource allocation where the asymmetry of information is the main bias to be corrected. Mechanisms of governance concerning the distribution of knowledge are part of a world of resource creation, where bad circulation (repartition and distribution) of knowledge is the main problem to be overcome. These two worlds are not of course disconnected. The mechanisms of governance of knowledge distribution are dependent on the mechanisms of governance of transactions and vice-versa. This conjecture leaves open a number of areas for research: for example one can put forward the hypothesis that the existence and generalisation of hybrid forms of governance in larger quantities than Williamson expects result in a need to compromise between the two contexts of governance.

But other risks, may be even more important, are inherent in the procedures of the "conversion" of knowledge (Nonaka 1994). The examples given below illustrate the inherent risks in the processes of creating and distributing knowledge and attempt to identify incentive mechanisms which are linked to these.

4. CIRCULATION OF KNOWLEDGE, MODE OF CONVERSION AND RELATIONSHIPS BETWEEN TACIT AND CODIFIED KNOWLEDGE

To analyse the risks inherent in the procedure of conversion of knowledge, we refer to the representation given by Nonaka (1994) of the different modes of "knowledge conversions" to interpret on-going changes in incentive and control mechanisms. The author puts forward two dimensions as conceptual foundations for his model. The first, called epistemological, concerns the classic distinction between tacit knowledge and codified knowledge, developed in particular by Polanyi (1966). The second dimension, called ontological, underlines the importance of the interaction between individuals.

The distinction is made between four types of conversion (knowledge creation): tacit to tacit (socialisation), codified to codified (combination), tacit to codified (externalisation) and codified to tacit internalisation (cf. Table 1).

a) Socialisation allows the acquisition of tacit knowledge, through shared experiences, trust and mutual understanding. By setting up teams, or a self-organised network of experts, the organisation endeavours to build, by these means, a base of common knowledge. This effort implies the creation of a context for social interactions where individuals are progressively brought to share their experience through continuous horizontal exchanges. These are interactive schemes in which individuals commit themselves both physically (being presence in the team and meeting with other persons) and intellectually (problem-solving with the team) in a process of mutual experience and collective learning. The incentive to co-operate remains here a key factor in the operation of such a scheme.

b) The combination of codified knowledge takes place between individuals. Communication networks (notably through intranet) are one f the ways of accelerating the accessibility and the transfer of this knowledge which can be centralised and shared by other individuals by promoting a dynamic process of knowledge creation through combination. It is a mode of knowledge transfer whereby experts' explicit knowledge is transformed into an explicit base of knowledge. For example, in the case of data bases (technical, commercial, etc.), we can see that electronic 'information and communication networks increase the speed of access to aid transfer of data which may be both centralised and shared. The capacity to share and to circulate is a determining factor in the setting up of this mode of knowledge conversion, which requires multi-agent interaction contexts where experts exchange and combine different types of explicit knowledge.

c) Externalisation starts when contradictions between individuals appear and slow down the firm's activities. The new codified knowledge then becomes a solution to these problems. This implies that an organisation is capable of devising a common knowledge base, which includes explicit elements derived from parts of its experts' implicit knowledge. This makes the experts' work significantly easier in as much as access to the knowledge base can eliminate the duplication of efforts when solving problems. Externalisation is important in as much as it allows experts to have access to other experts' knowledge within the organisation. This contributes to the efficiency of co-ordination schemes, given the possibility for individuals to share knowledge in explicit forms. This is, no doubt, the transfer mode which attracts the most interest these days due to the potential offered by these new means of communication (Cohendet *et al,* 1996). This transfer method also brings about deep changes in power relationships. Coriat and Dosi (1995) showed how the wave of externalisation, which accompanied the development of Taylorism, gave the hierarchy (here the planning department) the opportunity to "capture-" or control part of the knowledge which had so far been tacit : *"Indeed, the story of 'Scientific Management is precisely the story of the transformation of individual skills into organisational competencies codified into a hierarchy of routines".*

d) Internalisation refers to a learning process linked to repetitiveness of tasks (trial and error procedures) which allows tacit knowledge to emerge. Thus, new knowledge and skills linked to the firm's base of experience can originate from such a mode. It must be stressed that this conversion can be achieved when the co-ordination scheme allows for communication between individuals who share a common knowledge base (socialisation). As a result, the information and communication structure which shapes the exchange framework between individuals also influences the succession of different conversion modes.

Table 1.
Different modes of conversion of knowledge,
(Nonaka, 1994)

To : From :	Codified Knowledge	Tacit Knowledge
Codified Knowledge	Combination	Internalisation
Tacit Knowledge	Externalisation	Socialisation

The typology of knowledge conversion modes provides a better understanding of incentive mechanisms, which develop progressively to control the distribution of knowledge. Again, the hypothesis of a strong dependence of the mechanisms adopted on the type of dominant organisation seems valid to explain current trends. Western style companies seem to prefer incentive mechanisms, which correspond to an externalisation conversion mode, after having favoured the so-called "combination" type. The wave of codification of tacit knowledge linked to certification strategies (such as ISO) falls within this reasoning. Several specific incentive schemes accompany this wave (longing for acknowledgment, specific training courses, etc.). Japanese style companies, on the other hand, are pursuing an incentive logic, which favours more a change towards a conversion mode oriented towards "socialisation", after having favoured more "internalisation". "Peer pressure" and "reputation effect" type mechanisms further this type of knowledge conversion. However, these archetypal organisation schemes are, of course, only two extreme types of reference. Other mechanisms can be designed to facilitate the circulation of knowledge. Thus Nonaka (1994) advocated increasing circulation between tacit and codified knowledge in order to deploy learning in satisfactory conditions. At the same time, he stressed the extent to which incentive schemes themselves are part of a learning process and need progressive adjustment.

CONCLUSION

In this contribution, we have tried to some of the main features of the emerging evolutionary theory of the firm. This theory is still under construction, but we have tried to demonstrate that it already captures the main characteristics of the firm conceived as a processor of knowledge. The perspective, which is now fully opened, offers a renewed way to interpret the main theoretical mechanisms that are the basis of the functioning of the firm. However, on theoretical as well as on practical grounds, we are now facing two major visions of the firm: on the one side the firm as a processor of information, on the other side the firm as a processor of knowledge. The existence of these two alternative visions of the firm raises some fundamental questions: does the evolutionary approach brings a complementary or a competing view when compared with the traditional theories of the firms, in particular the dominant transaction based approach ? Which one of the two approaches is the best fitted to explain what Casson (1998) considers as being the main issues addressed by modern theories of the firm: 1) the boundary of the firm; 2) the internal organisation of the firm; 3) the formation growth and diversification of the firm, and4) the role of the entrepreneur ?

As Langlois and Foss (1996) pointed out, we are confronted with the choice between, on the one hand a traditional contractual approach based on transaction, where « firms and other institutions are alternative bundles of contracts understood as mechanisms for creating and realigning incentives », and on the other hand, « *a qualitative coordination, that is helping cooperating parties to align not their incentives but their knowledge and expectations* ». Further investigation and analysis should be made in reconciling these two approaches. The issue at stake is in fact to try to converge towards a coherent theoretical framework that reconcile the specific problem of management and creation of knowledge within the firm, with the traditional problem of allocating resources based on the transaction cost approach. This could be seen as a step towards the direction indicated by Milgrom et Roberts (1988) when they say, « *the incentive based transaction cost theory has been made to carry too much of the weight of explanation in the theory of organisations. We expect competing and complementary theories to emerge, theories that are founded on economising on bounded rationality and pay more attention to changing technology and to evolutionary considerations ».*

REFERENCES

Alchian A. (1951), "Uncertainty, evolution and economic theory", *Journal of Political Economy*, vol. 57, 211-221.

Aoki M. (1986), " Horizontal vs. Vertical Information Structure of the Firm ", *American Economic Review*, vol.76, 971-983.

Aoki, M. (1988), *Information, Incentives and Bargaining in the Japanese Economy*, Cambridge, Cambridge University Press.

Argyris C. & Schön D. A. (1978), *Organisational Learning: a Theory of Action Perspective,* Addison-Wesley Publishing Company.

Burkhart R., Cohen M.D., Dosi G., Egidi M., Marengo L, Warglien M., Winter S. (1996) : "Routines and other Recurring Action Patterns of Organizations : Contemporary Research Issues", *Industrial and Corporate Change*, Vol. 5, n°3, 653-698.

Casson M. (1998), "An entrepreneurial theory of the firm" presented at the Conference "Competences, Gorvernance and Entrepreneurship", DRUID, Bornholm, June 1998.

Chandler A.D. Jr (1992), "Corporate Strategy, Structure and Control Methods in the United States during the 20th Century", *Industrial and Corporate Change*, vol 1, n°2, 263-284.

Coase R.M. (1937), *The Nature of the Firm*, Economica, vol.4, 386-405.

Cohendet P., Kern F., Mehmapazir B. & Munier E (1997), "Organisation of Transnational Firms and Networks of Telecommunications" EMOT Workshop (European Science Fondation), *Learning and Embeddedness : Evoluting Transnational Firm Strategies in Europe;* Collingwood College, University of Durham Newcastle UK, 27-29 June 1996.

Cohendet P., Llerera P, & Marengo L. (1994), "Learning and Organizational Structure in Evolutionary Models of the Firm"; EUNETIC Conference Evolutionary of Technological Change, European Parliament Strasbourg, October 1994.

Coriat B. & Dosi G. (1995), "Learning how to Govern and Learning how to Solve Problems: On the Co-evolution of Competences, Conflicts and Organizational Routines", Luxenburg. Austria IIASA, Working paper 95-06.

Coriat B., Weinstein O. (1995): *Les nouvelles théories de l'entreprise*, Livre de Poche, Collection Références.

Dosi G , Egidi M, (1991), "Substantive and procedural uncertainty", *Journal of Evolutionary Economics,* 1, pp.145-168

Dosi G, Marengo L, (1994), "Towards a theory of Organizational Competencies", in England R.W (ed), *Evolutionary concepts in contemporary economics,* Michigan University Press

Dosi G., Teece D.J., Winter S.G. (1991), " Toward of Theory of Corporate Coherence ", in Dosi G., Giannetti R. and Toninelli P.A. (eds), *Technology and the Enterprise in a Historical Perspective,* Oxford, Oxford University Press.

Favereau O. (1989) : " Marchés internes, marchés exterrnes", Revue Économique, n°2, p. 273-328.

Favereau O. (1993): "Suggestions pour reconstruire la théorie du salaire sur une théorie des règles", WP Laedis, Uni. Paris X, April.

Favereau O. (1995): "Apprentissage collectif et coordination par les règles: application à la théorie des salaires", in , Lazaric N., Monnier J. M. (eds), *Coordination économique et apprentissage des firmes* Economica, Paris, pp. 23-38.

Foss N.J. (1996): "The 'alternative' theories of Knight and Coase, and the modern theory of the firm", *Journal of the History of Economic Thought,* Vol. 18, Spring,, pp. 1-20.

Fransman M. (1994), "Information, Knowledge, Vision and Theories of the Firm", *Industrial and Corporate Change,* vol. 3 n° 3.

Guilhon B. (1994), "Le processus d'apprentissage de la firme : contenu et limites", *Revue d'Economie Industrielle,* n° 74.

Hayek F.A. von (1937), " Economics and Knowledge", *Economica*, vol. 4, pp. 33-54.

Héraud J. A. & Garrouste P. (1993), "Auto-organisation et création technologique" in Ancori B (ed), *Apprendre, se souvenir, décider, CNRS* éditions, Paris.

Jensen M.C. and Meckling W.H. (1976), " Theory of the Firm : Managerial Behaviour, Agency Costs and Ownership Structure ", *Journal of Financial Economics*, vol. 3, 305-360.

Knight F (1921), *Risk,Uncertainty, and Profit,* Reprint 1971, Chicago, The Chicago University Press.

Langlois R., Foss N. (1996), "Capabilities and governance: the rebirth of production in the theory of economic organisation", working paper Uni. of Connecticut/Copenhagen Business School.

Levinthal, D. (1997), "Adaptation on rugged landscapes", *Management Science*, vol. 43, pp. 934-50.

Lesourne J. (1991), *Economie de l'ordre et du désordre,* Economica, Paris.

Loasby B. J. (1989), "Organization, Competition, and the Growth of Knowledge", in Langlois R. *(ed), Economics as process,* Cambridge University Press.

March J, Simon H, (1993), "Organizations revisited", *Industrial and Corporate Change*, 2, 3, pp. 299-316

Marschak J., Radner R. (1972), *Economic Theory of Teams*, New Haven, CT, Yale University Press.

Milgrom P., Roberts J. (1988), "Economic theories of the firm: past, present, future", *Canadian Journal of Economics*, vol.21, pp. 444-458.

Marengo L. (1994), "Knowledge Distribution and Coordination on Organization: On some Social Aspects of the Exploitation vs. Exploration Trade-off", *Revue Internationale de systèmique*, n° 1.

Nelson R. (1994), "The Co-evolution of Technology, Industrial Change and supporting Institutions", *Industrial and Corporate Change* vol. 3.

Nelson R. & Winter S. (1982): "An Evolutionary theory of economic Change", Belknap Press of Harvard, Cambridge.

Nonaka I. (1994), "A Dynamic Tbeory of Organizational Knowledge Creation", *Organisation science,* vol 5.

Nonaka I., Takeuchi H. (1995): *The Knowledge Creating Company,* New York, Oxford University Press.

Penrose E. (1959): *The theory of the growth of the firm*, Oxford Uni. Press.

Polanyi M. (1966), *The Tacit Dimension,* Doubleday & Co, Inc Garden City New York.

Postrel S., Rumelt R.P (1992): "Incentives, routines and self-command", *Industrial and Corporate Change,* vol. 1, n°3, 397-425.

Radner R. (1986), " The Internal Economy of Large Firms ", Economic Journal, vol. 96 (Supplement), 1-22.

Richardson G (1960), *Information and Investment,* Clarendon Press

Richardson G (1972), "The Organization of Industry", *The Economic Journal,* September.

Schelling T. (1978), *Micromotives and Macrobehavior, Norton.*

Simon H.A. (1957), *Models of man*, New York, Wiley.

Teece D. (1988), "Technological Change and the Nature of the Firm", in Dosi *et al. (eds), Technical Change and Economic Theory.* Frances Pinter, London.

Walliser B. (1988), "Systémique et Economie', *Revue Internationale de Systèmique,* op. 2, n°3, pp. 245-260.

Williamson O.E. (1975), *Markets and Hierarchies : Analysis and Antitrust Implications*, New York, The Free Press.

Williamson O.E. (1985), *The Economic Institutions of Capitalism : Firms, Markets, Relational Contracting*, London, Mac Millan.

Williamson O.E. (1993), "Transaction costs economics and organisation theory", *Industrial and Corporate Change,* vol.2, n° 2, pp. 107-156.

Williamson. 0. E. (1996), *Mechanisms of Governance,* Oxford University Press.

Zuscovitch E. (1993), " Evolutionary Economics and the Lamarkian Hypothesis : Towards a Social Imperfect Competition ? , *Revue Internationale de Systémique.* vol 7, n°5.

Chapter 8

INFORMATION IN THE THEORY OF ORGANIZATIONS

Jacques Crémer
Director of Research CNRS, GREMAQ and IDEI
University of Social Sciences, Toulouse

Since the beginning of the 1970s, the economic theory of organisations has made rapid progress, and the intuitions of Coase and Simon, which had, so to speak, remained in the collective unconscious mind of our science, were made explicit and integrated in the analytical corpus thanks to advances in the economics of information. The aim of this chapter is to throw some light on the reasons why the theory of organisations has become in great part a theory of information.

I will proceed in two stages. In the first part of the chapter, I will explain the basic methodology of the analysis of transaction costs, and will present its links with the theory used by Alan Kirman in his chapter in this volume. The second part will be less systematic. It will present some of the themes recently discussed in the academic literature, chosen because I feel that they illustrate in a specially useful way the links between the economics of information and the theory of organisations.

This way of proceeding, which might seem disorganised, has one objective: it tries to highlight what I will call the "not integrated" methodology of the theory of organisations. There is a general consensus among mainstream economists on the general way in which organisations should be studied, but "the" integrated model of organisations does not exist. Each specific concrete case must be interpreted at the light of many partial models, which each illuminate one aspect of the situation. We have many models we can use for this task, but there still is lots to do.

1. TRANSACTION COSTS AND MARKET IMPERFECTIONS

1.1 Coase and the concept of transaction costs

In his classical, and often cited, article of the theory of the firm, Coase (1937) distinguishes two types of "transactions": market transactions, between firms, and transactions within organisations. For instance, the seminar in which the ideas of this paper were presented at the French "Commissariat du Plan" was a market transaction, but, if I had presented it at the University of Toulouse, it would have been a transaction within an organisation. Coase considers the set of transactions as given, and tries to identify those that would be most efficiently

P. Petit (ed.), Economics and Information, 139–153.

conducted within a firm and those that would be most efficiently conducted through the market. Furthermore, he assumes that the economy will choose the most efficient mode of transaction.

For instance, a firm that needs computer chips for producing a scientific satellite must decide whether it is preferable to buy them from a subcontractor or to produce them in-house. There are costs in conducting this transaction through a market transaction, if only because these chips have a specific use, that we are faced with a bilateral monopoly and therefore that the welfare theorems which prove the efficiency of markets do not apply. There are also costs in conducting this transaction within the firm, for instance because there will be less effort in the factory that would produce the chip because the incentives to maximise profits would be weaker. Coase assumes that, in most cases, the technology does not depend on the mode of organisation that has been chosen (in our example, the same technology is available to the subcontractor and the satellite producer) and therefore that only the difference in "transaction costs" will influence the choice of one or the other solution.

Another example might be useful. In his very well-known discussion of the division of labour, Adam Smith gives the example of a pin factory. He shows that work can be more efficient when "one man draws out the wire, another straights it, a third cuts it, a fourth points it, a fifth grinds it at the top for receiving the head...", as workers become more proficient and more productive in the respective tasks. He concludes that firms appear in order to facilitate specialisation. However, one cannot jump to this conclusion. Indeed, one could imagine that each of the specialised workers could create his or her own firm, and that they coordinate through market transactions. One would buy wire, and would sell straighten wire to a second who would cut it and sell pieces of wire to the third... If we believe that the invisible hand of the market functions well, we must conclude that this organisation of production would be efficient. Intuitively, it is clear that this is not the case, and it is reasonable to think that, in this specific case, transaction costs would be lower within a firm than through the market.

Coase's analysis has generally been accepted in the literature, but the theory of organisation progressed slowly in the thirty years that followed the publication of his article, in great part because economists did not know how to identify and analyse precisely these transaction costs. (This summary is, of course, much too brutal. It should be softened by a discussion of the contributions of a certain number of authors, in particular Herbert Simon and the "Pittsburgh school".) It is only with the development of the economic theory of information and of contract theory that we have acquired the ability to study these phenomena in detail.

1.2 Organisation and market imperfections

From a methodological viewpoint the major contribution of Williamson in his programmatic book *Markets and Hierarchies* (1975) was to correctly tackle the identification of transaction costs – this is quite remarkable, as it is in some sense a synthesis done before the analysis had been conducted. Using results from information theory, Williamson realised that he could find there methods to better understand why markets can sometimes lead to large transaction costs. It is only later that contract theory explained – still imperfectly – why transactions internal to firms can avoid some of these costs. (The progresses of the theory of organisations give one more example of the stupidity of the too often heard claim that economic theory is sterile. Transaction cost theory could never have developed without general equilibrium theory, the introduction of time and uncertainty in that framework, and other organic developments of economic theory, such as the identification of the notions of adverse selection and moral hazard.)

In the next few pages, I illustrate through a few examples the most characteristic elements of Williamson's methodology.

1.2.1. In the beginning was the market ...

Williamson assumes that "in the beginning was the market". The analysis of transaction costs is done by first imagining a world in which all the transactions would be conducted through the market. Then, one identifies all the reasons why this market would not function perfectly efficiently. Very often, these reasons are linked to difficulties in the acquisition and the use of information, in particular, as explained by Alan Kirman, because prices do not convey all the information that would be necessary for the agents to take their decisions in a socially optimal way. The creation of an organisation is interpreted as a way to respond to these market imperfections.

Rather than proceed abstractly by listing the type of imperfections that one can find in market, I will present two examples of the use of this method of analysis.

1.2.2 First example: universities

My first example will be an example that I often use in my teaching, that of universities. Assume that we decided to organise a university system by using markets as much as possible, that is by maximising the proportion of transactions that are done through the intermediation of markets. (This is, of course, a pedagogical exercise, and not a proposal for managing higher education.)

Each professor will offer some courses, will announce prices, and the students will choose among these courses those that they believe offer the best quality/price ratio. We can imagine that a system for renting classrooms will evolve, and that the prices of courses will vary according to the number of students. I would announce a course on theory of organisations, would describe it, would rent a room (firms would specialise in the rental of classrooms) and would fix a price for the students that want to come. This organisation would have important benefits: the most important would be that improvements in my lectures would increase my income, more or less proportionally to the increase in the welfare of the students, and this increase will provide me with appropriate incentives.

On the other hand, a bit more thinking shows that difficult problems of access to information would arise. For instance, it is difficult for students to judge the quality of a teacher. They can judge the presentation and whether or not the professor keeps his class awake, but the scientific validity of the content is very difficult to judge. Market can treat these problems: specialised institutions evolve that treat information and spread it (for instance, in France, the "Guide Hachette des Vins" provides consumers with information that is less biased than the pitch of salespeople.) We know, however, that these institutions are always somewhat imperfect: technically, they do not yield the "first best" solution. In some cases, the creation of an organisation can improve the processing of information.

In order to better sell my course on the theory of organisations, I could create a club with some colleagues, through which we would guarantee to students the quality of our courses. The students would only need to verify the quality of our club, rather than the quality of each of us. Of course, for this advantage to obtain, we would have to put in place a system of internal controls, to avoid free riding on the effort of others. We already see the apparition of the notion of university, and we can deduce that one of the roles of a university is to guarantee the quality of professors, as it is more efficient that reputation be attached to the institution than to individual teachers.

Let us continue to think about this example from the viewpoint of the potential employers of the students. Before recruiting new employees, they want information about the quality of the teaching they have been subject to, the amount of work they have done, as well their natural gifts. In a totally decentralised system, employers would need practically the same information on the quality of the professors as the students need. Grades would be very difficult to interpret, and it would be difficult to make sure that they are given honestly and not only to increase the popularity of a course, and therefore the revenues of the teacher. For all these reasons informational costs would be very high, and one understands how an institution such as a university can improve the transmission of information through quality control.

I leave it to the reader to continue with analysis of this example. He or she can, for instance, think about the difficulties of coordinating schedules, or about the problem of prerequisites.

This example is a caricature. This has benefits: it shows in a very striking way that the organisation has a role in reducing the cost of processing information. This has costs: from an applied point of view the conclusions are totally obvious as it is clear that such an extreme decentralisation as the one described above would be inefficient (which does not imply that more decentralisation of higher education would not be a good policy in countries such as France). The next example will apply the technique of analysis to a more subtle problem.

1.2.3. Second example: conglomerates

Our second example will be conglomerates, an example discussed by Williamson (1975). It can teach a lot, despite the fact that these large firms, diversified across many industries, are no longer in fashion, at least in North America and in France, and that they have been going through severe crisis in, for instance, Korea. During the 1970s, the challenge was to explain their apparition and their success.

Williamson starts from the observation that capital markets are inefficient. Ideally, investment choices would be made in such a way that their marginal profitability would be the same in all sectors of the economy. An expanding sector has, on average, a higher marginal profitability, but it can be difficult to invest there. Indeed, it is not enough to decide to invest more in sector X. One must, within this sector, identify the most promising projects, but this is difficult because of the presence of asymmetries of information between investors and entrepreneurs, who know well the quality of the projects they are putting forward. It is clear that an investor whose only policy would be to invest in sector X will be offered many projects with a negative return.

According to Williamson, conglomerates help mitigate the negative consequences of these asymmetries of information. First, the definition of a conglomerate that we will use: it is a firm that has total ownership of subsidiaries in sectors between which there are no synergies, either commercially or industrially. As unique owner, the conglomerate has access to information that outside investors would not privy to, if a subsidiary were quoted on the stock market: one of the reasons for this fact is that it can impose on its subsidiaries management accounting systems that allow for a standardised measure of the productivity of capital.

As it owns subsidiaries in several industries, a conglomerate can easily use this information to allocate capital efficiently, and, actually, it is its only role. Indeed, the employees of the core of the firm, those that Williamson call the "elite staff" do not intervene in the day to day management of the subsidiaries. Their only roles are to provide incentives to their managers, and to measure the productivity of investments to transfer capital to the subsidiaries where it will be more useful. (The Boston Consulting Group used a framework that had some similarities with this analysis.)

From our viewpoint, it is important to note the methodology used: the creation of an organisation helps circumvent the imperfections of capital markets, imperfections created by the difficulties of transmitting information. The conglomerate can decrease the transaction costs associated with transferring capital from one sector to the other.

1.3 Limits of the methodology

It is important to understand that the assumption that "in the beginning was the market" is not a historical summary. To the contrary, the record is clear: since the Middle Ages, the market has invaded a word where organisation was king. (A similar phenomenon was observed in the Eastern European countries before the Fall of the Berlin wall: black or "grey" markets were appearing despite the authorities best efforts to forbid them.) From a theoretical viewpoint, we begin by studying the way in which a market would function for the simple reason that the analysis of market transactions is easier, or at least better understood, than the analysis of transactions within organisations. Indeed, we have all the tools of the theory of general equilibrium, with its extensions to dynamics and to uncertainty, as well all the tools of the theories of imperfect competition, of externalities, of public goods, to identify circumstances in which markets function satisfactorily and circumstances where they do not.

The main difficulty that one meets when applying this methodology stems from the fact that it is very difficult, both in theory and in practice, to measure transaction costs, and to compare the costs linked to different forms of organisations. More precisely, it is relatively straightforward to identify reasons why a market is not efficient (or at least would not yield "first best" optimality). If we assume that firms are managed perfectly efficiently, we come too easily to the conclusion that they are able to correct these inefficiencies in all circumstances. In reality, we know that intra-firm transactions also have costs – for instance, it is difficult to give "powerful" incentives to employees of large firms – but these inefficiencies are difficult to measure precisely. And the theory tells us that we must compare transaction costs in different organisational modes.

Furthermore, the theory assumes that, in a market economy, at equilibrium, the most efficient forms of organisations will emerge. One would like to understand in which circumstances this hypothesis can be deduced from a more fundamental theory of organisational choices in a market economy: we know that equilibria can often be inefficient. Because this theory does not exist, it is easy in applied work to fall in the trap of always assuming that the organisation that one sees is the most efficient. For instance, even though the theory of conglomerates that we have discussed is very seductive, in practice, conglomerates have not been able to play the role it describes for them. We would have liked the theory to help us predict this fact, but, even ex-post, it is difficult to understand exactly where the analysis that predicted that they were very efficient went wrong.

2. HIERARCHIES AND OPTIMAL ORGANISATION

At this point, a systematic discussion of the theory of organisations would list the different types of transaction costs in markets and would show how a firm can decrease these costs. This way of presenting things has at least two major disadvantages. First, it requires quite a lengthy theoretical discussion and a long catalog of the different reasons why markets can be inefficient, and postpones the discussions of concrete examples. Second, and I think more importantly, it gives too unified a view of organisation theory. In reality, we only have tidbits of theories that throw partial light on a number of important issues (and therefore lots of exciting work to do).

I will therefore continue by reviewing some recent themes in the literature, chosen in part because the role of information is specially clear, but also because I find them specially interesting and that I know them less badly than others. I will try to show how the comparison of the transaction costs induced by different organisational choices leads to interesting insights.

2.1. Theory of hierarchies

Nearly all organisations – public and private firms, government agencies, non-profits – have a hierarchical organisation.[1] Formally, one can represent the hierarchical position of their members by what graph theorists call a tree: there is a leader, and every employee, apart from this leader, has a hierarchical superior. Radically different methods of organisation, such as matrix organisations, have usually led to failures. An important branch of the literature, which has been very active in the first half the 1990s, takes its inspiration from analytical techniques used by computer scientists in order to study parallel computing and shows that hierarchical organisation can be explained as the optimal response to the problems of aggregation of information that firms must solve (see Radner (1990) and Bolton and Dewatripont (1995)).

In order to conduct the analysis, one represents the firm as receiving in each period of time pieces of information that it needs to aggregate. For instance, a bank receives regularly requests for loans. Each of the employees of the firm is subject to bounded rationality, which we will represent by assuming that they can only aggregate two elementary units of information in each period. On the other hand, the employees can share work. For instance, in a two employee firm, employee A and employee B could share information that arrives. Each would aggregate the information which she is handed; once this is done, they would have a new elementary unit of information, which would be the sum of the elementary units that they have been allocated. Employee A would transmit to employee B the sum she has computed, and employee B would be able to finish off the computation.

The problem becomes more difficult when there is more data to be treated, and there are more employees in the firm: who must receive the information coming from the environment? what must be done with the results of intermediate computations? Under rather strong hypotheses about the type of information and the type of computations that must be performed, one can show that the optimal organisation is a hierarchy, sometimes adapted. The lowest

---

[1]One of the difficulty of writing about the theory of organizations is the problem of avoiding expressions of the type "the organization of the organization", as in this sentence!

level employees each receive part of the information, and transmit the sum to their superiors. Each of these superiors aggregate the information received from his or her subordinates, and so on until the grand aggregates is indeed received by the head who can take a decision, on the basis of the whole set of information that the organisation has received.

This theory may seem a mere caricature, but it does have one great advantage: it allows for the computation of the production function of a firm from elementary data on the activities of each of its employees. One can draw conclusions on the relative efficiency of large and small firms, more precisely to study the returns to scale in the treatment of information – Radner shows that there are increasing returns to scale.

However, despite the elegance of this theory, one may wonder about the relevance of the description of the treatment of information:

- On one hand, modern firms do not try to accumulate information at the highest level, but, on the opposite, are trying to push it down the hierarchy.
- On the other hand, firms have lots of different tasks to accomplish, and the organisational problem is to coordinate these different tasks, not to coordinate employees participating to the same task. It seems to me that these theories of hierarchy have a somewhat too mechanical view of the firm.

2.2 Optimal organisation

I would like now to try to show how one can build a theory of the internal organisation of a firm that takes into account the heterogeneity of tasks. In practice, we know that one of the signs that a firm is badly organised is the fact that the top layer of management looses control because it becomes overwhelmed by too much information, and is forced to take too many decisions that should have been left to lower levels.

For instance, Chandler[2] (1962) studies the story of Du Pont de Nemours at the end of World War I, at the time at which this firm, which had been specialised in the production and sale of explosives and had excess capacity, tried to diversify. Du Pont had kept a "functional" organisation, in which marketing and production were separated from each other. The new products that it try to put on the market, such as dyes, required very close coordination between these two functions: marketing had to be able to reorient production towards products for which it had discovered high demand; production had to be able to provide information about the technical difficulties it was encountering and the fact that it could not fulfil some orders. Without an intermediate hierarchical level, the coordination between marketing and production can only be done at the highest level in the firm, and Chandler shows convincingly that

[2] Chandler's book is the first book which should be read by anyone interested by the study of organizations. The four case studies that he presents are fascinating, and throw light on numerous issues.

the fact that DuPont's organisation was not adapted to its new strategy required nearly continuous interventions by that highest level.

Facing this problem, Du Pont invented what has been called the multidivisional organisation in order to limit the cost of transmitting information. In this organisational form, the first hierarchical level is responsible for a product line. A division in charge both of the production and the sale of dyes solve the coordination problems that we have sketched above.[3] Notice this very important point: whereas economists normally ask the question "how should one facilitate the transmission of information?", in practice, firms try to limit the quantity of information that is transmitted.

A simple "team theoretical" model can illustrate this way of looking at the problem (see Crémer (1981)). One assumes that the firm is composed of groups of employees that perform an elementary task – we will call each of these groups a "shop". Choosing an organisation is equivalent to regrouping these shops into "divisions". We will make the hypothesis that communications are easy within divisions and very costly between divisions. Then, one can show that it is optimal to regroup within the same divisions shops that need to communicate continuously, that is that exchange among themselves goods and services (or, if we want to be more precise, which require a continuous exchange of information to determine the quantity of goods and services that they should exchange).

3. THE FIRM AS A STORE OF INFORMATION

The theories sketched in the preceding section consider the firm as an information processing machine, in a rather static framework as information is only used once. There is no accumulation of knowledge within the firm. In reality, firms have a history during which they accumulate information, habits, ways of doing things. In the present section, I would like to explore some of the ways in which the literature has thought about these issues.

3.1 Information capital

The expression "information capital" was introduced in 1980 by Prescott and Vissher. According to these authors, the production process generates not only products that the firm can sell, but also information that it can use later to increase its productivity.

More precisely, Prescott and Vissher focus on the information that firms acquire about the quality of their employees: just after they are hired, employees are assigned to tasks where it is possible to observe their comparative advantage in one or the other of two specialised tasks to which they will later be assigned.

---

[3] Of course, if the main coordination problems were problems of coordination between, for instance, the manufacturing of different products, this would not be the appropriate organizational form.

After a certain time, they are promoted in one of these two tasks. If the firm is growing very fast, employees spend little time at the entry level task, little information is gathered, and orientation is badly done. Efficiency suffers. On the other hand, if the firm grows slowly, employees spend lots of time in the entry level position and are better oriented later.

This model has quite a few interesting aspects:

- it highlights the fact that the firm, as an entity, has information that is valuable, as it helps decrease costs;
- it gives a concrete description of a specific process of accumulation of information – it is regrettable that more work has not been done in the same general vein, for instance by describing the information that firms acquire about their clients;
- it shows that the necessity of accumulating this information constraints the growth of the firm and explains the reasons for this constraint: Prescott and Vissher prove that as the firm grows faster its costs are higher, because employees are promoted in the "wrong" job. Although their model is very specific, one perceives that the phenomenon must be general and that similar constraints are imposed by the necessity of acquiring other types of information.

Other authors have studied similar phenomena. For instance, Harris and Hölmstrom (1982) have presented a theory of "career paths" which also rests on the accumulation of information of the capacities of employees. Chiappori, Salanié and Valentin (1995) recently presented a brilliant empirical test of this theory.

The notion, extensively used in economics and management, of "learning by doing", which expresses the fact that cost decreases with the cumulative production of a firm, rests on a similar intuition. By producing, the firm acquires information on technology, which helps decrease costs, but I know of no formal analysis that tries to link learning by doing to an explicit description of the way in which information capital is accumulated.

3.2. Corporate culture

Management textbooks and specialised magazines often discuss "corporate culture". This concept is often used in a not very disciplined manner, and one has the impression that it makes it a bit too easy to explain many phenomena: "the merger of these two companies did not have the positive aspects that we expected because their cultures were too different".

Yet, it is true that when he begins work in a firm, it is not sufficient for a new employee to learn the technology that it uses and the type of job that he must do, he must also learn the "personality of the firm". I seems to me important to try to see if it is possible to develop an economic theory of this concept.

I attempted this exercise in Crémer (1993) where I define corporate culture as the stock of knowledge which is shared between its different employees, and where I try to show that the fact that this knowledge is shared plays an important efficiency inducing role. Let us indeed think through a model of internal communications of firms in which employees are in contact not only with their superiors and their subordinates, but also with employees of other services, in a somewhat random manner depending on the decisions to be taken. For instance, a salesman from times to times needs information coming from the R&D department. In this case, he directly calls a engineer and will not go through the hierarchical channels. Because it would be costly for two employees who must take a common decision once a year to have to learn about the work habits and the techniques of communications of their partner, organisations will impose a certain uniformity in order to avoid at least some of these costs.

For instance, Arrow (1974) discusses the internal language of organisations, the "coding", that is the words that are either invented or used in a very specific manner by their members. This coding, which is part of corporate culture and of which Arrow insists that it is specific to the organisation, can only be important if the employees of the firm have a communication network that is relatively dense and diversified. Indeed, if employees communicated only with their superior and their subordinates, one does not understand why the firm would use a single code. On the other hand, if the communications of each of the employees are very diversified – they communicate with a number of partners – one understands the need to develop communications systems that are efficient.

One can further analyse corporate culture by showing that standardised behaviours can have the same function: they allow the members of the organisation to communicate better, because each of them understands better the constraints that bear on the decisions of the other. For instance, in a firm that has developed a culture in which a rapid response to clients is the rule, it is important that the R&D engineer knows this fact when the salesman gets in contact with him. The fact that he belongs to the "corporate culture" allows one not to repeat this fact every time there is some communication.

Much research remains to be done to understand non hierarchical communications within firms, at the same time in order to draw the contrast with the theory of hierarchies to understand better advantages and disadvantages of different communications networks, and to explore their organisational consequences.

Kreps (1986) proposes also a theory of corporate culture, but he stresses the knowledge that clients or suppliers of the firm have about its behaviour. He shows that reputation – that is the knowledge that the partners have of the past cooperative behaviour of the firm – can have a market value. Indeed, reputation implies that the firm has a clientele, and this clientele has value (for instance, restaurants and stores are sold, at least in France, at prices which are nearly proportional to their sales). Moreover, the fact that reputation has value serves as an insurance for potential clients, as they know that the firm has incentives to provide high quality goods or services in order to maintain this value.

4. INCENTIVES AND QUALITY OF INFORMATION

Since the 1970s and the development of the theory of contracts, the economic theory of information has focussed its attention on the problems of providing incentives when there is asymmetry of information, whether this asymetry relates to exogenous variables (adverse selection problems) or to actions of agents (moral hazard problems). It was natural for specialists in the theory of organisations to try to apply the results of the economics of information to their own field of research. How should one give incentives to employees when they know better than their boss some of the constraints that they face and that they cannot be under constant surveillance? How can stockholders give incentives to CEOs so that they try to maximise profits and not their private welfare?

This section tries to show the complexity of the study of the problems to be studied, by presenting two themes recently discussed in the literature. Once again, my aim is not to present a complete survey of the issues, but rather to give examples of how the analysis can be conducted.

4.1. Improving information can be counterproductive

Contract theory has typically tried to identify techniques through which one can give incentives to agents to reveal their private information, but there exist circumstances in which it is preferable for information not to circulate well. One can indeed show that having *less* information can make it easier to give agents more powerful incentives, closer to what Williamson (1986) calls "market incentives".

The following example, inspired by another example presented in Crémer (1995) provides some intuition. A doctoral student writes a term paper, and on the basis of the quality of that paper, the professor will decide whether or not she will accept to supervise her dissertation. Should the professor discuss with the student the difficulties that he is encountering while writing the paper?

1. Such a discussion has obvious benefits: a student can discuss the hidden difficulties in the topic which he has been given, and the choice of supervisors will be done on more complete information on their qualities and weaknesses. Hence, there are clear advantages in improving the quality of information.

2. However, there is also a cost. The students will be insured against the risk that they have been allocated too difficult a topic, will have less incentives to work hard, and, as a consequence, the quality of the work can suffer. One can show formally that the cost of effort will be higher: in order to extract a given amount of effort from the student, it must be the case that the value for him of writing a dissertation have to be higher when there is discussion of the difficulties as he is writing the term paper.

I have recently tried to apply this intuition to vertical integration, that is the merger of two firms of which one is the supplier of the other, and to try to describe the mechanisms by which mergers can make incentives less powerful. We are here back in the midst of the fundamental questions asked by Coase: under which circumstances are internal transactions less efficient than transactions between two independent firms? (The classical article on vertical integration is Grossman and Hart (1986)).

4.2 Control and creation of information

Riordan (1990) notices that the owner of a firm usually has control over its cost accounting system, that he can modify as he sees fit[4]. This has very important consequences on the way in which the firm is managed. Indeed, the cost accounting system has important implications at the same time for the allocation of resources within the firm and for the incentives of executives. This two types of uses can be in conflict with each other:

- the efficient allocation of resources requires as much flexibility as possible in the cost accounting system, as it must be possible to adapt to changes in the strategy of the firm or to changes in its environment;
- on the other hand, providing incentives to executives requires a way of measuring their performance that is as stable as possible, for two reasons:
- first, so that they can know how to allocate their effort among the different tasks that they must carry out ;
- second, so that they are protected against unilateral modifications of the rules under which they work and they are paid and which would be aimed at depriving them of the rewards to which they are entitled.

Riordan shows that a consequence of all this the transfer of the control over the cost accounting system has profound consequences on the incentives to reveal private information and to work hard. More precisely, he studies the purchase of a supplier by a firm. On one hand, the client firm has better information about the costs of its suppliers once it controls its cost accounting system and it can impose management techniques that are consistent with its own. On the other hand, it becomes impossible to use any type of measure of profits of the supplier to judge the quality of the work conducted by its executives, as the non availability of the profits measured by the standard methods of financial accounting implies that there is one less instrument available for non manipulable measurement.

---

4 A full discussion would have to be more careful. For instance, the valuation of stocks for financial accounting requires that certain rules of cost accounting be respected. Furthermore, a firm might have to justify the way it compute its costs, for instance if it wants to defend itself against accusations of predatory pricing, or if it wants to participate in public procurement.

CONCLUSION

The chapter has certainly not tried to present a survey of the whole economic theory of information (for recent and more complete discussions see the preliminary chapter of Tirole (1988) or the book of Milgrom and Roberts (1992)), but to show how modern economic theory has studied the firm as a locus of information processing. I hope that the reader will be attracted to this field of study, to my mind one of the most fascinating parts of economic theory, as the problems which are asked are problems of choice of the right model rather than the technical problems of solving problems that have already been well asked.

REFERENCES

Arrow, Kenneth J., (1974) *The Limits of Organization,* W.W. Norton & Co, New York.

Bolton, Patrick and Mathias Dewatripont (1994) « The firm as a communication network », *The Quarterly Journal of Economics*, 109, 809-839.

Chandler, Alfred D. (1962) *Strategy and Structure: Chapter in the History of the Industrial Enterprise.* Boston: MIT Press.

Chiappori, P.A., B. Salanié, and J. Valentin (1995) « Early starters versus late beginners: an empirical test of the Harris-Hölmstrom model of wage formation », mimeo.

Coase, Ronald (1937) « The nature of the firm », *Economica,* 4, 386-405.

Crémer, Jacques (1981) « A partial theory of the optimal organization of a bureaucracy », *The Bell Journal of Economics*, 11, 2, 683-693.

Crémer, Jacques (1993) « Corporate Culture and Shared Knowledge », *Industrial and Corporate Change*, 2, 3, 351-386.

Crémer, Jacques (1995) « Arm's length relationships », *The Quarterly Journal of Economics*, CX, 2, 275-296.

Grossman, Sanford J. and Oliver D. Hart (1986) « The costs and benefits of ownership : A theory of vertical and lateral integration », Journal of Political Economy, 94, 4, 691-719.

Harris, M. and B. Hölmstrom (1982) « A theory of wage dynamics », *Review of Economic Studies*, 49, 315-333.

Kreps, David (1986) « Corporate culture and economic theory », in *Technology Innovation and Business Strategy*, ed. M. Tsuchiya. Tokyo: Nippon Keizai Shumbunshas Press.

Milgrom, Paul and John Roberts (1992) *Economics, organization and management*, Prentice Hall, Englewood Cliffs.

Prescott, Edward C. and Michael Visscher (1980) « Organization capital », *Journal of Political Economy*, 88,36-461.

Radner, Roy (1990) « The organization of decentralized information processing », *Econometrica*, 61, 509-1046.

Riordan, Michael H. (1990) « What is vertical integration? », in *The firm as a nexus of treaties*, eds. M. Aoki, B. Gustafsoon, and O.E. Williamson. London: European Sage.

Tirole, Jean (1988) *The Theory of Industrial Organization*, MIT Press, Cambridge.

Williamson, Oliver E. (1975) *Markets and Hierarchies: Analysis and Antitrust Implications.* New York: The Free Press.

Williamson, Oliver E. (1985) *The Economic Institutions of Capitalism: Firms, Markets and Vertical Contracting.* New York: Free Press.

Chapter 9

ON THE CODIFIABILITY OF KNOWLEDGE : TECHNICAL CHANGE AND THE STRUCTURE OF COGNITIVE ACTIVITIES

Robin Cowan

MERIT Maastricht University
Professor Western Ontario University

Dominique Foray

Director of Research CNRS/IRIS
Paris IX Dauphine University

1. TACIT KNOWLEDGE AND CODIFIED KNOWLEDGE

My method, my routine ? Heel the circle and then the hollow. Always put the ball so that the valve is turned slightly to the left, like that, and then lean the nose of the ball slightly towards the goal post to give more momentum. Take aim, calmly. Note the wind. Stand straight. The left foot barely touching the ball, the right just behind it. Visualise the kick. Eye and foot on the same line. Rub your hands. Take exactly four steps back. Stop. Check. Visualise. Then two steps to the left if it's a Mitre ball like those we use in Bristol, one and a half if it's a Gilbert ball at Twickenham. They need more control, although they go further. Imagine the feeling in your foot. If you tried to write down exactly, with absolute certainty, everything you do when you kick a ball between two posts, it would be impossible, you'd still be here in a thousand years. But you just need to have done it once and your body-and-mind have the exact formula, ready to be repeated. (interview with J.Webb, British journalist, quoted in Mangolte, 1997, our translation).

The exchange, diffusion and learning of tacit knowledge require those who have it to take deliberate or voluntary action to share it. These operations can be difficult and costly to implement. Storage and memorisation of tacit knowledge are conditioned by the renewal of generation after generation of people who have such knowledge. In many fields, including those that seem the most rational and systematised, the risk of "disinvention" is great. As MacKenzie and Spinardi (1995) show, and contrary to common sense, it is possible to "disinvent" the bomb. In the field of nuclear weapons, studied by these researchers, tacit knowledge is so important that a break of a single generation of engineers would be enough to lose a large number of procedures and simply forget "how it's done".

But a "unique quality of man [is] being able to put his memory outside himself." (Leroi-Gourhan, quoted by Favereau, 1998). This is done through

P. Petit (ed.), Economics and Information, 155–165.

codification: transforming knowledge into a message which can be stored, recalled, processed or transmitted as information. This process, itself subject to economic considerations, transforms several fundamental aspects of the economics of production and distribution of knowledge. Codification consists of attaching knowledge to a medium and thus freeing it from all attachment to a person. Although it involves high fixed costs (discussed in Section 2), it also enables agents to perform a number of operations at a very low marginal cost.

One of the most important effects of codification, and very likely to have been the first, historical impetus for it, is that codification reduces the costs and improves the reliability of storage and memorisation. As long as the medium remains legible and the code has not been forgotten, codified knowledge can, theoretically, be stored and retrieved indefinitely. A decrease in the costs of other aspects of transmission — transport, transferral, reproduction and even access and search — follow from this. Because codified knowledge is easy to reproduce, "originals" need not be moved, and assuming the medium is not difficult to transport, dissemination and diffusion becomes straightforward (Simon, 1982).

Codified knowledge can also be commodified. Relative to tacit knowledge, it can be described and defined much more specifically in terms of intellectual property. When knowledge is codified it becomes transferable independent of the transfer of other resources such, as people, in whom tacit knowledge is necessarily embedded. This improves the efficiency of knowledge market transactions.

A lesser effect concerns the impact of codification on spatial organisation and the division of labour. The ability to codify knowledge enables firms to externalise knowledge production and to acquire larger quantities of knowledge at a given cost. It is no longer necessary to develop knowledge internally, for it can be bought. This effect is at the root of the growing trend towards out-sourcing in many industries. Not only is the production of elements and components externalised; but because planning and design can now be bought even they can be performed outside the firm.

A caveat to this rosy view of the brave new world of knowledge needs to be made. Some of the beneficial effects of codification are limited by the fact that certain aspects of knowledge remain "stuck" in people (Von Hippel, 1994) and are never free or fluid. Thus, in general the transfer of knowledge from one site to another, as well as its capitalisation, will always pose problems due to the irreducibility of the tacit dimension of knowledge. This irreducibility of tacit knowledge means that the codification process can never provide all the knowledge required to undertake an action; it can provide only incomplete solutions to the problem of expressing knowledge. That is why codification should not be considered simply as an operation of substitution of a codified element for a tacit element. It consists rather of the construction of new sets of tacit and codified knowledge. Once the codified message has been received by an economic agent, that agent has to mobilise additional knowledge in order to exploit it.

This is not to say that there are always huge costs to using codified knowledge. In the case of regular exchanges of messages in a stable community of agents, the mobilisation of additional knowledge can be minimal. What this implies though, is that all the advantages described above are only potential. Important conditions have to be met before they can materialise. The realisation of these benefits requires an irreversible initial investment in the training of a community of agents capable of deciphering and using the codes. And some set of agents has to make the investments that permit them to codify the knowledge that they and others use.

2. FRAMEWORK

The three aspects of codification

There are three aspects to the codification of knowledge and expertise (Cowan & Foray, 1997): modelling tacit knowledge; developing a language; and writing and storing a message.

Codification results in the formulation of a message imprinted on a base or medium. This process involves the mobilisation of tools and techniques. From the invention of writing to its mechanisation and from copyists to the electronic printer, the extent of progress in printing technologies has been vast. But, as Hatchuel and Weil (1995) show, codification almost always involves knowledge creation. In general this includes modelling the tacit knowledge that is being codified. In order to make tacit knowledge explicit it is necessary to analyse it, to break it down into microelements and even to reformulate it. This means that codification is not simply a matter of transferral but also one of creation, involving other instances of decomposition and recomposition of knowledge. Two main forms of modelling can be mentioned here: the construction of automatic behavioural sequences, and the theorising of practices learned, so that they can be described and generalised. It is the modelling of knowledge that explains why the codified knowledge base never entirely covers the tacit knowledge base that it is supposed to replace.

Finally, codification is based on the creation and development of a language. Sometimes a natural language or another existing language (symbolic, numeric, etc.) is enough. Often, however, it is necessary to create new elements in the framework of an existing language (jargon) or to produce an entirely new language with which to express the model.

This concept of a language leads us to the problem of initial investments, so crucial for understanding the question of the social value of codified knowledge: to be able to be a potential user of codified knowledge, it is necessary to master the language used. This is true both for a natural language or a computer or mathematical language. In other words, knowledge will be easier to codify and disseminate in a community whose members share the language used. Thus, the diffusion and use of codified knowledge is based on the initial irreversible investments required to construct a community of agents, a "clique" or network whose members can "read" the code (Arrow, 1974).

Hence, codification is based on the three poles indicated below.

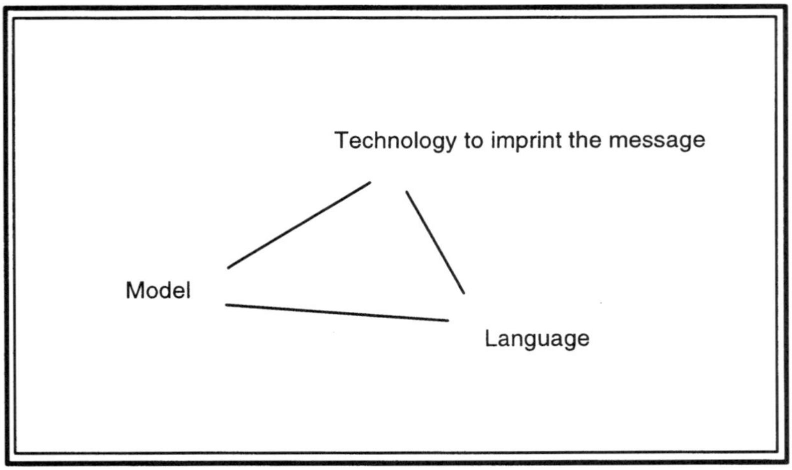

3. THE ENDOGENOUS BOUNDARIES BETWEEN TACIT AND CODIFIED KNOWLEDGE

In a recent paper, Cowan *et al.* (2000) criticise the position that the classification of knowledge into main types is an exogenous question, a matter for epistemologists, cognititians or psychologists, essentially predetermined by non-economic factors affecting the supply of knowledge. Such a position overlooks the importance of a set of factors that influence the demand for codified knowledge, including institutional arrangements affecting the structure of incentives for codification activities. They also concern the state of technology, which determines codification costs. This position on the endogenous nature of boundaries between tacit knowledge and codified knowledge and the importance of economic determinants is in fact very similar to that of Nelson & Winter (1982).

4. CASES FOR ECONOMIC CHOICES: "CODIFIABLE" KNOWLEDGE

Of course costs and benefits will explain the decision to codify only in the case of codifiable knowledge. The economic question is therefore the following: how do economic agents decide whether or not to codify "codifiable but not yet codified knowledge"? This is where price considerations come in. If, instead, we took the case of tacit, non-codifiable knowledge (considering the state of printing, modelling and language technologies) — for example those concerning the recognition of a perfume — there is obviously no possible choice or discussion on costs. For the firm, the only way of managing knowledge is by resorting to the internal labour market. If this firm has a vision of its future it will perhaps be able to allocate resources to a R&D programme for developing the complex tools to make this knowledge codifiable in the long term (which is in fact happening in the development of an artificial nose capable of recognizing and analysing smells!). But in the short term the knowledge remains tacit, without that being the consequence of an economic choice. By contrast, a computer technician may choose either to codify his or her knowledge in the form of a manual or expert system and then to exploit its dissemination, or else to keep it tacit so that users continue to buy the technician's repair services.

Thus, the economic analysis of the choice to codify concerns only that which is codifiable in a given historical context. This "codifiability" depends on the existence of appropriate languages, printing technologies and modelling capabilities for the knowledge under consideration.

In the next section, we argue that the codifiability of a given piece of knowledge depends upon two factors: the level of technology and the cognitive structure of the knowledge considered.

5. THE EXTENT OF CODIFIABILITY OF KNOWLEDGE

In the discussion that follows we consider three types of knowledge activities.[1] The purpose of distinguishing among these activities is to identify different ways in which knowledge is used, or purposes to which it is put. That said, we should emphasise that the types of activities we identify are not mutually exclusive. Indeed, most activities use knowledge in many different ways. But it is worth distinguishing to a certain extent in order to understand different issues in codification. Many activities require the use of data or facts — declarative knowledge — as input. Examples are countless: making a telephone call requires knowing the number; planning a journey requires knowing distances, speeds and times; making a product requires knowing where to get raw materials and so on. The second category we consider are activities that involve some process. An industrial process, for example, has an identifiable end goal, and knowledge is used in various ways to achieve it. Simply planning a production process; maintaining capital equipment; identifying activities that will increase profits all involve combining knowledge of various types into a coherent package that furthers the goals of the organisation. Finally, consider knowledge activities that are aimed at creating (or finding) new knowledge. With the recent emphasis on innovation as recombination, finding (pertinent) knowledge becomes an important feature of industrial activity. But finding knowledge has more prosaic uses in consumption as well.

---

[1] In keeping with Cowan et al. (2000) we try to avoid discussion of types of knowledge and focus instead on knowledge activities. It is only through its use in economic activity that knowledge is of interest to an economist, thus whether or not certain types of knowledge can be codified seems less germane than whether the possibility of codification changes certain activities.

6. TECHNICAL CHANGE, CODIFIABILITY OF KNOWLEDGE AND THE USE OF FACTS

The invention of writing permitted a significant change in human ability to extract value from declarative knowledge or "facts". To put it in the words of Jack Goody: "there are two main functions of writing. One is the storage function, that permits communication over time and space, and provides man with a marking, mnemonic and recording device." When writing is common, the problem of memory ceases to dominate intellectual life. "[T]he second function of writing ... shifts language from the aural to the visual domain, and makes possible a different kind of inspection, the re-ordering and refining not only of sentences, but of individual words." (Goody, 1977). The creation of lists, tables formulae and so on are all greatly facilitated with writing technologies. But further, writing or codification in general, permits us to remove knowledge from its context and to apply it in different, novel contexts.

From the invention of writing, the French historian Roger Chartier derives three lines of progress that have an impact on the economics of codification (but not so much on the codifiability of declarative knowledge):[2]

- evolution of the physical support: from rolls to codex (the modern book) and finally to electronic books. On this line, it is useful to note the technical progress that was made on books even before the invention of printing (quality of paper, reduction of size and illumination and, above all, creation of analytical systems such as abbreviations, contents pages and indexes), and which opened the age of manuals (Le Goff, 1985).
- evolution of the modes of production: from the manual copy to the collective or "industrial" organisation of copyists in the "scriptorium", to the printing press and finally electronic printing (Eisenberg,1980; David, 1988)
- evolution of the relationship of people to the writing. There is for example the evolution from voice aloud reading to silent reading; another major evolution nowadays is provided by electronic document which allows the reader to write not only in the margin but in the text itself.

Of course, all of these changes are very important but as far as the impact of these changes on the *codifiability* of declarative knowledge is concerned, the invention of writing (achieving the two major functions) is the decisive event. Later developments — the successive inventions of paper, the book, the printing press, and finally the electronic storage of information — are, of course, essential developments allowing productivity gains in the process codification

---

[2] There is a subtle point here. Whether or not knowledge is in principle codifiable is a technical question: Does today's technology permit us to turn this knowledge into a code? But if the answer is yes, this does not imply that the knowledge is codified. Whether or not it is codified depends on the costs and benefits of doing so. What is described in this section is the decrease in costs and increase in benefits to codification of factual knowledge. The "in principle" question is not alluded to here.

of this type of knowledge, and changing the costs of it. But, they improve the *codifiability* of declarative knowledge only marginally.

7. TECHNICAL CHANGE, CODIFIABILITY OF KNOWLEDGE AND INDUSTRIAL PROCEDURES[3]

Since the beginning of the industrial era automation has been one important part of technical change. Today there are many attempts to automate through knowledge codification. Many industrial activities use knowledge to produce goods or to plan their production, and the advances of the last decades in computer technologies, hardware, software and algorithms, have permitted the emergence of expert systems which are developed to reduce the extent to which these activities depend on human experts. There is a spectrum of activities here, and we mention three points in that spectrum: activities that can be successfully automated almost in their entirety; those that can be partially automated; and those that seem to withstand automation attempts.

Planning and executing a linear process with a fixed goal is relatively easy to automate with an expert system. The steps of the process and the stages in planning the process have simple interaction, with no feedback, and thus "backward chaining" from the fixed goal through the various stages needed to reach it is feasible. Modern expert systems handle this task well. It is the fixity of the goal, and the linearity of the process to achieve it that make this possible.

Pattern recognition, categorisation and generalisation is more difficult. The industrial process where these activities are most prominent is in fault diagnosis or repair. Expert systems developed for fault diagnosis are moderately successful but have great difficulty when they encounter situations that are significantly different from those they have seen in the past. The difficulty here lies in the novelty of situations and in trying to draw analogies to other situations. What makes a repairer good is that he has internalised some of the logic of the system he is repairing and can use this in drawing the analogies he needs when faced with new situations. But this logic is highly abstract, and difficult to codify. Current technology is still weak at drawing analogy, so it remains something at which human agents provide superior performance. Codifying what an expert knows is useful in training new repairers, and in helping repairers work more quickly, but in general it is not yet possible to automate the diagnosis and repair activity.

Finally there is activity which does not involve stable goals. In one sense for any firm the final goal is fixed (for an economist), namely to maximise profit. But often the link between actions that can be immediately taken and the final goal of profit maximisation is highly tenuous and difficult to discern. In this case, intermediate goals are then put in place, to which the connection is tighter. For instance, maximising profits of a conglomerate is reduced to maximizing the

---

[3] This section draws heavily on Hatchuel and Weil (1995) and on Cowan (2001).

profits of its subsidiaries. But when this is done, the intermediate goals can, and often do conflict. Part of the process of deciding which actions to take involves a negotiation (whether actual or metaphoric) over the different intermediate goals. The activity here involves a simultaneous definition of means and ends, which, as yet, is beyond our technological capabilities, and must remain in the hands of human experts and thus part of the body of uncodifiable knowledge.

8. TECHNICAL CHANGE, CODIFIABILITY OF KNOWLEDGE AND FINDING INFORMATION

Finally, knowledge that allows access to other knowledge has remained largely uncodifiable for a long time. Address books or "yellow pages" are used to structure information (or facts) without codifying the "know-how-to-find-information". It is only with the development of artificial exploration agents operating on electronic networks, that this type of knowledge becomes more efficiently codifiable. However the codifiability of this kind of complex knowledge is still far ahead. The best agents would not only be efficient in finding all the information corresponding to a certain question but they will take into account the peculiarities of the user and situation. In this sense, an agent should fill the role of what some experts call a "digital sister-in-law" (Bradshaw, 1997): when I want to go out to the movies, I ask my sister-in-law who is an expert on movies *and* an expert on me. Thus she will not inform me about the thousand movies showing this week in Paris but with the 10 that she knows I would enjoy seeing. In fact, a useful agent is often one where expertise on a certain topic is mixed with knowledge of you. A good travel agent blends knowledge about hotels with knowledge of you. And that of course puts strong limitations to the codifiability of this kind of knowledge.

9. THE IMPACT OF NEW INFORMATION AND COMMUNICATION TECHNOLOGIES

New information and communication technologies (ICTs) have had a decisive impact by substantially expanding the fields of codifiability and increasing the profitability of codification. ICTs have three effects on the codification of knowledge.

First, the new ICTs are changing "the economics of writing" and thus have a strong impact on the process of codification of declarative knowledge. For the first time in the history a technical change causes a major modification at the three levels simultaneously: on the structure of the support (electronic books and paper), on the mode of production (electronic printers, document creation and formatting software) and on the relationship between the text and the reader. Thus, they reduce the cost of codification of simple knowledge and introduce major changes.

Secondly, by permitting the formulation of new languages (for artificial intelligence for example) and substantially increasing the capacity to model complex phenomena, they expand the field of codifiability, supporting the codification of more and more complex knowledge or expertise.

Thirdly, by providing a medium for a new electronic communication infrastructure, the new ICTs enhance the economic value of codification since electronically codified knowledge can be diffused rapidly to huge numbers of agents; and agents can search much more effectively through the world's codified knowledge stock.

These effects can help to introduce dynamic interdependence between the growth of ICT capacities and the increase in resources allocated to codification. ICTs raise the value of codified knowledge, which increases private incentives to codify knowledge and results in an expansion of the codified knowledge base. This can, in turn, affect the demand for ICT (to access the newly codified knowledge) and supply of it (if codified knowledge is used in development and production of ICT), and so on. A virtuous circle of positive feedback is established.

It is, however, advisable to qualify this view of the impact of technological progress on the value of codification. There are at least three kinds of issues about the costs of codification.

The first issue deals with the fragility of digital memory. Because paper has a low acid content, printed books and journals can last for centuries. Physically, they deteriorate slowly and because the language in which they are written evolves very slowly, the interpretation of even very old texts remains relatively easy. This is not necessarily true for documents stored on magnetic or optical mediums. Magnetic tapes deteriorate quickly physically and, given the rapid changes in software technology and computer hardware, languages can disappear just as rapidly. The problem is that with information technologies, what we record are not documents but sets of instructions that have to be interpreted and managed by appropriate equipment and software before the information they contain can be used. Thus, although short-term storage and data retrieval costs have decreased, long-term storage (i.e. archiving) and access to old documents clearly remains (or has become) a problem.

The second issue deals with the problem of organising information in storage units, which can generate substantial costs (see Steinmueller, 2000, for analysis and overview of this problem). If the net benefits of codification increase, we are likely to find ourselves faced with more of it, or at least want to have useful access to more of it. This demands organisational abilities or technologies that have not been seen previously. How to enter knowledge or information into our non-mental memories, both the technology of data-entry, and its storage, becomes more important in our codification activities and in the economics of them.

The third issue deals with the organisational rigidity that codification can generate while increasing communication and transaction efficiency. Codification can become a source of "lock-in" to obsolete conceptual schemes and to technological and organisational systems that are built around them

(Cowan et al., 2000). Because of the investments necessary to create both codified knowledge and a community of users of it, a certain amount of path dependence will emerge. It can be different to switch from one mode of operation to a different one which better suits both internal and external contemporary realities.[4]

10. LIMITS TO CODIFIABILITY AND THE NEED FOR OTHER "TECHNIQUES" OF KNOWLEDGE MANAGEMENT

As policy makers become more interested in knowledge codification, and the ways in which codification improves storage, retrieval and most importantly distribution of knowledge, it may be important to point out that there are limits to what can be codified. That is to say, codification is not the answer to all problems.

There are two key issues here that impinge on whether knowledge can be codified, or more precisely whether an activity can be automated through some form of knowledge codification. First is whether the immediate goal changes as the activity proceeds. If so, codification is likely to fail. The key to making this insight operational is being able to identify the immediate goals of the activity (every firm activity has the final goal of increasing profits, let's say; but lots of activities do not aim explicitly at profits, but rather some intermediate goal, since the connection between whatever actions are available and firm profits is too distant), and to see whether they change as agents pursue their activities. The second issue is whether the activity demands some deep, relatively abstract understanding of the processes involved. If so, we are still unlikely to be able to automate the activity successfully. This sort of knowledge tends to be tacit because it is difficult (or perhaps impossible) to articulate. In either case, codification is not the (complete) answer to the problems being faced by a firm. Codification can help, but there is likely to be crucial tacit knowledge that remains part of the operation. This is a reason why in most cases "codification-only" cannot be taken as a strategy of knowledge management. This is an important aspect, but it must be combined with heavy investments in building networks of people and other means for transferring tacit knowledge. Changes in the economics of codification do not imply the death of older knowledge management techniques. What they may imply is a challenge for these older techniques to adapt and take advantage of new technologies and the new abundance of codified knowledge to make themselves more efficient.

---

[4] This adaptability is one of the advantages often cited of the weak codification aspect of common law as opposed to systems in which the legal code is more completely, and thus rigidly codified.

REFERENCES

Arrow, K., 1974, *The limits of organization*, Norton, New York

Bradshaw, J., 1997, "An introduction to software agents", in J. Bradshaw (ed.) *Software Agents* MIT Press, Cambridge MA.

Cowan, R., 2001, Expert Systems: Aspects of and Limits to the Codifiability of Knowledge, *Research Policy*, forthcoming.

Cowan, R. and Foray, D., 1997, "The economics of codification and diffusion of knowledge", *Industrial and Corporate Change*, vol 6

Cowan, R., David, P.A. and Foray, D., 2000, "The explicit economics of knowledge codification and tacitness", *Industrial and Corporate Change*, vol 9, 2

David, P.A., 1988, Information technology, social communication and the wealth and diversity of nations, CEPR Discussion Paper, n°148, Stanford University

Eisenstein, E., 1980, *The printing press as an agent of change*, Cambridge University Press

Favereau, O., 1998, "Notes sur la théorie de l'information à laquelle pourrait conduire l'économie des conventions", in P.Petit (ed.), *L'économie de l'information*, La Découverte, Paris

Goody, J., 1977, *The domestication of savage mind*, Cambridge University Press, Cambridge.

Hatchuel, A. and Weil. B. (1995) *Experts in Organizations*, de Gruyter, New York.

Le Goff, J., 1985, *Les intellectuels au Moyen Âge*, collection Histoire-Point, Seuil, Paris

MacKenzie, D. and Spinardi, G., 1995, "Tacit knowledge, weapons design and the uninvention of nuclear weapons", *American Journal of Sociology*, 101

Nelson R. and Winter, S., 1982, *An evolutionary theory of economic change*, Harvard University Press, Cambridge, MA

Simon, H., 1982, *Models of bounded rationality: behavioral economics and business organization*, vol.2, The MIT Press, Cambridge, MA

Steinmueller, W.E., 2000, "Will new information and communication technologies improve the 'codification' of knowledge", *Industrial and Corporate Change*, vol 9, 2

Von Hippel, E., 1994, "Sticky information and the locus of problem solving: implications for innovation", *Management Science*, 40.

Chapter 10

THE EUROPEAN POLICY OF PROMOTION OF THE INFORMATION SOCIETY

Michel Catinat[1]

DG III European Commission
EEC Brussels

The current technological change linked to the Information and Communication Technologies (ICT) is exceptional by nature. It cannot be compared to previously observed technological change, with the only possible exceptions being printing, steam power or electricity.

The change underway, sometimes labelled as a revolution, is based on information, itself the source of human knowledge. Technological progress achieved to-date, notably through digitalisation, enables us to process, store, retrieve, and communicate information in whatever form it may take - oral, written or visual - almost without any constraint of distance, time and volume. This revolution adds new opportunities and broad capabilities to human intelligence. Information when easily and pervasively used is similar to any raw material like energy or capital. In this context, it should be no surprise if we try to monitor, control, or even own information, and adapt our social and economic organisation, which governs the way we live or work together, entertain or train ourselves. The current technological wave - the third one according to the Toffler A. (1995) - affects all industrial structures and social relations.

Most analysts, thinkers, and advisers share the same vision in Europe, in North America and in Asia. Like the industrial revolution in the nineteenth century, the emergence of the information society will generate economic and social progress. The first nations to enter the information society will reap the greatest rewards. But nobody can know accurately what the shape of the future information society will be. Uncertainty about its precise characteristics and dynamics is as great as certainty about its arrival and its potentialities. Even now, when certain nations in the vanguard, such as the USA or northern European countries, are foreshadowing what might become the information society, the path ahead is still too long to be able to predict its main patterns. It is difficult to minimize uncertainty, because it is inherent to the process itself. The emergence of the information society will be chaotic, resulting from

[1]Michel Catinat is advisor to the Director General of the Directorate General for Enterprise, European Commission. The views expressed in this article reflect the author's and in no way commit the European Commission.

P. Petit (ed.), Economics and Information, 167–187.

economic successes and failures, social acceptances and refusals, structural adaptation or maintained rigidities, policy support and impediment. Its evolution seems particularly rapid, yet the transition may last several generations.

This article will not aim at synthesising the debate about the likely shape of the information society, or even information societies. Its aim is to achieve a better understanding of the economic and social changes underway, to recall the main issues raised, and to describe the policy implemented by the European Union with a twofold objective: firstly to speed up the arrival of the information society in the European Union, and secondly to alleviate its economic and social costs. The EU's policy will be briefly presented in the context of this short article (see Catinat M. (2000) for further details) Its rationale and objectives will be analysed while attempting to indicate where further economic research proves to be necessary to provide decision makers with a firmer economic foundation.

1. FEATURES OF THE INFORMATION SOCIETY REVOLUTION

A revolution of technological origin, but of economic foundation

The technological progress observed in the field of ICT during the last thirty years has been exceptional in its speed and its scale. Since the 'sixties, the speed of processing information and the capacity of storing it have roughly been multiplied by one hundred every ten years (Moore's law). There is no other example where technological progress has been as rapid and sustained. The magnitude of change is difficult to take in. Suppose that the same progress had happened in transport, the railways for instance: the time taken to travel by train between Paris and Marseille would have been reduced from about ten hours in the sixties to six minutes in the seventies, four seconds in the eighties, and four hundredths of second in the nineties. At the same time, the number of passengers in each train would have been multiplied by about one million within the same time period. By comparison, how tiny the technological progress actually achieved by the TGV ('high speed train'), regarded as exemplary, appears ! This trivial analogy, despite its obvious limits, highlights the exceptional nature of technological progress achieved in the domain of ITC and enables us better to perceive how deep and structural the impact of the new digital world may be on our societies.

This impact, although of technological origin, is of economic foundation. Market competition for the information technologies industry, by contrast with a monopolistic situation for telecommunication operators, has resulted in translating technological progress into price decreases for forty years. This decrease in prices has been of a magnitude similar to the rise in technological progress : the price of processing and storing a bit of information has been roughly cut by hundred every ten years. An aggregated and accurate measure of change in prices is particularly hard to achieve by statisticians, so difficult is it to disentangle volume from price within the value of information technologies products. However, experts generally agree on the aforementioned order of magnitude, and measurements made on some specific products such as personal computers, hard disks or active components confirm this[2]. Whatever the actual reduction in prices, nobody contests its exceptionally high order of magnitude. This has generated a virtuous circle between price, demand, production and technological progress, and triggered a positive dynamic.

There is no evidence that ICT technological progress might slow down in the medium term. Indeed integration on silicon chips has a physical limit (assessed to be 0.12 microns for the CMOS[3] process technology). But this limit should not be reached before 2005-2010 and new lithography technologies are being developed. Research projects such as the projects MEL-ARI in Europe or SCALPEL in the USA are being carried out to perfect extreme ultraviolet, X-ray, electron-beam or ion projection lithographic tools. Additionally, progress on computer architectures (parallel or neuronal architecture, networking) and software (object-oriented software) may compensate for an eventual slowing down in the integration of electronic components. In the domain of telecommunications, recent progress on physical supports (for example, fibre optics), transmission and switching (for example, compression and high speed ATM[4] switching technologies), and signalling is promising. In brief, no disruption in ICT technological progress is foreseeable in the medium term: Moore's law is not yet dead.

The sharp reductions in prices entail two major economic outcomes.
On the one hand, markets for ICT products have developed more rapidly than most other markets: 10% rate of growth for the Western Europe ICT market during 1995-2000 in value terms, as opposed to 4.3% for nominal GDP. ICT products have increasingly penetrated most human activities, from the home to work, from healthcare to entertainment. The ICT industry has become the most significant industrial sector overtaking the automotive, steel, and aeronautics sectors combined. In 1999, the European ICT market, including the Western and Eastern Europe, reached 493 billion Euro, to be compared with 564 and 171 for the USA and Japan respectively (Source: EITO). The breakdown of the European ICT market is the following for 1999:

[2] see EITO (2000)

[3] Complementary Metallic Oxide Semi-conductor

[4] Asynchronous Transfer Modem

European ICT Market

(in billions Euros)

Computer hardware	80.7
Office equipment	10.0
Data communication hardware	12.1
Software products	44.3
Services	79.3
Total information technology	**226.4**
End-user equipment	35.3
Network equipment	25.9
Carrier services	205.4
Total communication	**266.6**
Total ICT	**493**

Source : EITO (2000)

The value-added created by the ICT industry accounts for between 4 and 5% of European GDP. Its direct contribution to wealth creation and employment[5] is thus particularly high.

On the other hand, ICT gives rise to a high and increasing level of innovation, either process innovation (for instance, computer-aided manufacturing and design), product innovation (for example, the ICT components integrated in a car are currently worth 25% of its total cost), or organisational innovation (for example, strategic information systems[6]). These features of ICT are economically crucial: they are an endogenous factor of growth through innovation.

In addition to these two mechanisms, a third one should be mentioned. Users have progressively become more mature: they have greater knowledge and awareness of digital systems, and consequently they become more demanding and more receptive to new products and applications. The ICT market can no longer be regarded as a supply-led and technology-driven market. Nowadays users are experienced enough to select useful applications, reject useless ones,

---

[5] See "Job opportunities in the Information Society" COM(1998) 590 final and "Strategies for jobs in the Information Society" COM(2000) 48 final

[6] See C. Wiseman (1988) or H. Tardieu and B. Gutheman, (1991).

and to express their requirements accurately. This user maturity forces suppliers to offer products which are more user-friendly, more interoperable, and more focused on users' requirements. Consequently, the supply and the demand sides of markets match far more closely, and ICT market develops more smoothly and efficiently.

Most economic conditions are therefore in place to allow ICT to be the driver of growth for our industrialised countries: mastery and dissemination of information, which can be capitalised as any physical investment, sharp reduction in usage prices of information, and increasing maturity of users.

2. SOME ECONOMIC FEATURES OF THE REVOLUTION UNDERWAY

The revolution underway has the following main economic features :

- It is global and has an impact on all regions. The ICT markets are planetary. These technologies are able to fit regional specificities. Integrated in the process of production, they are more and more capable of allowing both the individualisation of products and the exploitation of economies of scale.
- It is fully pervasive; it affects most economic sectors, human activities, and social structures.
- Unlike previous technological waves, it will not only displace workers in manufacturing industries but also in services, and not just the clerical worker but also the more highly skilled. It is in contrast with the industrial revolution, where job destruction was concentrated in agriculture and compensated for by job creation in manufacturing industries. All sectors, from industry to services, may increase their productivity significantly. The flows of employment will happen between different skills rather than between different sectors.
- The speed of ICT dissemination may become an issue. Structural change, which can (for example) help companies using ICT to increase their competitiveness, is slow to come about. In the usual process of 'creative destruction' fostered by technological progress, the rapidity of ICT dissemination may give rise to growing fears that job destruction will overtake job creation in the short term and create political reluctance by raising the already high rate of unemployment.
- ICT makes work more exportable. Whereas the industrial revolution has shifted workers from home to factory, the information society may set the inverse process in motion. Teleworking is bound to develop.
- This revolution is market-led. Fighting against it is a dead-end. The first countries to enter the information age will reap the greatest rewards. Being an insider and speeding up the arrival of the information revolution by effective policies is regarded by governments as the best recipe for grasping opportunities and mastering the risks for their countries.

In short, analysts and decision-makers are in agreement over their forecasts of significant impacts on the economy and society as a whole. Profound structural, cultural, and mental changes are required to realise the opportunities created by the information society - but these take place too slowly.

The list of new ICT applications and 'tele-products' lengthens every day. Uncertainty about future markets, their size, content, and development, remains high. This is inherent to the very process of the emergence of the information society. The products that will emerge will be tested, then selected by the market through a complex process of interaction between supply and demand for new applications. Users will accept, refuse or force them to be adapted according to their own requirements. Uncertainty also arises from the magnitude and the nature of change necessary to take advantage of new applications. Change may concern new skills for workers, new productive organisations for companies, or new kinds of partnerships between the private and public sectors. Instead of proceeding at the margin, the information society will proceed through rupture and structural and organisational discontinuity. The development of new applications will stem from a process of 'social adaptation', which means the satisfaction of users' requirements as well as the adaptation of socio-economic structures to take advantage of new applications in appropriate conditions. This interactive process of selection is extremely difficult to forecast. The successful nations will be those whose agents are risk-takers and whose structure is sufficiently flexible and adaptable to the new context. In a sense, the USA benefits from its greater potential, notably by comparison with Europe, even if the gap is narrowing.

THE INFORMATION SOCIETY : A PRIORITY FOR POLICY AGENDA

The emergence of the information society is an irreversible process. All interested parties act towards the same objective and their actions reinforce each other to speed its arrival.

Firstly, industry actively supports and promotes the information society. A strong industrial interest progressively strengthened in the triad both from the supply side, with continuous double-digit growth in ICT markets, and from the demand side, e.g. all those industries which have learnt from best practices how to use ICT to improve their competitiveness. The growth of electronic commerce is accelerating the process. The numerous mergers and agreements, and the explosion of start-ups witness the dynamism of the productive fabric and the strategic importance for companies to hold on to the leading edge and use ITC in the best ways.

Secondly, governments in most developed countries have begun to implement comprehensive policies to promote the information society. They share the same vision that global growth, employment and prosperity will result from this revolution. During the G7 ministerial conference held in Brussels in February 1995, the leading countries agreed on joint objectives and common principles for their own policies. Five years later, the shared policy agenda is still valid and many measures have been implemented: liberalisation of the telecommunication markets and strengthening of competition, removal of barriers to trade for ICT products, adaptation of the regulatory and legal framework notably to ensure the fair protection of intellectual property and privacy, promotion of universal access to infrastructures, and co-operation for standardisation. As a result, the emergence of the information society accelerated and electronic commerce triggered a further evolution. Some preliminary expected benefits of the information society, notably the strengthening of growth and job creation, have already been reported by governments[7].

THE POLICY OF THE EUROPEAN UNION

Since the end of 1993, the European Union has taken a wide range of initiatives to promote the emergence of the information society in Europe. They rely on several basic reports[8].

The European policy of promoting the information society has been implemented in three stages.

The first stage has been mainly aimed at building up a vision and identifying the issues to be tackled; the second stage is to implement an action plan and speed up the emergence of the information society; and the third stage is to gauge social reluctance and seek to alleviate it.

3. THE VISION

A great number of documents[9] have contributed to improving the vision of the future information society. At the Community level, two reports in particular are worth mentioning:

Firstly, the *White Paper on Growth, Competitiveness and Employment* prepared for the European Summit of December 1993. This policy report was

---

[7] "The Emerging Digital Economy" and "Digital Economy 2000", reports of the Department of Commerce, USA, 1998, 1999 and 2000. "Job opportunities in the Information Society" and "Strategies for jobs in the Information Society", Communications by the European Commission, 1998 and 2000 (see infra).

[8] "White Paper on Growth, Competitiveness and Employment", European Commission, Office for Official Publications of the European Communities, 1993

"Europe and the Global Information Society - Recommendations to the European Council", Bangemann report, Brussels, May 1994

"Europe's Way to the Information Society : an Action Plan", communication of the European Commission, COM(94) 347 final

"G7 Ministerial Conference on the Global Information Society", Ministerial Conference Summary, Office for Official Publications of the European Communities, February 1995

Green paper "Living and Working in the Information Society : People First", communication of the European Commission, COM(96) 389 final

"A European Initiative in the Domain of Electronic Commerce", Communication of the European Commission, COM(97)157

"*e*-Europe – An Information Society for All", communication of the European Commission,, COM(1999) 687 final

[9] See Dyson E. (1997), Alvin and Heidi Toffler (1995), Negroponte N. (1995), Bell D. (1973).

the first attempt to articulate a comprehensive vision at the Community level; it introduced the concept of the "Information Society". By contrast with the USA, which developed its policies in the context of the concept of a *National Information Infrastructure,* and Japan, with its programme *Advanced Information Infrastructure*, Europe has from the outset considered the phenomenon as a societal process. The key issue is not so much the "pipelines", even if their availability and access are a necessary condition for the provision of new applications and services; rather, it is the content transmitted and the effect of ICT on growth, competitiveness and the standard of living for Europeans. The impact on societal organisation and general welfare has always been at the forefront of debate in the European Union.

A second key document was the report entitled *Europe and the Global Information Society*, often known as the *Bangemann Report*, prepared in response to a request from the European Summit in Corfu in June 1994. Prepared by a group of nineteen independent European CEOs under the chairmanship of Commissioner Bangemann, this report confirmed the vision of the White Paper and proposed priorities for action to the European Union for the creation of favourable market conditions and to foster the emergence of the information society.

These thoughts and visions have been broadly debated, progressively refined and directly confronted with evidence; their content is now sufficiently known and does not require any further presentation. It is striking how convergent are most of these analyses, whether carried out in Europe, or in the USA, Japan, Canada, Australia, or in other regions. All convey the same political message: progress brought about by ICT is changing our way of living, working, making business, educating our children, studying, training, carrying out research and entertaining. No human activities escape. The proposed vision is positive, sometimes particularly optimistic. It is rarely based on sound theoretical economic analysis, but rather on "elaborated common sense"; yet it is scarcely criticised. Politicians have adopted this vision because of its forward-looking, modern and pervasive flavour. Opportunities are regarded as limitless, and, when adequately seized, might tackle many problems facing our societies today.

The analytic and theoretical basis for most statements and perspectives is rather frail. In most visions, it is implicitly assumed that there exists a positive correlation at the macroeconomic level between technological progress due to ICT, gains in productivity, growth and employment. Yet for instance, since the famous "Solow paradox", the supposedly positive correlation between ICT dissemination and overall gains in productivity is questioned and, to date, no sound evidence has been produced to close the debate definitively. Applied research, notably by the OECD mandated by the G7 meeting in Detroit, has been carried out in order to understand better the economic mechanisms involved. Numerous issues remain unanswered on the functioning of an economy where information with its characteristic of "public good" becomes a central product, used both as an intermediary and as an investment good by the productive sphere, and as a consumption good by consumers. Theoretical analyses are currently being developed under the label of the "new economy", and have begun to give rise to new explanations and models, but there is still more to be achieved.

4. THE EUROPEAN ACTION PLAN

The second stage of the European policy consisted in implementing a coherent and co-ordinated set of policy measures at the Community level. The Commission proposed a complex set of actions in its Communication to the Council entitled *Europe's Way to the Information Society: an Action Plan* in July 1994. The wide range of actions proposed was the result of a number of factors: Firstly, the emergence of the information society is basically market-led and is complicated by the number and importance of issues at stake. The responsibility for investing, innovating, and offering new multimedia applications falls to decentralised private agents. Consequently, the role of the public authorities can only be indirect and catalytic. It should aim at implementing a favourable legal and political framework, in a context of high uncertainty as to what the future shape of markets and their conditions of development will be. Secondly, there was a need to strike the right balance between conflicting interests so as to ensure market development and simultaneously a sufficient level of safeguards, for instance, protection of intellectual property, privacy or public security. Finally, the multiplicity of domains affected – technological, legal, normative, industrial and social – is in itself a complicating factor.

This action plan is composed of four priorities: the adaptation of the legal and regulatory framework, the promotion of networks and new applications, the raising of awareness, and promoting an understanding of the social and cultural aspects of the information society. Most actions taken in the European Union since the mid-nineties have fallen into one of these categories.

THE ADAPTATION OF THE LEGAL AND REGULATORY FRAMEWORK

The liberalisation of telecommunications markets

Technological progress in the field of telecommunications has been very similar to that achieved in the field of information technologies. In spite of this, the price of transmitting a bit of information has not decreased in the medium term with the same speed as has been observed for processing and storing a bit of information. The monopolistic situations which have profited the incumbent telecommunications operators in Europe for a long time led to tariffs for telecommunications services evolving in step with the prices of services in general, i.e. bearing no relation to the drastic decrease in prices observed for information technology products. The level of telecommunications tariffs has long been higher in Europe than in the USA, notably for the most advanced services, for which a ratio of one to five could still be observed some years ago. With the liberalisation of telecommunications markets in Europe since the first of January 1998, the average gap has reduced significantly: for some services, the gap has now disappeared, whereas for others differences remained high, such as leased lines, to the detriment of European Internet service providers.

This relatively high level of telecommunication tariffs is detrimental to Europe and slows down the overall usage of ICT. With technological convergence between telecommunications and information technologies, it becomes a seriously binding factor for the emergence of the information society. Now computers are multimedia, computer architectures are distributed (client-server architectures), telecommunication technologies use digital signals more and more, and the Internet belongs both to the worlds of computers and of telecommunications. The revolution underway calls for low prices in both telecommunications and information technologies. In this context, telecommunications liberalisation was particularly welcome and its downward pressure on tariffs was expected to enable the revolution to "run with two legs": IT and C. One might even argue that the acceleration of the emerging information society currently being observed is partly due to the telecommunications liberalisation reinforcing other factors such as the Internet and E-commerce.

With this economic rationale in mind, the Commission in its *Green Paper on telecommunications liberalisation*[10] proposed to open up fully telecommunications markets to competition within the European Union. The proposal was unanimously endorsed by the European Council at the end of 1994 and the decision was taken to liberalise the telecommunication markets of both services and infrastructures by the first of January 1998, with some additional time granted to the few Member States which requested longer transitory periods[11]. Interestingly, all these countries have unilaterally decided to liberalise their telecommunications markets ahead of negotiated deadlines because of the social and economic advantages this would bring.

Since then, the Commission has put in place a comprehensive regulatory framework allowing competition to thrive. As regularly analysed in annual reports[12], this policy has had a major impact on the development of the telecommunications market in Europe (more than 10% per year), contributing to the emergence of a strong European communications sector, and allowing consumers and business users to take advantage of greater choice, lower prices,

---

[10] Green Paper on the liberalisation of telecommunications infrastructure and cable television networks, European Commission, Part I COM(94) 440 final and part II COM(94) 682 final

[11] a supplementary delay of 2 years for Luxembourg and 5 years for Greece, Ireland, Portugal and Spain

[12] Annual reports on the implementation of the telecommunications regulatory package, European Commission, 1995 to 1999

and innovative services. Successive layers of regulation, technical convergence and the Internet overturning traditional market structures to a large extent brought the European Commission to propose a comprehensive review of its regulatory framework[13] with a twofold objective: depart from regulation implemented as a proxy for competition and thus limit regulation to those areas where policy objectives cannot be achieved by competition alone; create a coherent regulatory environment for all electronic communications infrastructure and associated services.

Standardisation

Standardisation raises the traditional issue of "common ownership": a cost of dissemination close to zero and gains that cannot be fully internalised by the companies holding the standards. Market failure or segmentation by standards is a danger and calls for specific government actions. In the European Union, this role is indirect: some European standardisation organisations (CEN-CENELEC, ETSI) have been set up, which involve companies in the establishment of standards. European standardisation activities are monitored by the Commission with the aim of achieving "competing, but not conflicting standards", ensuring the establishment of open standards and defending European interests within international standardisation bodies. Mandates may be given by the Commission to channel standardisation towards key areas, for instance critical interfaces within digital systems or standards for access to communications infrastructure such as GSM or UMTS[14].

With the emergence of the information society and the increasing rapidity with which the markets impose *de facto* standards, a new standardisation policy was deemed necessary in Europe so to counter the criticisms addressed to it, namely its slowness and its insufficient relevance to market requirements. Change in the European standardisation policy hinged on the following principles:

- the possibility to integrate *de facto* standards or "publicly available standards" into the traditional *de jure* approach;
- reinforcing the free market; notification of any national standards likely to erect barriers to trade; priority for the establishment of open standards for 'critical interfaces'[15] in order to ensure the interoperability of networks;
- the possibility to launch calls for technology; strengthening relations between pre-normative research and the standardisation process;

---

[13] "Towards a new framework for Electronic Communications infrastructure and associated services", communication of the European Commission, COM(99) 539

[14] GSM and UMTS stand for Global System for Mobile Telecommunication and Universal Mobile Telecommunications System respectively. They are reference standards for mobile telephone systems.

[15] e.g. interfaces between the different parts constituting electronic systems (devices, software, networks) or within these parts (for instance between different application software)

- improved integration into the world standardisation system.

European standardisation policy is subject to competition policy that ensures non-discrimination through norms.

The protection of intellectual property

This area is the most complex one from both theoretical and applied points of view. Conceptually, the basic question is mainly to determine what principles should govern the exchange of information in an information society and notably its prices while taking into account the features of this good (public good and difficulty for the users to know its value before having access to it). Pragmatically, the ICT enables anybody to access information easily and to copy it at almost no cost, indefinitely and anonymously. The Internet, for instance, only knows the plugged-in computer not the connected individual.

For the legislator, the difficulty lies in striking the right balance between conflicting interests: on the one side, information providers whose activity requires payment, and on the other side, users who often innovate from accessible information and provide new services to final users. In order to develop, the market simultaneously needs to protect information and to provide easy and cheap access to it.

To date, the Commission has adopted a careful approach to adopting a legal framework: it released a *Green Paper*[16] in October 1995 with the objective of spurring a broad debate in Europe and to better identify the necessary adaptations. Then, it issued a proposal for a Directive on copyright and related rights in the information society. A political agreement between the Commission, the Council and the European Parliament was finally attained in the summer of 2000. The whole exercise had taken place within the framework of the new WIPO treaties[17] negotiated at the end of 1996 with the European trade partners. In substance, the Directive ensures an adequate protection of music, films, videos and all materials protected by copyright throughout the internal market, and will consequently facilitate cross-border trade in protected products. Network operators and service providers have the benefit of an obligatory exception for technical copies on the net. It also provides an exhaustive list of exceptions to copyright, for instance schools and libraries in the case of teaching, which Member States may decide provided that copyright holders receive fair compensation.

---

16 Green Paper on copyright and associated rights in the information society, European Commission, COM(95) 382 final

17 Concluding seven years of work in the World Intellectual Property Organisation (WIPO), two new treaties were signed in Geneva in December 1996, which clarified the international protection regime and adapted it to the digital world: the "WIPO Copyright Treaty" and the "WIPO Treaty on Performances and Phonograms".

The approach remained very legal and insufficiently economic. Intense lobbying from interested parties led to compromise and margins for manoeuvre and for interpretation for Member States.

The protection of privacy

The issue of personal data has traditionally been of great concern in Europe. Fears amplified with the capabilities offered by ICT to merge databases at distance, extract private information at low cost and exploit it for commercial, political or other purposes. Its extraterritorial dimension has brought the Commission to propose an integrated legal framework for the whole European Union[18]. Common rules now apply to all Member States. They must adapt their legal frameworks so as to ensure the right of any individual to access any private data on himself; the right to know their origin, use, and identity of users; the right to correct them; the right to refuse their use in certain circumstance such as for commercial canvassing; and the right to appeal. For specific kinds of information, for instance religious, political, medical or racial data, the explicit agreement by concerned individuals is required before integrating them into any databases.

The most delicate issue concerns the transfer of data to third countries and the necessity to avoid circumvention of EU legislation from abroad. The Directive stipulates that free transfers with non-EU countries are conditional upon their legislation ensuring an equivalent level of personal data protection. It raised difficulty with the USA because of the skimpiness of their privacy protection (see Catinat M. (1998)). The USA are now ready to put in place an arrangement known as the "safe harbour" under which companies would adhere to a set of data protection rules through codes of conduct and related enforcement requirements and consequently would be authorised to access European personal data.

Electronic signature, liability and security

The required adaptation of the regulatory framework definitely concerns other legal domains. Electronic signature had to be recognised to be as legally binding as any physical signature, and rules for conclusion and validity of electronic contracts to be harmonised throughout the European Union. The Internal market principles for information society services have been enforced ensuring free movement of on-line services, freedom of establishment, clarification of liability of intermediaries and improvement of cross-border dispute settlement[19]. So as to contribute to building trust and confidence in on-line services, markets for cryptography software have been liberalised in all Member States and an action

---

[18] Directive 95/46/EC of 24 October 1995 on the protection of individuals with regard to the processing of personal data and on the free movement of such data, European Commission

[19] "Ensuring Security and Trust in Electronic Communication – Towards a European Framework for Digital Signatures and Encryption", communication of the European Commission COM(97) 503 and Directive on the electronic commerce, May 2000

plan has been enforced at the Community level to protect security of citizens and fight against new forms of digital crime.

5. THE PROMOTION OF NETWORKS AND NEW APPLICATIONS

Networks

The information infrastructures are composed of numerous networks interconnected and interoperable between themselves: a 'network of networks'. Every network with its own communication technology will be less and less dedicated to a specific service as was the case in the past: for instance, twisted wire networks and circuit switching to vocal telephony, or coaxial cable networks and hertzian waves to television. Technological evolution, notably digitalisation, enables independence between networks and services or, in other words, universality of support networks through which the services flow whatever their kind.

In the field of networks, European policy aims at promoting the modernisation of existing networks, generally of good quality and advanced technology in most European regions, as well as the implementation of new infrastructures. Its role is simultaneously regulatory, legal, and normative. The main initiatives worth being mentioned concerned the extension of ISDN networks, the implementation of a broadband ATM backbone, and the deployment of infrastructure for mobile and satellite communications.

Research and technological development (RTD)

Specific RTD programmes have been co-funded by the Commission to support research projects and promote trans-European co-operation in the field of ICT. The most well-known programmes are ESPRIT, devoted to information technologies, ACTS (communication technologies) and TELEMATICS (ICT applications in utilities: health, transport, education, libraries, etc). With technological convergence, they became more and more linked to each other: since the adoption of the Fifth Framework Programme (1998-2002), they have been regrouped in a unique programme dedicated to information society technologies with a total budget of about 3600 billion Euro.

The content industry

The development of new digital applications on a large scale is characterised by high uncertainty on market acceptance, the complexity of mastering all the necessary know-how, and the difficulty in reaching 'critical thresholds', all of which impedes the taking-off of markets below a certain number of users (the so-called 'network effect'). These market failures and imperfections call for government action, and notably a catalytic role of promoting test beds with the objectives of testing the value to the user and the economic feasibility of the information systems, fostering partnership, and reaching critical mass. Of course, the diffusion of the Internet made less relevant the rationale of critical mass for government action; indeed global markets are directly accessible to any new application provider. But the other reasons still remain valid.

A number of initiatives have been undertaken by the Commission, all of which cannot be described here. Amongst the most significant or innovative initiatives, the following ones should be mentioned: the *INFO 2000* programme aiming at promoting European start-ups for multimedia products; the *MEDIA* programme, the objective of which is to tackle two weaknesses of the European audio-visual industry, namely the commercial distribution of audio-visual products to television and film programmers, and the training of professionals in new technologies; the setting up of the *European multimedia Forum* at the beginning of the nineties, regrouping about one hundred European multimedia companies to ensure the convergence of views and interests between the different industrial segments of multimedia; finally the *Task Force on multimedia education software,* gathering the software industry and representatives of education systems in order to develop new pedagogical multimedia applications.

Pilot applications

Industry representatives gathered to prepare the Bangemann Report for the G7 countries during the ministerial conference in Brussels agreed on the economic interest to launch pilot applications. In substance, these initiatives were to regroup industrialists and users, identify the needs, check the economic sustainability of new applications, and, on this basis, help raising awareness, disseminating best practices, and levering markets. The issues proposed in the Bangemann report and by the G7 countries broadly overlap and thus bear witness to a comforting convergence of views on the needs to be satisfied as a priority and with the catalytic support by governments (see the table below).

6. PILOT APPLICATIONS

Domains	Bangemann report	G7 projects
Infrastructure	City Information Highway Network for Universities and Research Centres	Global Interoperability for Broadband Networks
Education and culture	Distance learning	Cross cultural Training and Education Electronic Libraries Electronic Museums and Galeries
Transport	Road Traffic Control Air Traffic Control	Maritime Information Systems
Healthcare	Healthcare Networks	Global Healthcare Applications
Enterprises	Telematic Services for SME's Teleworking	Global Marketplace for SME's
Administration	Electronic Tendering Trans-European Public Administration Network	Government On-line
Environment		Environment and Natural Resources Management Global Emergency Management
MISCELLANEOUS		Global Inventory

The fate of these pilot applications was varied. Some reached their objectives successfully, such as teleworking, global marketplace for SMEs or infrastructural projects, although one can wonder whether the markets alone should not have supplied these applications even without any governmental support. Some others experienced significant difficulties in their launch. Generally, the success of and the interest raised by these pilot applications remained far below expectations. In fact, new applications today were mostly developed through innovation often based on the Internet. Few new applications followed the expected path: large scale applications, fully innovative, in rupture with and substituting for previous applications. New applications were market-led, often marginal, without any technological breakthroughs. Most of them have been boosted by the Internet and electronic commerce, both far more catalytic than any pilot application.

The e-Europe initiative

This initiative launched by the European Summit at Lisbon in March 2000 lies within the lineage of European policies of promoting the information society. It expresses the political will to invigorate policies underway by advancing certain policies ahead of the current schedule and better co-ordinating European and national policies through dated targets and benchmarking. Its main contribution is to streamline a whole set of scattered measures under the heading of eleven priorities: cheaper and faster Internet access; faster Internet for researchers and students; secure networks and smart cards; European youth into the digital age; working in the knowledge-based economy; participation for all in the knowledge-based economy; accelerating e-commerce; government online: electronic access to public services; health online; digital content for global networks; and intelligent transport systems.

7. AWARENESS RAISING

In the European context where citizens generally express distrust, even fear, with respect to technological progress, raising general awareness and ensuring that change towards the information society is cohesive, not divisive, is a prerequisite for change to be accepted socially.

The social and cultural aspects

The arrival of the information society appeared to be less rapid than expected. Rigidities and social reluctance, sometimes refusal, slowed down the necessary cultural, structural and institutional adjustments.

Three types of concerns are generally expressed in Europe: the risk of a two-tier society, the risk of dissolution of cultural diversity, and fears of job destruction or change in working conditions.

The risk of social exclusion covers different concerns. The future knowledge-based society will require highly qualified IT-literate employees. The main danger lies in the creation of a two-tier society of 'haves' and 'have-nots' where only the 'haves' will have the capability to benefit from new digital devices and services. Even worse, some services would only be accessible through computers or other digital-human interfaces, thus excluding the 'have-nots' from services they could access previously. Other concerns are also expressed: fear of loneliness, individualisation, disappearance of existing communities or furthermore rupture with the real world.

Europe is diversified from a cultural and linguistic point of view. European citizens attach great importance to this diversity. Concerns expressed highlight the risk of homogenising European cultures through the filter of the Internet or computers, as well as the fear of dominance of the 'American model', imposed by market rules, and in particular leading to the supremacy of American films.

Finally, the impact on job creation raised many questions. This essentially pessimistic view, even if it is plausible at a first glance, does not stand up to either sound economic analysis, nor empirical evidence. The technological waves underway generate gains of productivity which have an impact on the whole economy through the returns on factors of production or decreases in prices; dynamically, they trigger innovation and investment. All the economic ingredients are gathered so the dissemination of ICT creates growth and, at the end of day, employment. A cross-border comparative study[20] shows that the countries which witnessed the highest total factor of labour productivity rates in the medium-long term also benefited from the most sustained growth and the most numerous job creations.

Potential for job creation would be all the more significant if two conditions are fulfilled. On the one side, a shift in skill structure that requires an adaptation in the education and training systems. The objective is not to train anybody as a computer scientist, but to make any user IT-literate and informed about best practices and ways to access useful applications. On the other side, new form of company organisation. Running a company without using ICT became inconceivable. These technologies enable companies to aim at a complete integration of their different functions in time and space, as well as their integration in the business environment. The use of ICT, globalisation and international competition forces them to deeply restructure their productive organisation to ensure flexibility, innovation and access to crucial information, for instance about their competitors. The companies have to take profit of strategic opportunities and react to their business environment. The challenge is not so much to be the best ones in absolute terms, but just to be more competitive than their competitors in relative terms. With the development of electronic commerce, issues at stake intensified for the companies: time to react shortened, opportunities to offer new products multiplied, and change in existing positions sped up. Generally their reorganisation cannot be marginal but must be deep, and driven by the need to be adaptable. The conditions of success for

---

20 "Information Technologies, Productivity and Employment", working paper of DG Industry, European Commission, January 1996

company reorganisation are conceptually well known. The up-to-date business process reengineering approach is based on a triptych: adequate strategy, adapted organisational structure and support provided by information systems. Though genuine progress in concepts, there exists no universal, prescriptive recipe. Each company is a specific case, which, beyond cultural synergy, explains the relative slowness of current company restructuring.

Whatever the relevance or importance of these fears, they have to be taken into account by European policies. From the very beginning, a broad social acceptance was regarded as a prerequisite for the emergence of the information society. A better understanding and assessment of social impacts was sought. Two independent reports were prepared to that end: firstly, the report[21] of the 'Information Society Forum', regrouping all the different components of the society and set up to advise the Commission, and secondly, the report of the 'Group of Social Experts'[22] established by the Commission to analyse social impacts of the information society. The scope of these reports is fairly broad: it encompasses issues such as employment, the work organisation, the work conditions, training, the social cohesion, the medias, culture, etc. On this basis, a *Green Paper on the Social Aspects of the Information Society* has been written down by the Commission with the usual objective, in such a context, to clarify the debate, define priorities, and propose consensual measures. Such an approach is necessary in the European context to break down resistance and avoid block just because of false perception or overvaluation of risks. The European interest is of course to master its future by striking the right balance between risks and opportunities. Its interest is to remain an insider and to shape change towards the information society according to its own social and cultural features.

CONCLUSION

No doubt, the emergence of the information society will deeply affect European society and the economy. By nature, it will create many opportunities of all kinds, which will require structural and organisational change if they are to be seized properly.

In fact, there exists no alternative. This technological wave is market-led, and most of the private actors in the developed countries invest consequently.

Forecasting what will be the precise shape of the future information society is particularly difficult, even impossible, for the shift will be an interactive and complex process. The only certainty is likely to be the unpredictability of change. In this context, the key role for economists is not to predict: it is to

---

21 "Networks for People and their Communities – Making the Most of the Information Society in the European Union", first annual report of the Information Society Forum, June 1996

22 "Building the European Information Society for Us All", intermediary report, DG V for Employment, European Commission, January 1996

understand better the economic mechanisms that will drive the information society, and identify the conditions for a successful emergence. The policies, which are being implemented in Europe to meet all the concrete challenges, require sound analytical and theoretical support.

REFERENCES

D. Bell (1973) *"The Coming of Post-Industrial Society : a Venture in Social Forecasting",* New York, Basic Books.

Catinat M. (2000) "La politique Européenne de promotion d'Internet", *Revue du Marché commun et de l'Union européenne*, no 435, February.

Catinat M. (1998), "The National Information Infrastructure Initiative in the US – Policy or Non-policy ?", *Computer and Telecommunication Law Review*, Volume 4 : Issue 3 (Part I) et 4 (Part II), Sweet and Maxwell, April and May.

Dpt of Commerce (1996) *"The Unpredictable Certainty: Information Infrastructure through 2000"*, Washington, DC: National Academy Press.

Dyson E. (1997), *Amongst American Visionary Work : "Release 2.0: A Design for Living in the Digital Age*", New York, Broadway Books.

EITO (2000) European Information Technology Observatory, Statistical Outlook, Lyoner Str. 18, D-60528, Frankfurt/Main, ISSN 0947-4862.

Negroponte N. (1995) *"Being Digital",* New York, Alfred A. Knopf.

Tardieu H., Gutheman B. (1991), *"Le triangle stratégique"*,Paris, les Editions d'Organisation.

Toffler A. and H. (1995), *"Creating a New Civilization: The Politics of the Third Wave"*, Atlanta, Turner Publishing, Inc.

Wiseman C. (1988), *"Strategic Information System",* New York, IRWIN books.

Chapter 11

SCREENING THE INFORMATION ECONOMY THROUGH THEORIES OF INFORMATION

Pascal Petit

Director of Research
CNRS CEPREMAP Paris

1. WHAT IS AN INFORMATION ECONOMY ?

In what sense can we qualify contemporary developed economies as information economies ? Does it amount to the same thing to speak of economies based on knowledge ?

The answer to the question requires us to clearly grasp the different ways according to which information and knowledge condition economic relationships. It is with this goal in mind that we have decided to go through various approaches to the notion of information in economics. It will not be our objective to establish a new (and impossible) general theory. But the diversity of theoretical approaches to information considered constitutes a reading framework, a screen bringing out the multiplicity of questions raised about the role played by information and knowledge in our economies.

The notion of the information economy, in its everyday use, often emphasises the scale and diversity of application of an entire range of new technology, so-called information and communication technology.

It would be misleading to base the characterisation of information economies on the distribution of this technology alone. First of all because even if one observes the presence of this technology in all economic activities, in the form of computers or telecommunications products, the sum of tangible investment which they represent remains modest. Furthermore, because this equipment has probably less importance in itself than the organisational transformation which goes with it. Whether it is the intangible investment which its use implies (perfecting of software and complex automatic control systems), or all forms of reorganisation of production activities which intend to make use of the new possibilities of distance control, information storage or instantaneous processing. Finally, and above all, this appreciation, founded alone on the localisation of the distribution of ICT (Information and Communication Technologies), would omit an important characteristic of our economies linked to the development, accumulation and distribution of skills and knowledge which subtends everything related to information.

The distinction between information and knowledge, which is more or less explicit according to the approaches presented, is, moreover, a key element in

P. Petit (ed.), Economics and Information, 189–216.

appreciating the contemporary phase of development. It is clearly because certain economies seem to have accumulated more skills than others for processing and disseminating information, for generating and accumulating knowledge, and for appropriating it, such that one has the impression that forms of new growth are emerging.

These capacities imply not only the education and training systems of the countries studied, but also the internal organisation patterns of companies, like the logistics of the big intermediation networks which their economic activities rely on.

We can try to analyse the dynamic of these economies in the framework of a pattern of growth, articulating the ways in which: 1°) productivity gains are generated in production activities, 2°) then divided between the involved parties and finally 3°) determine the different components of demand, whether for investment or consumption (see figure11.1).

An information economy might then be understood as an economy where information and knowledge played a particular role in the different stages of the growth pattern referred to above: the organisation of production activities, the functioning of the markets and the fulfilment of lifestyles and consumption.

The order in which the different parts of the present work are presented takes account, precisely, of the reading framework proposed above. If the three first chapters are transversal in character (aiming the foundations of the notion of information), the three following ones (chapters 4, 5 and 6,) deal with the functioning of the markets and the three last ones (chapters 7, 8 and 9) deal with the organisation of production activities. These different chapters thus contribute to the characterisation of the development mode of the so-called information economies.

2. LESSONS OF THE THEORETICAL APPROACHES : THE CONTRIBUTION OF THEORIES OF INFORMATION

The three approaches to the theory of information in the strict sense (chapters 1,2 and 3) present transversal problematics which concern the market behaviour as much as organisations.

2.1. *Economics of Information or Economics of Information System ?*

(Jean Louis Le Moigne, chapter 1).

Information is not a simply given naturally. We must recognise its ternary character, combining a sign (the syntactical component), a meaning (the semantic component) and a context of action (the pragmatic component). To integrate this complexity in the field of economic analysis, Jean Louis Le Moigne makes use of three lines of investigation. The first, the code/channel dialectic, suggests reflecting conjointly on the problems of encoding and transmission, in a perspective close to Shannon's theory of information (developed in chapter 2). The questions of signification are *a priori* excluded but the choice of encoding implies not only the nature of the channel (with its own qualities) but also the respective knowledge and skills of the sender and the receiver. This brings us back to the economic and social context of the action as well as to the agents' capacities (including their powers of memorisation).

The second line of investigation or heuristic considers the way in which information received from outside conditions the organisation of the system. Let us note that Jacques Crémer (chapter 8) addresses the related problem of the circulation of information inside an organisation. These two lines of investigation overlap but one analyses organisational contexts and proposes operational modes in the following of the New Industrial Economy while the other followed by J.L. Le Moigne adopts an evolutionist position where the interactions with the outside milieu constantly modifies the organisations. The references to biology are very present but the operational applications to the economy are quite limited (as Pierre Garrouste points out in chapter 2).

In his third heuristic, Jean Louis Le Moigne proposes to analyse the economy of the information system as a new area of activity developing information products. It is difficult to delimit such a sector, for the current evolutions are disrupting the frontiers between activities and consequently broadening the sphere of information producers including the producers and distributors of knowledge and skills. On a more micro-economic level, this heuristic has the merit of asking the question of the functioning of an information system with the problems of reproduction, diffusion and archiving which that represents. Hence the importance of context (which makes information more or less intelligible and applicable) and the capacity to use and to deliberately distribute this information. These questions affect the processes of accumulation and transformation of information in knowledge, skills and information "of greater value". However, the tools required to conceptualise these functions of contextualisation or deliberation are lacking and it is difficult to deal with these questions outside of their specific context as they are so firmly fixed in economic and social issues.

The problem then is to define adequate intermediary levels so as to be pertinent, specific and integrable in the development of a theory of the economy of information systems. The stakes are all the higher in that it is clear that the ICT and the codification practices which accompany them, no doubt profoundly modify these economies, a question which is at the heart of Dominique Foray and Robin Cowan' contribution in chapter 9.

That being the case, Jean Louis Le Moigne's contribution allows us to give back its ternary complexity to the notion of information, which can be applied to a number of productions where the "content" in information is important. Indeed, if the sign is the equivalent of the objective characteristics of a production, to distinguish the meaning of the product from the context in which it occurs, facilitates the apprehension of cultural barriers (barriers of meaning) which condition the diffusion of numerous innovations produced.

2.2. *What Economics Borrows from the Statistical Theory of Information* (Pierre Garrouste, chapter 2)

Pierre Garrouste presents the statistical theory of information such as it was developed immediately after the war by Shannon and Weaver and follows its different filiations. The notion of information is strictly limited to its role as signal. At the time, Shannon sought to evaluate the properties of the transmission of signals: questions of the reliability of the channel, the reconstitution of the entering message. But his work on signs and their transmission quickly became inseparable from fundamental problems of meaning. Shannon has difficulty himself in limiting the reading made of his work to questions of transmission. He introduces problems of recognition, the reconstruction of signals, which relies on the contexts and opens the way to questions on meaning (a little like the decoding of an unknown form of writing).

This shifting from signals to semantics of the messages also explains the attraction there was at the beginning of the 50s for this theory which was contemporary to the beginnings of computers and cybernetics[1]. But once its fashionable character had worn off, by the beginning of the 60s, this theory of communication seems to have only significantly marked certain developments in biology, psychology or linguistics (see for example Dion 1997). The applications in economics, as Pierre Garrouste recalls, conserve a rather narrow statistical character, from Theil's work on the distribution of industrial labour force to those of Thionet on surveys. The developments in the theorisation of an economy with perfect information, which culminated with the works of Arrow and Debreu on general equilibrium, concealed promising elements in the dynamic of a broadened approach to Shannon's work. This does not exclude the development of an entire information economy, as the works of Marshak, Hirshleifer, Radner and Arrow illustrate, but without reference to the statistical theory of information (STI) which has the drawback of speaking of entropy and redundancy without pointing out the utility of signs for the various agents. Arrow (1974) is moreover very explicit regarding the limited applications of the statistical theory of information in economic analysis where the rational and well informed agents are only marginally troubled by rumours and uncertainties[2].

The second filiation of STI presented by Pierre Garrouste leads to the central models of biology where uncertainty and the weight of milieu play a dominant role. Patterns of self organisation developed by Varela or Atlan in biology then quickly find an echo with economists refusing analysis in terms general equilibrium. In fact, this filiation has two modalities according to the reading of

---

[1] Weaver, then director of the Rockfeller Foundation, understood the value of this pedagogy straight away (going from an analysis of signals to elaborate an effective theory of information); it was also the case of a whole group of intellectuals enthused by the theory of the decision and the modelisation of human behaviour, from Von Neuman to Savage and Wiener, as Pierre Garrouste's text reminds us (see also Lancry (1982) and Dion (1997)).

[2] In the middle of the 70s Shannon's theory of information seemed to have lost its attraction, re. the elements of the debate related by Lancry (1982) and Rene Thom's highly critical remarks (1975).

the notion of redundancy. On the one hand, Von Foerster's patterns of self organisation, postulate the growing capacity of institutions to efficiently manage the "information" coming from outside. On the other, the patterns elaborated by Henri Atlan, where organisational capacities are limited by the internal possibilities of the system (the means of redundancy are exhausted in the creation of a certain order). Thus a number of categories introduced by Shannon such as that of redundancy continue to produce various readings. Chapter 3, evoking game theory and the formation of beliefs, suggests that these effects of redundancy, rumour and ambiguities can be created or manipulated by the agents.

The analysis must therefore concern the capacities of redundancy, the rate of exhaustion of these capacities and their ability to regenerate. All the configurations seem to exist, which may also reveal a relative disorder.

Hence a certain scepticism with regard to the use of the statistical theory of information in economics. However, one of the major interests of this approach is to bring to light problems of meaning through an economy of signals. The analysis of the markets in an over-informed world (a state which the statistical theory of information can help us to see) can benefit from this Shannonian theorisation.

The same thing goes for the analysis of any organisation broadly open to information from outside (firms or other institutions). These considerations are close to those in the contribution Olivier Favereau, no hazard if one notes that his theorisation of information relies on the developments of experimental psychology, another scientific field where the statistical theory of information has led to fertile developments.

2.3. *Structure and Role of Information and Beliefs in Game Theory* (Bernard Walliser, chapter 3)

Bernard Walliser's analysis of the elaboration of information and its use in game theory is quite complementary to the preceding approaches. We can restore this complementarity in the framework of the post war debates which we have just mentioned. In a certain way, the era fully legitimises a reflection which is concerned with both economic regulation to avoid crises (leading to war) and individual liberties (touchstone of the Western world). Developing a theory of individual decision fits naturally into this perspective by focusing on an individualist methodology.

In contrast, the theory of information favours operational considerations more (as does a whole series of contemporary research of the same name) by specifying a situation and a type of problem without specifying the place and the motivation of the actor. For game theory, this choice of perspective implies a certain typology of information distinguishing structural information, which defines the states of nature and the players' characteristics (their beliefs and preferences or the cognitive and instrumental rationality of their decisions), from factual information about the playing of the game (the players' states of nature and actions in each period, retrospective or prospective factual information according to whether it relates to past or future states).

The notion of structural uncertainty is added to this dichotomy of information types, supposing that the agents do not have all the structural information. They will therefore use their (retrospective) factual information to reduce this structural uncertainty, in particular by revealing the type of information held by others through his actions. But this process of constituting knowledge becomes complicated as soon as the other player, whose interests are antagonistic, anticipates this process of revelation and acts in accordance. We end up all the more quickly with complex situations because these games of crossed anticipations can involve several players over several periods. Game theory will therefore try to frame the analysis of such sequences of strategic behaviour.

Let us point out first of all that the apparatus organising the information structures which surround the actor's decision is rather elaborated, with several strata of structural information, concerning the state of the actors' worlds and fundamental situations, and more or less retrospective and prospective factual information (with the uncertainties that that implies).

Information remains quite abstract and only takes on meaning through the evoked contexts. This is not without analogy to the semantic developments which can be drawn from the statistical theory of information through its investigation into the structure of signals. Admittedly, information (or information structures) have a certain utility for each agent but this utility is not socialised (as goods or a service can be). Bernard Walliser points, out; moreover that in game theory, information can have a negative value for all the players at once. Lacking a more precise economic contextualisation all cases remain possible. This structuralist perspective will allow for the description of different situations of knowledge sharing, from situations where knowledge is diluted (a piece of knowledge cannot be exhibited except by pooling particular skills) to situations of shared knowledge (where everyone possesses the knowledge in question and knows it) as well as shared knowledge of the k-order (reflexivity of the proposition where each player knows that the others know). This structuring of information space in shared knowledge is all the more relevant in that a society multiplying its means of processing and communicating information has to take into consideration that this knowledge is not accessible to all and that more or less visible cultural barriers can develop. This elaboration of shared knowledge can explain certain cognitive mechanisms leading to Nash's equilibrium, that is to say, to situations of stationary games where it is common knowledge that no player has any interest in being alone in changing strategy. But this application is rather static and requires moreover unrealistic conditions where all the players are rational and Bayesian (maximising their utility) in an ensemble of possibilities which they are perfectly informed about[3]. The

[3] Freeing oneself from these hypotheses would only serve to make even more ad hoc the eventual definition of an equilibrium obtained in this non standard context.

application of the axiomatic to the illustration of processes of the revision of beliefs appears more realistic. The methods of possible revision are, *a priori*, numerous and respect a certain number of principles. Thus, the players have initial knowledge and receive a message which will take precedence (principle of priority) in case of contradiction; but which will also be taken to be without effect if the initial knowledge is not affected (principle of economy). To which strictly Bayesian methods of revision are added in probabilistic universes where received information allows to rectify the initial probabilities.

The revision methods can clearly be multiplied; here again we face the empirical question of knowing the effective practices of revision of beliefs. Game theory also distinguishes the case where the player doesn't benefit from playing the game to increase his information and revise his beliefs but himself creates conditions for experimentation (active experimentation) to acquire information. This acquired information can then be used strategically and be revealed or not to the other players. In the same strategic line, the players can "bluff" about the information they have acquired. This possibility of revision also has the great interest of introducing learning processes. The panoply set up by game theory is therefore important and relevant. The criticisms that it receives, as Bernard Walliser reminds us in his conclusion, bear essentially on the difficulty in itemising and contextualising these models in an ensemble of realistic patterns which take account of all the perturbations such as the comprehension difficulties, divergences in interpretation, screening and phenomena of erosion which punctuate communication and information in socio-economic relationships.

The structuring of information which the perspective of the actor and action retained by game theory leads to a series of totally relevant notions emphasising the strategic dimensions and the factors at stake. This is doubly important, both because the great actors of the modern world, company directors or governing powers, largely occupy the media with their great strategic manoeuvres, furthermore because technology and learning favour the greater diffusion of such strategic behaviour to all levels of economic activity, from the small "dynamic" entrepreneur to the "new" consumer, as well as the "expert" civil servant.

This being the case, these constructions are complex and one has reason to be surprised by the weak operational character of this theoretical equipment. Game theory seeks less to provide a means of grasping reality and explaining behaviour than provide new tools allowing to widen the already wide range of strategic options. The normative value of this extended game theory is therefore intrinsically weak but its contribution to the variety and complexity of behaviour is far from being negligible by favouring, among other things, the construction of a common language, which is all the more remarkable for in these developments as in those which precede, information didn't have a meaning.

For information to have meaning, we must place ourselves in more specific contexts.

3. LESSONS OF THE THEORETICAL APPROACHES : ON THE FUNCTIONING OF MARKETS

3.1. *Information and Prices* (Alan Kirman, chapter 4).

In pure and perfect Walrassian economies (free competition, perfect information) prices constitute a minimal and efficient structure for informing agents and provoking transactions balancing supply and demand on the markets in a sufficiently satisfying way so as not to be contested by all the agents. The optimal character of the signal which prices represent is appreciated from the minimum number of messages addressed to carry out exchanges. Let us note in passing that this approach by "signal" is close to that which the statistical theory of information starts from.

Alan Kirman's contribution seeks to show how and why this optimal character of prices is illusory. The reasons advanced are of two types. On the one hand the signal price can be disturbed because it must itself vary with the evolution of the fundamentals. On the other, all questioning of the genesis of the signal-price leads to very strongly doubting that a real process might allow to converge on a "correct" signal-price.

This second aspect of Alan Kirman's questioning constitutes a new element in our perspective: a reflection on the genesis of the signal, therefore on its signification for the agents. In fact, as soon as one wants to analyse the formation of prices and/or their diffusion on a market, the role of expectations is one of the "concrete" conditions of functioning which not only hold the attention of the economist but quickly turn out to have devastating effects for the credibility of the Walrassian model.

The financial markets which confront evaluations of assets (or fundamentals) carried out by agents, who are not instantaneously perfectly informed, are, as it happens, subjected to phenomena of crossed anticipations, factors of instability or sub optimal results. In other words, the investigation of the genesis and/or the diffusion of prices suffices to establish that prices cannot be the only signals and that in consequence the Walrassian model is incomplete. This demonstration brings us back to Hayekian problematics. Either it is possible to define a minimal structure of information (in addition to prices) and on this basis re-establish the theory of a market economy, or else one postulates from the outset that in the great complexity of information exchange the optimum set up is obtained when all holders of information can act consistently. This last proposition is used by Hayek in his debate with Lange on the advantages of the market against planning[4].

---

[4] In relation to this debate between Hayek and Lange, one can refer to Arrous (1990, 1995)). However, whereas Lange (1967) saw the increased use of the computer (in the 60s) as something

The anticipation patterns which Alan Kirman retains suffice to call into question the Hayekian postulate according to which the increasingly "freed" market remains the most suitable form of organisation for transactions in order to draw benefit from all the local information which agents possess. Kirman reminds us in fact that patterns of anticipation can have the perverse effect of blocking learning processes and keeping sub optimal technology in place.

The application to contemporary markets is, however, not quite that simple. One is obliged to take a closer look at the functioning of the various markets. The ICT greatly facilitate accessibility, but can also complicate the definition of products... precisely because they broaden product contours (packaging of goods and services, uses on various levels of "intelligent" products...) and consequently make the perception of their qualities more difficult.

Another factor of eventual disturbance is the agents' strategic use of computerised market systems. Computerised air reservation systems give classic examples of such strategic behaviour[5],... which we find again with electronic commerce. This discussion of Walrassian markets raises the question of the origin of price-signals and underlines the need for signals and consequently the need (a necessary but not sufficient condition) to have information products.

Throughout the following contributions we will come back to this information product of bizarre algebra (as pointed out by Arrow (1994)). This need for information also leads to a need for various intermediations and Alan Kirman, like André Orléan in the following contribution, reminds us that it implies an aversion to risk and induces imitation in behaviour (in seeking out average behaviour).

3.2. *The Self-centred Logic of Financial Markets* (André Orléan, chapter 5).

This contribution fully illustrates the proposition according to which prices do not fulfil the role attributed to them by Walrassian theory as soon as information is itself the product of either economic activities or social interactions of various types. The example of the financial markets therefore shows how opinions sometimes unconnected with the fundamentals are formed. This querying of the origin of information brings us closer to questions raised in Le Moigne and Walliser's contributions on communication and beliefs. If prices are seen as signals, then information can be conceived as means of correcting eventual faults.

The adjustments carried out by the most highly informed agents will, in particular, lead to even more marked movements on the behalf of the other agents, which might explain the great variability in the prices of financial assets

---

which supported his theses in favour of a command economy, there are many, who, in the 90s, made the opposite hypothesis according to which the ICT shared out information more uniformly between the agents and favoured a more competitive functioning of the markets. It is true that the use of ICT has, thirty years later, become a lot more decentralised!

[5] On the conditions for the development of these systems re. G. Dang Nguyen (1996).

with regard to smaller scale evolutions of the fundamentals which determine them. But this dichotomy between informed and non informed simplifies a reality where a whole series of representations and intermediations contributes to forming market opinions.

In the case of the financial markets, the conventions which rule opinion are strongly self-centred. The need for liquidity which founds finance, conditions the evaluation of the fundamentals by reducing its links with reality to the benefit of increased attention to shifts of opinion. The effects of imitation are going to hold an important place for objective reasons already emphasised by Keynes in his analysis of financial speculation. From this particular disposition emerges a propensity to develop conventions particular to the milieu which plays the role of veritable cognitive rules justifying the agents' evaluations at a given moment. Imitative behaviour can lead to speculative bubbles and financial crises. New technology appears as cognitive apparatuses capable of influencing behaviour in different ways. The control of practices (prudential regulations) plays a major role in this evolution, to the detriment of restrictions on the fields of activity which predominate in the legislation inherited in the post-war period. The concrete conditions for the functioning of markets (either the temporal and spatial realisation of operations, as M. Allais underlined, at the end of the 80s in relation to computer trading) are decisive. But as Olivier Favereau's contribution shows, the modalities in behaviour on complex markets, even if just as imitation, are very diverse.

Moreover, if this trend for mimicry is for some devoid of strategic intention, it is not the case for other participants where this strategic dimension is very present and adds to the complexity of markets.

Finally, let us note that the notion of information which has been considered up to this point is quite unidimensional, whereas the introduction of various types of knowledge would allow to differentiate the positions of the speculators in relation to their learning abilities for tacit knowledge (expertise on the financial markets) or their ability to access codified knowledge (computerised markets and monitoring equipment)... distinctions which Cowan and Foray return to in their contribution.

3.3. *Theory of Information: from Bounded Rationality to Interpretative Reason* (Olivier Favereau, chapter 6).

This contribution plays a pivotal role. First of all it constitutes the first attempt to deal with the semantic aspects of information and its economy. Secondly, it puts itself at the point of articulation between what are referred to as market problems (an individual in a complex multiple universe, from which he receives and from where he emits signals) and those referred to as organisational problems, where the relational context is defined to such an extent that it is inseparable from a hierarchical relationship and therefore a relationship of power.

This quest for meaning, for the construction of meaning, in a universe of communication, is introduced by Olivier Favereau, taking a certain cognitive realism as a starting point and taking the hypothesis of the limited rationality of the agents very seriously. If the agents conceive that they cannot resolve everything in an immediate manner, in particular because there is a level of unpredictability (future states which one cannot anticipate), what can the precepts of efficient decisions be? There is no miracle remedy to this situation of uncertainty and limited rationality, one simply observes that the purpose of a certain number of cognitive apparatuses seems, precisely, to confront this situation. Olivier Favereau gives some examples of these "activities of understanding, memorisation and inference".

We find the merits of a certain redundancy being referred to (a phenomenon which is seen on the level of the signal, but which quickly leads, as we pointed out, to semantic questions), but also the interest of models and patterns which facilitate a certain memorisation of information.

In fact, a number of these cognitive apparatuses underline the particularities of a an economy of information management having to allow each receptor to retain and classify it, and give it its value in a scale of value which is at the same time personal but in constant reference to those of the world to which the individual belongs. Resistance to change, the cultivation of a relative availability are part of this same personal economy of information of the receptor, with its own scales of reference. Olivier Favereau draws on the works of cognitive psychology to highlight the existence of different levels or regimes in this process of creating meaning, of classification/memorisation, but also the hierarchical character of the classifications carried out to compensate for the complexity of the problems dealt with. Attention and routine thus appear like two polarising regimes of this process, a distinction where attention is of course the regime used with caution[6] (which the economy of the interpretation process applies to).

Olivier Favereau goes from the individual processing of information to deal with the processing of information in a hierarchical organisation. Power relationships will become directly readable.

In setting out to introduce the notion of meaning, this contribution significantly broadens our approaches to information, all the more so as this method is clearly inscribed in the extension of a questioning which was perceptible from the very mechanical processing of signals by Shannon. This broadening remains, at the same time, somewhat partial and open where the description of certain cognitive apparatuses encourages us to know the entirety of the "cognitive" environment better. The key is to be able to have an operational theory, that is to say one allowing to define a small number of decision-making patterns of the economic agents characterising the regime according to which information finds itself integrated and processed in the development mode of contemporary economies.

---

[6] We would prefer to speak of a regime used cautiously rather than as a rare resource as Olivier Favereau does.

How information can become merchandise in the interactive game of these individual processes is part of this querying. To deal with this, perhaps merchandise and information should not be opposed with regard to quality as Favereau does: the quality of merchandise, as that of information, *is* information. In an economic sphere where prices no longer carry all the information required for transactions to take place correctly (which, in the jargon of economists, is expressed as the rise in non price competitiveness) so information on merchandise can also be considered as an element from a different level of logic[7]. With this last extension the range and the forms of merchandising information become very broad. And an evolutionist and institutional theory of information has to combine both approaches well, the merchandising of information and the power relationships which organise the circulation and the processing of information in hierarchical organisations.

4. LESSONS OF THE THEORETICAL APPROACHES: ON THE FUNCTIONING OF ORGANISATIONS

4.1. *Information, Knowledge and Evolutionary Theory of the Firm* (Patrick Cohendet, chapter 7)

Patrick Cohendet's contribution, which focuses on the firm, clearly breaks with the essentially "individualist" perspective of the three previous contributions. He distinguishes the "traditional" vision of the firm as an information processor and that of the evolutionist theory where the firm is above all processor of knowledge. This substitution of the term "knowledge" with that of "information" manifests the desire to introduce the semantic dimension which gives information its price. The evolutionist approach opposes a perspective where the appropriation of information implies, as with Favereau, an economy of learning processes and an economy of information processing to an entire series of approaches to the firm as a more or less specific processor of information (from Alchian to Williamson), which could be read in the immediate extension of a Shannon type reading of communication[8]. This parallelism which *a priori* is fruitful, nonetheless has its limits. For example, there will be a strong temptation to assimilate collective learning and individual learning by an anthropomorphic reduction of the collective under study. How can we go about this question of collective learning differently? The immediate transpositions like those of routines for example, distinguishing routines of exploitation and exploration are very interesting and relevant, but not specific to collectives. We need to grasp both the internal interactions of the group and reactions to the outside environment. The notion of skill, with what it expresses of the collective's capacity to act/react in relation to the outside and to others is certainly important,

---

[7] The similarity will appear all the stronger if, instead of merchandise in the strict sense, the product in question is a service (a specialised and complex service as found with services to companies).

[8] The firm then appears as a solution to particular problems of circulating and processing information, initially fluid but eventually submitted to the hazards and interference that occur during processing.

but how is it constructed? How does it maintain itself? In relation to this point, Patrick Cohendet speaks of the firm as an "emergent property of dynamic interactions". This perspective remains too general to be operational. Moreover, the notions, which deal directly with the collective, like those of centralisation/decentralisation, remain difficult to define for being too closely linked to the circulation of information and not the transfer of knowledge. The risk of this evolutionist perspective would then be to render the notion of knowledge too fluid, simplifying the problem of transfers. In fact, the perspective requires that one strictly differentiates the circulation of information from the transfer of knowledge. It is ambiguous to speak of the circulation of knowledge, without specifying if this circulation is linked to the mobility of people or to a learning process. These diverse questions can only be clarified in terms of heuristics. The brief inventory of "risks" which a collective learning process incurs, is revealing in this regard; it underlines the importance that the dissonance between collective learning processes and individual learning processes can have. If the relationships between these two levels of learning are at the heart of the querying of the evolutionist firm, how are we to define its modalities? The capacity of organisations which leave a certain local autonomy to individual learning processes, to adapt to small scale evolutions in the environment, is often highly thought of, but how can we read collective learning into this? And how does shared knowledge develop in this process? A symmetric question could be asked in the case of highly hierarchical organisations on their aptitude to resolve challenges of a certain size. The distinction between tacit and codified knowledge is in this respect crucial, to the extent that the term "codified" already implies something shared... but in the instance of a scale which often surpasses that of the organisation considered. It will probably be necessary to broaden the use of this notion to specific cases of shared knowledge in such and such a type of firm. In his contribution, Bernard Walliser envisages such shared knowledge of different types. The distinction of transfers of knowledge between tacit and codified levels proposed by Nonaka (1994) is interesting but often one does not know if it is transfers of knowledge between individuals or between organisations (or even within the same organisation). At some point the codified/tacit distinction also returns to the one between syntax and semantics (which subtends the majority of the contributions). To conclude, the transfer modalities proposed by Nonaka are of importance in themselves and very different in nature: externalisation (passage from the tacit to the codified) referring to a process of accumulation of knowledge; internalisation (passage from the codified to the tacit) allowing itself to be read above all as the second stage of the same process (codification frees fields for the constitution of new knowledge) which is not, strictly speaking, a transfer of knowledge[9].

---

[9] The two other modes are still further from what is understood as a transfer of knowledge: combination (passage from codified to codified) likened to a syntactical reconstruction; socialisation

It is also necessary to highlight the role played by representations of the organisation to subsume individual learning processes into a collective process. It follows that the emergence of collective learning processes comes through the existence of a suitable representation of the learner organisation. Moreover, all querying on the subject of the firm combines a question on the manner in which diverse individual knowledge and skills are rendered coherent with a question on the collective ability to produce and manage. In other words, the social relationships of production, and the power relationships that they imply, cannot be separated from the co-ordination of skills upon which a the evolutionist analysis of the firm tends to focus. There are power relationships in a collective organisation like a firm and all attempts to set up the equivalent of collective learning cannot free itself from this hierarchy[10].

The modalities of all these learning processes are transformed with the means used for processing and circulating information, as is attested to by the very contemporary theme of the dissolution of the firm's frontiers and the redefinition of sectors of activity. The shift from an approach to the firm towards a theory of organisation is thus objectively founded and favours the emergence of an entire theoretical corpus dealing with situations where the particularities of the distribution of information determine the forms of organisation which are retained.

The theory of organisations dealt with below appears to some extent complementary by providing, in normative terms, a range of patterns which the evolutionist approach can combine to describe heuristically the collective learning process which it seeks to define.

4.2. *Information in the Theory of Organisation* (Jacques Crémer, chapter 8).

In Jacques Crémer's paper, it is less the firm than the general form of organisation which is analysed as resulting from certain constraints to obtain information or to make it circulate. The nature of information is not specified, but it is very specific and plays a strategic role in the decision-making situations studied. The objective is that a decider organises his relationship with a person or a collective of persons (whose relations with the rest of the world remain rather undefined), so as to either obtain strategic information that he needs on the outside world, or to check that the actions of these same agents conform with what was agreed upon.

Jacques Crémer thus distinguishes a certain number of problematic situations... which economists have learnt to schematise and resolve analytically. One can appreciate the value of such a method for producing "operational" results by emphasising the optimal character of such and such a different form of

(passage from tacit to tacit) standing out like a solid black box!

[10] Here we find once again queries on the technical or disciplinarily character of the division of labour (illustrated in the 70s by the works of Gorz and Marglin).

organisation. The set of cases that can be dealt with does not claim to be exhaustive, but the method develops progressively throughout the cases so we learn to deal with a theory of organisations. This method is more radical, because normative, than Coase's positive approach, for whom the observed form (firm or market) minimises *de facto* the costs of the transaction. For the tenants of this new theory of organisations (NTO), hierarchical organisation is founded only when this primary mechanism, the market, turns out to be unworkable. This frontier of impracticability is not, however, clearly explored and a number of organisations find themselves in limbo, between the market and form of organisation (whose optimality is recognised).

A major advantage of the propositions of the new theory of organisations is to do with the fact that the schemas used succeed in showing that they allow for an optimal circulation of information. It remains to appreciate the realism of these patterns with regard to the analyses produced in other related disciplines like sociology, psychology or management, interested first and foremost by these organisation questions (and the difficulties that there are in removing them from their contexts).

The specificity of the questions dealt with has to do with the fact that the agents considered are already engaged in a "hierarchical" contractual relationship, of the principal/agent type, with the principal task of defining the terms of the contract. Two types of contract are then envisaged according to whether they have to compensate for eventual dissimulation on the states of nature or on the actions of the agents. These patterns at the basis of the theory of incentives finally raise the problems of organisation in terms of the possibilities for the more or less costly transmission or emission of a signal from an agent to a principal. This pattern type and the extrapolations which it gives rise to represents something like a cognitive apparatus (syntactical in nature) with which the NTO can describe a whole series of organisations, all the broader because one can consider that the conjunction and the concatenation of such relationships opens the way to the analysis of more complex hierarchical organisations. This presentation, without exaggerating the unity of the NTO approach, following Jacques Crémer's warning, nonetheless highlights both the syntactical character of the developments and the semantic dimensions which they establish when dealing with questions of the training of skills (culture, knowledge) and complex organisations (with hierarchies and information selection). Here again, the elaboration of a syntactical nature ends up introducing a semantic dimension, explaining the interest aroused by this theory, a little similar to that aroused by the statistical theory of information in its time.

The interest for the NTO must also be read on two levels. On the one hand, its schematisation gives an account of certain realities which can be drawn up sparingly, on the other, their normative aspect helps the actors themselves to construct representations which will influence choices of organisation. We have already insisted twice (chapters 6 and 7) on the importance of such representations for actions, and the necessity to accord them with the technological and social conditions in which economic activities develop. It is for this reason that specialists of management sciences emphasise that situations of the principal/agent type (with asymmetries of information) have multiplied in our contemporary economies.

The last contribution analysed extends this questioning by looking directly at the contemporary evolution of forms of knowledge.

4.3. *On the Codifiability of Knowledge : Technical Change and the Structure of Cognitive Activities* (Dominique Foray and Robin Cowan, chapter 9).
The analysis of the relationship between information and knowledge, central to dealing with relations between economic agents, is approached here through an analysis of the relationship between tacit knowledge and codified knowledge. This in fact requires specifying what codified knowledge is, and the nature of the process that leads to it.

To what extent is a piece of information codified knowledge or codifiable? In what way does new technology and new knowledge allow to extend or to transform the domain of codified knowledge? What are the hazards which govern these processes? What are the eventual consequences for the extension of knowledge?

The position taken by Foray and Cowan is quite cautious[11]: codification is presented as a process which has always existed, which new technology certainly transforms, but by implying an extension of knowledge itself. Codification has therefore three pillars: a language (signs), a modelling of concerned knowledge (a meaning) and a technology of transmission (a channel). In this respect we come back to the ternary structure of information put forward by Le Moigne (chapter 1). This will allow to highlight certain specificities of the codification processes.

A first aspect of codification seems clearly to be its duality, between openness and secrecy, between the will to diffuse and transfer knowledge more broadly and that of restricting access to it. The result of codification is in fact that access requires the possession of an access code (language) which can be shared knowledge, but also the privilege of a small number. This first remark on the codification processes implies the existence of at least two networks, those who had access to the tacit knowledge before codification and those who will have access to the knowledge after codification[12].

Another important element is that the codification of knowledge transforms it into different knowledge. According to the nature of the codification processes, tacit and codified knowledge will differ more or less strongly. One can even see paths of the "progression" of knowledge in this transformation. The works of

---

[11] The first version, presented during the seminar, was a lot less cautious, suggesting a relative growth of the stock of codified knowledge in regard to tacit knowledge (which explains certain of the questions expressed during the discussion, transcribed in appendix to Foray and Cowan's text).

[12] One could add two other networks, those in fact possessed by the tacit knowledge considered and those possessed by codified knowledge.

Hatchuel and Weil (1992) on expert systems are abundantly quoted by the authors to illustrate the force of this dialectic. An important question is then to know if an acceleration/extension of the codification processes translates itself as a movement of the same nature in the universe of knowledge (whether tacit or not). Technology extending the field of codification would then accelerate the progression of knowledge. The response is quite naturally conditional, all the problems which the economy of information raises highlight the eventuality of numerous faults (saturation, duplication, obsolescence, contradiction, cacophony,...). Hence the interest of defining these processes, while clearly distinguishing the evolution of the elements that support the process of codification in the strict sense.

On this basis, the codification of knowledge is, for Foray and Cowan, the creation of a message through a modelling of the knowledge expressed in a certain language. This ternary language/model/message structure attempts to give an account of the passage from knowledge to information/signal here referred to as the message. *A priori* the process taken as reference is that of the expert capable of analysing the structure of tacit knowledge so as to make a model of it. To situate these three moments of codification in relation to processes of decision-making analysed in other chapters (whether these are patterns of representation, with Favereau, the firm information processor with Cohendet, the principal elaborating the terms of its contracts with Crémer or the ternary structure of information with Jean Louis Le Moigne) it is necessary to point out who the actors of this codification are. Whether they are management experts (constructing expert systems) or scientists or engineers, developing theories or methods, they are all manipulators of symbols (in the sense that Robert Reich (1992) gives to this term) of a certain stature. They in fact require to be capable of model and using or creating a language in which they can transcribe their patterns. Let us note in passing that the realisation of these codifications can be carried out by a planning department within a company (like in the good old days of Taylorian automation) or a group of such codifying agents when then address themselves to a community of agents carrying out transactions of the same nature or between each other.

The questions of the compatibility, cumulativity and durability of this codified knowledge then arises. The interest of a code depends on its rate of use in the population of potential users. Codification implies a certain investment, mostly immaterial (but large in terms of qualified work hours); but codification processes are not unrelated among themselves. There are points of connection, economies of varieties, external aspects to networks which are probably difficult to delimit, but which appear in the numerous reuses and combinations of models and language which can be observed (re. David, Foray, 1995)[13].

---

[13] See also the evolution of software engineering which is trying to favour modular constructions so as to escape from codification which is too dedicated (re. Gibbs (1994)).

It is also on this level, which overall is difficult to gauge, that the diffusion of information technology, the development of knowledge in relation to modelling, and the mastery of new languages, could have the most structuring effects. One has difficulty following the codification dynamic and the extension of knowledge which our store of tacit and codified knowledge allows for and the "support" technology of messages which we possess.

The pattern of diffusion used in Foray and Cowan (1997) follows the more classic structure, combining the receptivity of the agents (or the capacity to understand the code) with their connectivity (that is to say the probability of two agents being in relation for the type of transaction envisaged). This pattern of diffusion can quickly become complicated if one takes into account the interdependence of codification processes, and the similarities existing between receptive capacities such as the dynamic of connection between agents.

Learning processes and habits (at the origin of what the evolutionist economists call increasing yield of adoption) tend, for example, to favour keeping codification, which is moreover surpassed by new possibilities of model; from expressing itself in a new language, or even transmitting on new supports. One can imagine that in a world where relations between codification are numerous and multiform, the identification of such developments remains difficult.

Similarly, by emphasising the networks (and the external elements which they generate) a whole interweaving of social and economic links appears. Codes and codification break up the heterogeneous ensemble of relations between economic agents in different ways. A number of them are shared knowledge but this cannot be generalised (distinctions like those introduced in Bernard Walliser's contribution between shared knowledge of various types could be of use in carrying out this description).

This vision where economic and social relations cannot avoid being submerged or more exactly mediated by an ensemble of codes and codification processes in constant evolution is not without paradoxes. In particular, the frontier between tacit knowledge and codified knowledge is no longer as assured if none exists in a pure state and if what distinguishes them has more to do with the proprieties of the codes and codification processes which found them as knowledge (that is to say a social construction which is transferable to some extent even if its conditions are highly varied). Codification can then be assimilated to translation facilitating the passage of one "code" to another, which is *a priori* more accessible or, more exactly, easier to transfer. Indeed, in the economics of codification we come back to an analogy of all the problems of translation (change in meaning, lighter version, more accessible or idiomatic style,..). As, moreover, those who use this distinction between tacit and codified knowledge have a tendency of assimilating codified knowledge and information, one might be led, to the great displeasure of the above, to observe a certain continuum between knowledge of all types and information. This paradox has, relatively speaking, the same origins as the semantic shift which led the Shannon type analysis of signals to develop notions which were somewhat loaded with meaning. The economics of codification can thus develop, and in a non exclusive manner, either towards a rather "statistical" theory of the diffusion of signals in complex reticular "milieus", or towards a theory of the modelling of complex tacit knowledge. In the first case, the economics of codification would deal with problems of switching between networks. In the second case it is more specific questions of organisation that we would be dealing with.

Whatever the extensions, this economics of codification gives relevant clarification to some of the mutations of knowledge and skills of contemporary companies. The approach could be quite complementary to the previous ones provided the organisational problems which go hand in hand with the application of these diverse forms of codification are specified. More generally, one shouldn't underestimate the progress that has to be made before we have an economics of codification which is sufficiently effective to give account of important movements of innovation and obsolescence, diffusion and concentration, which constantly agitate our store of knowledge.

5. RESULTS AND IMPLICATIONS

5.1. *On the approach*

A first lesson of the assessment which precedes is that it brings out the proximity between methods of processing information according to the arbitration which they carry out between the syntactical dimension and the semantic dimension. According to a first schema (the approaches in the first part), the processing of information is above all the transmission of a signal (conditions of emission, transmission and reception). This syntactical analysis, in becoming more sophisticated, more or less takes on semantic value, as is attested to by the evolutions of the statistical theory of information. These syntactical approaches thus pass from signal to sign, which, from a linguistic perspective, combines signifier and signified (therefore meaning).

In contrast, the other approaches seek to introduce a semantic content of messages from the outset. But this semantic dimension seems to be taken into account in only two ways. One either specifies the cognitive processes by which individuals give meaning to information (the approaches of part 2 of the present work), or the contexts of decision making in which the agents are going to use the information (the approaches in part 3, and in this case one can speak of a pragmatic perspective). This double manner of introducing the semantic dimension returns *in fine* to the classic distinction between methods of processing information considered as psychological phenomena or as modes of organising or giving form to possible[14].

Finally, we end up with a ternary structure which first of all passes through the dialectic opposition between sign and meaning, then decomposes questions of meaning either in the contexts of relations between people, or in cognitive process through which individuals structure and interpret the information which they receive.

This structure allows to position the different approaches. Roughly speaking, the so-called theories of information (first part of the book) have above all a syntactical dimension. The so-called market approaches (second part of the book), where individuals seek to interpret signals, have a semantic dimension inscribed into cognitive processes, while the analyses of organisations (third part) privilege a semantic approach limited to certain relational contexts. The relevance of an "economic" theory of information thus seems all the greater for being significantly represented in all approaches. While this point of reference allows to roughly position the fields covered by a theory of information and to appreciate its relevance, it can also be applied to characterise the relationships of information in a firm, on a market, or even on the scale of a whole economy.

Contemporary developments in the means of processing, handling and storing codified information have increased the syntactical dimensional of relationships to information on all levels (the firm, the branch of activity, the market). Many uses and populations of users thus find themselves specified, which raises the question of the access conditions and the evolution of these specifications. The maintenance of certain codifications can limit abilities to adapt to new situations. The rigidity of certain access conditions, whether financial or cultural, can hold back extension and interconnections between networks of users. The reality of these risks of increased rigidity depends on the appropriate character of the concomitant extensions of the semantic dimension of relationships to information.

These extensions come, as underlined above, in two forms, one relating to the diversity of forms of organisation and to a greater control over their implications in terms of the processing and circulation of information. This supposes a certain organisational learning, which can very well be founded on the dissemination of management sciences (with what that implies in critical attention to lessons of experience, the construction of models and expertise) and on the development of an entire logistics of consultancy services and the professionalisation of management and communication trades.

But this dynamic, and consequently that of codification, remains conditioned by the evolution of information relationships in the third dimension, that of meaning, such as is perceived on the level of individuals themselves.

---

[14] Ifrah (1994) (chapter 34) thus attributes the first perspective to Couffignal and Schutzenberger (the semantic dimension lending itself to assessment through a psychological phenomenon) and the second to the "repentant" cyberneticist Brilloin (the "neguentropic" or organising effect attests to the semantic dimension of the information).

One can suppose that here also a certain learning process might improve the ability of each individual to interpret the information he or she receives. But the essential of the dynamic along this "semantic" axis has less to do with the eventual improvements of individual abilities than with structuring processes and the accumulation of individual knowledge. The development of education with the prolongation of school years (and even more the development of life long learning schemes) is a major component of this but it is not the only one, and the role of the media is potentially important in this structuring of the sharing of knowledge which allows individuals to give meaning to the signals which they encounter in the sphere of economic activities. This understanding goes from the appreciation of the characteristics of the highly differentiated products offered on the markets to the understanding of the procedures and patterns which organise productive activities or the use of certain services.

Here we catch a first glimpse of a frontier where the absence of comprehension (which is distributed very unequally) comes to limit the complex and overlapping developments of codification (concerning signals) and patterns of organisation (concerning the specification of contexts). This underlines the determining role of the interpretation process in so-called information economies, that is to say of the structuring process and the accumulation of knowledge in our meta-system of information[15].

A new perception of risk in economic activities is no doubt one of the first aspects of the new situations created by the evolution of the "meta-system of information".

5.2. *Facing risks and radical uncertainty.*

The evolution of knowledge and its distribution leads in the first place, to a greater awareness of a certain number of risks and instances of interdependence within our economic activities. By the interplay of market competition, legal and political relations, the agents extend their strategic horizons. But this extension, as the development of new knowledge, itself leads to new risks. This rise of a new "economy of risk" manifests itself in the development of legal activities, insurance and finance. Its traces are less visible on the level of individual behaviour, where it is true to say that we don't know how to spot the evolution of the cognitive patterns used by the agents in contexts where the multiplicity of networks, the rapidity of the flow of information, the extent of compatibility problems and difficulties in accumulating codified knowledge complicate and extend the strategic universe of decision making. Changes in behaviour are real nonetheless.

As one of these recognised modifications of behaviour, we will note the more widespread desire to make calculations and to ask for explanations of agents

---

[15] To designate the entire spectrum of information processing and exchange which take place during multiple economic activities. This term is a counterpart the to the neologism proposed by Edgar Morin (1977, t1, p. 317) when he noted that a theory of information, to be complete, syntactically as well as semantically, has to be a meta-informational theory.

with certain responsibilities (accountability) and a more systematic search for information on the contexts of the action, whose links with the environment are more clearly perceived. Works on the agents' behaviour on the financial markets as those dealing with the construction and implementation of skills within firms, allow us to perceive such evolutions. Indeed, for the agents, it is a question of constructing informed representations which, out of quite deliberate convention, can then serve as a framework for individual actions. This approach is no longer the privilege of the central state or the result of long traditions. As Mirowski (2001) points out, it was the Chicago financiers who went looking for economists' models (and not the opposite) to agree among themselves on the modalities for the functioning of their market. Telecommunications provides another good example of the "new" behaviour which presides over various institutional changes. At the beginning of the 1980s, the deregulation of this activity in the United States based itself on a pattern of separating activities requiring heavy investments (but freeing economies of scale) from other activities of services using the same equipment (with rather decreasing yields). The frontier established on this basis of representation was, however, quickly to be upset, both by the evolution of technology (in particular through Hertzian telecommunications) and by the learning processes of new operators (the Baby Bells in the example of the United States) on their new markets, leading to a revision of rules and representations. The institutional changes in these companies which inform themselves and learn, thus have to be both more precise in their decrees and capable of adjusting more quickly to internal and external evolutions (learning processes).

This perspective which bases a new institutional dynamic on a concomitant evolution of individual behaviour is opposed to the one constantly advocated by Hayek (1948,1988) according to which all these institutional changes, deliberate and of a certain scale, can be taken to be dangerously illusory. From this perspective there could be no deliberation and meaning on this level, and only tradition would be able to make relevant use of the necessary selections. This is forgetting that the existence of such possibilities of deliberate choice on a more decentralised level is itself the result of an historic evolution with numerous roots which constantly pushes back frontiers and transforms the nature of the markets.

Current changes, as much in the organisation of productive processes as in demand, attest to the advances and deadlocks of this process.

5.3. *Reorganising productive processes and lifestyles*

In the contemporary transformation of the meta-system of information under consideration, the firm is led to considerably change its way of envisaging its role and specificity. It presents itself as an instance of co-ordination, favouring the constitution of particular skills which can easily spread towards other companies, even other fields of activity, the whole following the rhythm of the changing incitements of the markets and financial institutions.

Here the firms have to go through a heavy process of re-learning their role of "constructor of the future". Nor is it enough to take cognisance of the scale of the task and the duration of such systematic learning processes[16], for such adjustments do not seem to be the sole domain of companies. Deep evolutions of wage relations and lifestyles have to accompany these transformations. For the moment, these adjustments seem to be oscillating between the concern to control cost by putting pressure on jobs and salaries and the will to develop skills which guarantee advantages outside of costs.

This can be to do with the markets for the products, the company's organisational ability, but also the labour market, that is to say with modes of training and mobilising individual skills. Time and the modes of adaptation of new technology can also be called into question. How can eventual deadlocks be compensated for ? How can new co-ordinated transformations of these diverse spaces be favoured ? Our reflections on the role of information only suggest premises, underlining the importance of representations, from type situations to recognised solutions, the shaping or codification of information flow favouring the constitution and the transfer of knowledge on various levels,...

The issue is not only controlling this information flow to increase knowledge, it is also to have a active, innovative role in these market spaces, not only in the conception and in the making available of products but also in the conditioning of the markets[17]. From this perspective, the economy of information corresponds to a deep transformation of the markets' mode of functioning, where relationships are more constructed, differentiating the exchanges (between standard products and made to order services), spreading them in space and time (local relations, durable relations) according to not only companies' but also individuals' strategies, as consumers, workers and citizens.

But the necessary co-ordination cannot take place on this scale unless the objectives of learning processes and work are not only made legitimate for their economic efficiency but widely desirable in terms of lifestyles, and throughout the entire duration of the latter. In a world where information circulates widely, where knowledge is disseminated and renewed, the representation which individuals make of their place in the company is deeply changing. The "acceptable" forms of the diffusion of ICT in the public and private services but also in domestic uses, are part of this representation and condition the level of employment and the work status to come. Demand has often been given a passive role, considering that access to information and the accumulation of

---

[16] P. David (1991) suggests, in comparing the "diffusion" of the computer to that of the dynamo, that this period could last half a century.

[17] In the marketing sense of the term.

knowledge differentiate tastes, while allowing to condition this demand. Things are not as simple and this conditioning must be understood as a need for intermediation.

The function of intermediation is central in a market mechanism; it not only appears through the activities which make the products available (transport and retail) or help to finance their purchase (banks and insurance), but also in the whole range of mediations which inform and/or transmit the knowledge of what the products are, key parameters of the purchase decision. This transmission can take place in multiple ways in which the producers can intervene. This being the case, the credibility of this transmission of knowledge, therefore its efficiency, also depends on its relative autonomy in relation to the producers. The importance of this function of intermediation leads to the recognition of a ternary aspect of the market, a mediation (from many aspects) assuring the "acknowledgement" of what one party is offering to others. The evolution of relationship with information, its enrichment but also its increased complexity have an impact on this function of intermediation. In the first place, as we have already indicated, it multiplies the possibilities of new markets, but with regard to access, these markets are not universal and depend on each individual's ability to benefit from these mediations. Culture, language, education, experiences will play discriminating roles. This is particularly obvious for everything concerning the distribution of new goods and services directly linked to communication and information technologies. Sociologists and anthropologists[18] emphasise, for example, the potential for interactivity which these products can present for those who do not have access "with full knowledge of the facts". The products are thus differentiated, perhaps more than in the past, in accordance with the user's ability to develop its uses. Such an evolution can lead to a new social fragmentation which neither the progressive growth of revenue, nor the programme of initial training would reduce.

Indeed, the efforts made where education is concerned have constantly raised the average level of training while seeing the number of failures increase (the scale of the return to illiteracy, gaps between training received and training required or used in the job, the difficulties of continued training throughout working life, difficulties getting out of unemployment,...). A re-appreciation of investments in human capital is needed, specifying the needs and the way of responding to them, taking account of the entire duration of working life but also of the impacts and interactions which link professional experience and abilities to manage consumption and lifestyle.

Manifestly, transformations and learning processes taking place in the field of consumption are closely linked to those observed in productive activities.

[18] Re. for example the work of Ehrenberg (1995) or Levy (1990).

5.4. *On structural adjustment policies*
Two orientations of "structural" policy emerge at the end of our analysis of the approaches to the notion of information in economic theory. The first concerns the function of intermediation, the other, social cohesion.

If the major questions raised in these economies of information focus on problems of co-ordination, decentralised organisation, normalisation, risk management and representations and certification of production, then it is up to public authorities to favour the development of adapted logistic supports on various levels. This concerns both the major intermediation service-networks (transport, banks, communications, commerce,..) but also an entire range of specialised consultancy services to companies and finally the network of research and educational institutions around which professional expertise is constituted. All these activities remain, by nature, quite regulated, whether their fields of activity are segmented or their operative modes are subject to precise precautionary rules. Moreover, as a result they possess a still quite marked national dimension, even if a process of international harmonisation, through deregulation, has been underway since the 80s. It is true that the strong cultural dimension of many of these activities contributes to the maintenance of national specificities.

Structural policies have to be able to both take these national specificities into account and innovate in the structuring of these "logistics" which constitute the true framework of the economic transactions of production and exchange. A guiding principle of policies for the setting up of these structures has for a long time been to guarantee universal access. One could account for the greatest interactivity between elements in a transaction by having the objective of making this access be accompanied by certain skills of making the most of this available potential. This depends largely on the structure of intermediation, on its ability to differentiate its services and to propose qualifying uses, that is to say to allow access to a certain level of skill. A major challenge is to coordinate these logistics at regional level and Michel Catinat in chapter 10 outlines the efforts of the EEC to achieve such enlarged networking which would benefit all member countries.

The other orientation in policy is to some extent the immediate correspondent of the preceding one on the side of the consumers and citizens. It is about monitoring that origins and individual experiences do not lead to reinforcing a latent dualism in quite non egalitarian societies where social cohesion is largely founded on the sharing of a social project, or more prosaically, on an idea of economic and social progress. This dynamic has for a long time had two pillars, access to higher and higher levels of education and consumption. Both strongly risk being called into question by the relative incapacity of the education system to guarantee access to jobs when having the qualification required, and by the division of consumption norms which the clear gaps in the mastering of knowledge and new technology risk to induce. The objective of the policies would be to compensate these two drifts by monitoring, on the one hand, a new synchronisation between the functioning of the labour market and the education system and, on the other, by favouring all mediations (including through a certain use of the education system) to avoid a marked divergence, subjected and not chosen, between the consumption projects. The two objectives are related. First of all because they both imply a renewal of the education system. But above all because this renewal cannot be envisaged without taking into account the entire duration of individuals' lives and all their activities (both in and outside of work). In the reading which we have made of the economies of information in gestation referred to, the interdependence between all of these spheres of activity finds itself notably increased; in particular because a greater valorisation of knowledge of all types goes hand in hand with their more rapid obsolescence, encouraging a permanent reconstitution of these skills.

The contributions in the present book have shown the multiple dimensions of economic activity implied in our relationship with information and knowledge. The evolution of this relationship, which is beginning to take shape, is assuredly complex, leading to the growth and diversification of information and knowledge but also to obsolescence and hyper-specialisation. This book has tried to show that it was possible to classify the questions and develop a framework of analysis facilitating the identification and explanation of the problems encountered. The itemisation of these different perspectives is only outlined in a book whose objectives are quite theoretical, but sufficiently outlined, all the same, so as to perceive that it is possible to go further and that the screen used constitutes an appreciable tool for analysing the metamorphoses of the relationship of our economies to information and knowledge.

REFERENCES

Arrous J. (1990), Socialisme et planification: O. Lange and F. A. Hayek, *Revue Française d'Economie*, vol. V.2, printemps, pp. 61-84.

Arrous J. (1995), L'utilisation de l'information dans la société: vers l'économie mixte. document travail BETA n° 9510, Strasbourg.

Arrow K. (1962) The Economic Implications of Learning by Doing. *Review of Economic Studies* XXIX (2), pp. 155-173.

Arrow K. (1974) *The Limits of Organization*, Norton, New York.

Arrow K. (1994), Information and Organization of Industry. Rivista Internazionale Di Science Sociali. Occasional Paper. Pp. 3-8. April

Brousseau E., Petit P. and Phan D. (eds.) (1996), *Mutations des télécommunications, des industries et des marchés* ENSPTT-. Economica, Paris.

Dang Nguyen G. (1996) Les systèmes de réservation aérienne et l'économie des réseaux. in Brousseau E., Petit P. and Phan D. (eds.)

Dion E. (1997), *Invitation à la théorie de l' information.* Collection Points Seuil, Paris, March.

David P. (1991), "Computer and Dynamo : the Modern Productivity Paradox in a not too Distant Mirror" , in OECD ,1991.

David and Foray D. (1995), "Accessing and Expanding the Science and Technology Knowledge Base", *STI Review*, N°16, OCDE, Paris.

Ehrenberg A. (1995), *L'individu incertain*. Calman Lévy, Paris.

Foray D. and Cowan R. (1997) "The Economics of Codification and the Diffusion of Knowledge", *Industrial and Corporate Change*, vol 6, N°3.

Foray D. and Lundvall B.A. (1996), "The Knowledge-based Economy : From the Economics of Knowledge to the Learning Economy", OCDE, Paris.

Gibbs (1994) « Software's Chronic Crisis »,*Scientific American,*271(3), 86-95.

Hatchuel A. and Weil B. (1992), *L'expert et le système*. Economica.

Hayek F. A. (1948) *Individualism and Economic Order,* London, Routledge&Kegan Paul, Ltd.

Hayek F.A. (1988) *The Fatal Conceit: the Errors of Socialism,* London, Routledge.

Ifrah G. (1994), *Histoire universelle des chiffres*. Robert Laffont, Paris.

Lancry P.J. (1982), *Theory of information et économie.* Economica, Paris.

Lange O. (1967), *The Computer and the Market,* in C. Feinstein, (ed.) Capitalism, socialism and economic growth. pp.158-61.

Levy P. (1990), *Les technologies de l'intelligence. L'avenir de la pensée à l'âge de l'informatique,* Paris, La Découverte.

Mirowski P.(2001) Alice Trough the Liquid Crystal : A Different Perspective on IT and the Economy, january, mimeo

Morin E. (1977) *La méthode.* Tome 1 :La nature de la nature. Editions du Seuil, Paris

Nonaka I. (1994), A Dynamic Theory of Organisational Knowledge Creation. *Organisation Science*, Vol. 5.

Reich R. (1992), *The Work of Nations : Preparing Ourselves for the 21st Century*, Vintage Books, New York

Walliser B. (1994), *L'intelligence de l'économie*, Odile Jacob, Paris.

INDEX

A

Accountability 210
Action plan 175
Adverse selection 129, 141
Asymmetries of information 129, 143
Attention 98, 199
Availability 96, 199

B

Backward induction 55
Bayesian
    game 52
    logic 103
Bayes rule 55
Belief 14, 38, 49, 54, 55, 84, 86,87, 193
Beauty contest phenomenon 68
Bubbles 66, 198

C

Canal of information 40
Capabilities 126
Centralisation 128
Channel 22
Coasian approach 123
Code 22, 35, 125
Codifiability 15, 159, 204
Codification 156, 164, 204
Coding 149
Cognition
    distributed 108, 111
    distributive 106
Cognitive
    artefact 104
    capacities 124
    justification 54, 58
    mechanism 89, 121
    processes 109, 198
    realism 115
    resources 94
    structures 109
Cognitivist paradigm 49
Collective action 112
Complexity 18, 35
Communication
    statistical theory of 38
    theory 34
Commutativity 56
Competence 121, 126
Competitive equilibrium 49
Complex systems 100
Connectivity of the graph 72
Contextualisation 114
Contract theory 141, 150
Conventions 54, 84, 89, 198
Conversion of knowledge 130, 131
Co-ordination 104, 114, 121, 124, 202, 211
Corporate culture 148

D
Decoding 15
Deliberation 25
Development modes 190, 200
Digital sister in law 162
Disinvention 155
Dissonance 201
Diversity 129
Dualistic slide 13

E

Economics of
    communication 17
    electronics 17
    immaterial 28
    organisation 17
    transmission 17
Electronic commerce 173
Electronic signature 179
Emotion 99
Energetics of knowledge 28
Entropy 34, 192
Epidemics of opinion 77
Equilibrium
    general 74, 93
    Nash 54

rationalisable 54
self-confirming 58
sub game perfect 55

Equivocation 42
Evaluation 90 (see also financial)
Evolutionary
game theory 38
theory 15, 122, 125, 126, 200
Evolutionist paradigm 49
Excess volatility 65
Expectations 196, 197
Expert systems 161, 205
Externalisation 132, 201

F

Financial
conventions 86
evaluation 83
markets 66, 83, 198
Framing effect 114
Functional complementarity 108

G

Game 22
theory 14 , 49
Governance 128, 129, 130

H
Hayeckian approach 126, 196, 210
Herd behaviour 67
(see also imitation)
Heuristics 14, 21, 23, 24, 93, 96,102, 106, 114, 191
Hierarchy 100, 127
theories of 145
Hierarchical organisation 145

I
ICTs Information communication technologies 162, 167, 189
dissemination 171
Idempotence 56
Imitation 14, 87
Incentive schemes 129, 203
Incompleteness 94, 107, 108
Inflation 75
Information
capital 147
categories 33
content 35, 52, 97
loss of 42
notion 11
optimal structure of 40
processing 147, 168, 200, 208
product 197
quantity of 35, 36
taxonomy 50
structural/factual 50, 193, 194
Information society 172
Information structures 124, 194
Information systems 26
Informational cascade 67
Informational costs 142
Informational econometrics 37
Intellectual property 173, 178
Interaction 105
Intermediation 212, 213
Internalisation 132, 201
Interpretation 95, 102, 209
Interpreting 99, 107
Introspection 52
Institution 111, 126

K

Know
How 20
What 20
Who 20
Why 20
Knowledge 122, 124
accumulation of 147
codified 131, 156, 201, 204
collective 125
common 49,53
diffusion 53
distributed 121
shared 53, 194
tacit 131, 155, 201, 204

L

Learning 99
Single loop 111
By doing 148
distributed processes121
organisational process 127
processes 195, 200
Liberalisation 172, 175
Liquidity 85
Lock in effect 70, 130, 163
Logistics 213

M

Market
efficient 65, 83
organisation 76
processes 33
Meanings 18
Media 180, 195
Memorisation 25, 94, 156
Memory 94
Message 22, 42
Mimetic 87, 89
Miniaturisation of micro processors 12, 169
see also ICTs
Modeling 157
Moral hazard 129, 141
Multidivisional organisation 147

N

Network 180, 204, 206
ISDN 180
modelling 22
relational 72
random 71
of rules 107
structure 70
New Industrial Economy 15
Norms of evaluation 84

O

Objects 105, 106
Obsolescence 214
Opinion
collective 88
epidemics of 77
logic of 83
market 87
Order from noise 41
Organisation
control based 26
informing 27
hierarchical 203
memory based 26
theory of 139, 140, 144
new theory of 203

P

Phase of development 12
Peirceian triangle 19
Pension funds 86
Pilot applications 181
Positive feed back 163
Possible worlds 51
Power 108,109, 110, 113, 199, 202
Prediction 37, 66, 69
Price mechanism 63
Principal agent theory 123, 203
Principle of energy conservation 44
Privacy 174
Processor
of knowledge 121
of information 121
Probabilities
subjective 38
Productivity gains 13, 190

Q

Quanta of data 17

R

Rationality
bounded 93, 94, 95, 104, 114, 199
procedural 23, 112
reversal 96
substantive 94
temporalised 94
Redundancy 34, 43, 94, 192, 193, 199
Regulations 177

Representations 204, 210
Reputation 149
Research and technological development 180
Rest-points 73
Risk 183, 201, 209
Role 111
Routines 109, 110, 121, 125, 126, 127, 128, 199
Rules 102, 105,106, 121, 125, 126

S

Salient characteristics 105
Shannonian conception of information 40
Self –organisation 23, 41, 44, 73, 127, 192
Self referential character 98
Semantic content 97, 198, 208
Signals 21, 39, 107, 123, 192, 196, 208
Significance of information 45
Signs 18
Simonian vision of the firm 123
Social acceptance 185
Social cohesion 213
Social exclusion 183
Socio economic engineering 27
Speculative self referentiality 86
Standard theory 93, 94
  of decision 101
  extended 93
Standardisation 177
Stationary states 54,
Statistical theory of information 14, 34, 192
Stochastic graph approach 71
Stock markets 85
Storage 160
Strategic dimensions 14
Strategic use of information 56
Sure thing principle 57
Syntactical dimension 208
Systemic modelling 27

T
Tatonnement process 64
Technological wave 167
Teirceity 19
Telecommunication markets 175
Telecommunication operators 175
Ternary scheme 20, 205
Ternary complexity 191
Theory of teams 123
Traders 66
Trading relationship 72
Transaction costs 122, 124, 139, 140, 144, 203
Trust 112, 113

U

Uncertainty 209
  measure 38
  prospective/retrospective 50
  structural 50, 194, 199

V

Virtuous circle 169
Vision of society 174

W

Walrassian
  equilibrium 14, 111
  model 61, 196
Welfare theorem 61, 140

Y

Yield management systems 26